D1095111

NORMAN
THOMAS

NORMAN THOMAS

A Biography

HARRY FLEISCHMAN

W · W · NORTON & COMPANY · INC ·

New York

To all those, young and old,
unfortunate enough not to know
Norman Thomas

Contents

CONTENTS

Illustrations

9

ILLUSTRATIONS

An off-the-record "Political Rally"
Sketch of Thomas by Miriam Troop
Weekly radio program
Thomas chats with Robert Frost and Henry Wallace
Trade union leaders in Japan
Seventieth birthday party
Seventy-fifth birthday party
Thomas with Harry S. Truman
United Auto Workers luncheon meeting
Thomas exhibits film clips
Sympathy picket line in Birmingham

Preface

◦§ WHEN MY DAUGHTER Martha was three years old, I took her to New York's Museum of Natural History. Gazing in awe at the whale, she exclaimed, "He's almost as big as Norman Thomas!"

Martha's perception of size might have been inaccurate but her instincts were sound. I have never known a man with a bigger heart or one who worked harder for decency and justice than Norman Thomas. Some, therefore, may object that I am not an unbiased biographer, and I plead guilty. However, I have tried to present all the facts as objectively as possible.

I must confess that in 1931, when I became a Socialist at the age of sixteen, I had a different view of Thomas from the one I hold now. At that time I accepted him as the Party's public spokesman and propagandist, but he wasn't a strict Marxist—in fact, with the arrogance of youth, I considered Thomas a mere activist and probably a petty-bourgeois opportunistic humanitarian Socialist. Having hurriedly devoured the works of Marx, Engels, Bernstein, Lenin, Trotsky and Hillquit, my ideological bellyache convinced me that my militant young Socialist comrades and I had all the answers.

It took me a few years and much living to discover what Norman Thomas always knew: that truth does not come wrapped in neat, simple packages; that life is complex; and that easy answers should be viewed with a jaundiced eye. Not that I came to the conclusion that Norman Thomas was infallible. He made many mistakes, but somehow my own were worse. Years passed before I could appreciate his brand of socialism which, as *The New York Times* put it, consists mainly of "jumping in wherever he thinks human beings are abused or human rights ignored, and doing something about it."

I have been fortunate enough to have worked closely with

11

Norman Thomas for the past three decades, both in the Socialist Party and in assorted liberal groups. As former Party national secretary and campaign manager for Thomas in 1944 and 1948—his last two campaigns—I shared the many frustrations and occasional joys which came our way. I would not have missed a minute of these experiences. Working with Thomas bolstered my conviction that, next to equality and justice for all, the most satisfying thing in life is fighting for those ideals.

Several years ago, when I started taping biographical interviews with Norman Thomas, it was not with the intention of writing his biography. Instead I hoped that the tapes would provide valuable raw material for some noted historian and writer. Then two of Thomas' children, Evan and Frances, urged me to undertake the task myself. I suggested that a more prominent and skilled author could undoubtedly do a better job. They insisted that my long friendship and close association with their father would give me insights unlikely to be shared by others. I allowed myself to be persuaded, but only you who read this biography can determine whether or not the decision was right.

I should like to thank the American Jewish Committee for granting a short leave of absence to carry on basic research, and the J. M. Kaplan Fund, Inc., for generous financial assistance, which furthered the completion of the research activity. I am indebted to Mrs. Terry Corum, who transcribed the many, many hours of tape recordings; to my wife, Natalie; to my editors, Carol Houck and Eric Swenson; and my agent, Nannine Joseph; all of whom improved the style of the book considerably. My thanks also to my sister, Mrs. Lillian Schiff, for her help in research; and to Mrs. Susie Waldman for her assistance in proofreading. Other acknowledgments appear in the sources for this book.

While Norman Thomas cooperated closely with me, answering all my questions and providing me with a variety of original source material, the book is in no sense an official biography and I, alone, am responsible for any errors in fact or judgment.

Wantagh, New York   Harry Fleischman
July, 1963

Sources and Acknowledgments

My main source material in the writing of this book has been Norman Thomas himself. He was willing at all times to answer frankly and honestly the multitude of questions I asked not only about his political actions but about his family, his views on religion and other private matters. He also made available to me the Norman Thomas Papers in the Manuscript Division of the New York Public Library, more than 150 file boxes which contain the bulk of his political correspondence from 1932 to the present day. These papers also include manuscripts of speeches, press releases, articles, books, pamphlets and minutes of Socialist Party and other organization meetings. Although very little correspondence of a personal nature was included, Norman Thomas and other members of his family contributed a number of letters which I was privileged to read.

During the course of my research, I have interviewed Norman Thomas on tape many times, the transcript of which runs to about 325 pages. In addition, I have gone to him repeatedly for clarification of points that were unclear. A great boon was the opportunity to study his unpublished autobiography, which he wrote primarily for his children. At one point he considered publishing it but decided against it because autobiographies, he wrote, are "too often a form of fiction which I have preferred to read rather than to write." That autobiography, begun in December, 1944, and completed in March, 1946, was invaluable in writing the early chapters of this book.

Another source of considerable value was the transcript of "The Reminiscences of Norman Thomas," interviews compiled by the Oral History Project of Columbia University. I am particularly indebted to the Library of the Tamiment Institute in New York City and to its librarian, Louise Heinze, for making available a great mass of material about Norman Thomas, and for permitting me to make my home virtually a branch of the library for three years.

Thomas, of course, has written almost as much as he has spoken. He founded and edited *The World Tomorrow*, a Christian Socialist and pacifist magazine (1918–34, title varied). He edited the *New York Leader*, a daily labor and Socialist paper, for six weeks in 1923, and then wrote weekly in the *New Leader* from 1924 to 1935. When that publication became the factional organ of the Old Guard in the Socialist Party, he switched to the *Socialist Call*, which was founded by the militant caucus but soon became the Party's official organ (1935–60, title and format varied). In 1960 the *Socialist Call* gave way to *New America*, and Thomas continued his regular column. These Socialist papers carry a vast amount of material about Norman Thomas. Thomas has also written frequently in the last two decades both for *The Progressive* and the *New Leader*. My thanks to these publications, to the Socialist Party, Post War World Council, League for Industrial Democracy and Workers Defense League for permission to use their material freely.

Since the 1948 presidential campaign, Thomas has written twice-weekly columns for the *Denver Post*, also carried much of the time by a group of other papers in the West, represented by the *Times-Mirror* Syndicate of Los Angeles. I have used these columns liberally as background material.

Then, of course, there are more than a score of Thomas books which I reread with deep interest. I also found Murray Seidler's *Norman Thomas: Respectable Rebel* (Syracuse University Press, 1961) provocative and rewarding, particularly in its description of the internal life of the Socialist Party. I had the opportunity to read a number of chapters of a fascinating monograph on "Norman Thomas and the Socialist Party of America," by M. S. Venkataramini, head of the Department of American History and

14

Institutions, Indian School of International Studies, New Delhi, India. This monograph was scheduled for publication late in 1963 under the auspices of the Indian School. Incidentally, Venkataramini's study of the internal workings of the Socialist Party, U.S.A. in the thirties was so thorough that I found in his notes new items about Thomas and even reminders of some of my own obscure activities which I had long forgotten.

I have interviewed all the Thomas children, sons Evan and William, and daughters Frances (Mrs. John Gates); Polly (Mrs. Herbert C. Miller); and Becky (Mrs. John Friebely); as well as Thomas' five brothers and sisters—Ralph, Evan, Arthur, Agnes and Emma. Talks with all of them were invaluable. It was also my good fortune to interview four of Norman Thomas' Marion High School friends: Harvey Gracely, Joseph Neidhart, Henry True and Homer Waddell.

Many people, most of whom worked closely with Norman Thomas in some socialist or liberal cause, gave me their impressions and anecdotes, either verbally or in correspondence. For this valuable aid, I should like to thank: Marie H. Allen, Henry G. Alsberg, Angelica Balabanoff, Roger Baldwin, Gregory and Bea Bardacke, Irving and Jean Barshop, Daniel Bell, Paul Blanshard, Fenner Brockway, Irving Caesar, Alfred T. Carton, Travers Clement, Elizabeth Coleman, Louise Crane, Franz Daniel, Martin Diamond, Leon Despres, Judah Drob, Tilford Dudley, Les Finnegan, Hy Fish, Samuel H. Friedman, Erich Fromm, William Gausmann, Maurice Goldbloom, Frank P. Graham, Senator Ernest Gruening, Albert W. Hamilton, S. Ralph Harlow, Donald Harrington, Michael Harrington, Mary and John Herling, Al Herling, Sidney Hertzberg, John Haynes Holmes, Darlington Hoopes, Senator Hubert H. Humphrey, Harold R. Isaacs, Newman Jeffrey, Anna Kethly, Peter Kihss, Maynard and Elsie Krueger, Harry W. Laidler, Alf M. Landon, Aaron Levenstein, Alfred Baker Lewis, James Lipsig, Jay Lovestone, Sidney Lovett, Leonard Lyons, Frank Marquart, Lenore Marshall, Frank McCallister, Roy McCorkel, Krishna K. Menon, Morris and Grace Milgram, Naomi Mitchison, Amicus Most, Emanuel Muravchik, James Myers, Robin Myers, Reinhold Niebuhr, Liston M. Oak, Sam Oshry, Don Peretz, Hilda and Paul Porter, Robert Repas, Fania and Roy Reuther, Sophie and Victor

15

Reuther, Lydia L. Rickman, Vera Rony, Nevin and Kathleen Sayre, Ben Segal, Joel Seidman, Clarence and Ruth Senior, Brendan Sexton, David A. Shannon, Leonard and Eleanor Shatzkin, Hugh Sheehan, Mulford Q. Sibley, Paul Sifton, Upton Sinclair, Stephen Siteman, Tucker P. Smith, William A. Spurrier, Mel Stack, Lee Stanley, William Stark, Mark Starr, John C. Stevens, Irwin Suall, Frank and Helen Trager, Purshottam Trikamdas, Walter H. Uphoff, Louis Waldman, Henry A. Wallace, Margaretta B. Wells, Murray A. Weisz, Frank Winn, Morton Wishengrad, Bertram D. Wolfe, Frank P. Zeidler, Miriam Troop Zuger, and William Zukerman. And to those whose names may have been left out inadvertently, my apologies.

Since this book was written for the general public, I have dispensed with footnotes, and where possible, have included my sources directly in the chapter.

Quotations from the following works are copyrighted and have been included with the gracious permission of the copyright holders:

Edward Angly, *Oh Yeah,* Viking, 1931.
Daniel Bell, *The End of Ideology,* Free Press, 1960.
Claude Bowers, *My Mission to Spain,* Simon and Schuster, 1954.
Irwin Edman, "To Some Bloodthirsty Writers," *The New Yorker Magazine,* 1943.
Malcolm Hay, *Europe and the Jews,* Beacon, 1950.
Herbert Hoover, *The Memoirs of Herbert Hoover,* Vol. 3, Macmillan, 1951–1952.
Cordell Hull, *The Memoirs of Cordell Hull,* Vol. 1, Macmillan, 1948.
Harold L. Ickes, *The Secret Diary of Harold L. Ickes,* Simon and Schuster, 1954.
Morris H. Rubin, *The Progressive,* September, 1948.
Arthur Schlesinger, Jr., *Crisis of the Old Order,* Houghton Mifflin, 1957.
——— *The Coming of the New Deal,* Houghton Mifflin, 1959.
David A. Shannon, *The Socialist Party of America,* Macmillan, 1955.

David A. Shannon, Ed., *The Great Depression,* Prentice-Hall, 1960.

Norman Thomas, *As I See It,* Macmillan, 1932.

Norman Thomas, *Is Conscience a Crime?* Vanguard, 1927.

Norman Thomas, daily columns during political conventions, *Denver Post,* 1948.

Norman Thomas, twice-weekly columns, *Times-Mirror* Syndicate.

Norman Thomas and Thomas Brooks, "Socialized Advertising," *New Republic,* April 21, 1952.

Paul Willen, "Who 'Collaborated' With Russia?" *Antioch Review,* Volume XIV, Number 3, Fall, 1954.

NORMAN
THOMAS

In the Beginning

ↀ "You're worse than Gene Debs. If I had my way, I'd not only kill your magazine but send you to prison for life." These were the words with which Postmaster General Albert S. Burleson greeted Norman Thomas in the summer of 1918. Thomas, the editor of *The World Tomorrow*, had wrested this comment from the Government's top thought-controller in the first World War because his magazine consistently defended civil liberties, even in war-time, exposed government mistreatment of conscientious objectors and dared to question other government war policies. What particularly drew Burleson's fire was an article by Thomas called "The Acid Test of Our Democracy," which vigorously protested American military intervention against Soviet Russia in Archangel and in Siberia.

How did it happen that Norman Thomas, a respectable Republican Protestant minister, son and grandson of respectable Republican Protestant ministers, was called a "subversive" in World War I and then moved on to become the presidential nominee of the Socialist Party in six campaigns? What was there in his heredity and environment to cause this particular development of his life?

On both sides of the family Norman Thomas was descended from hardy, pioneering stock. Grandfather Thomas Thomas was born in the township of Llanon, Cardiganshire, Wales, on June 14, 1812. In 1824, after the harvest was over, the Thomases and some other Welsh families sailed from Liverpool on the ship *William Burns*. After a six weeks' voyage they reached New York and the Thomases found lodgings on Water Street. At first the

Welsh immigrants huddled together, working at whatever was available, but by 1825 they were so homesick for the hills of their native Wales that they finally selected some very beautiful land in the hill country of Bradford County, Pa., and moved there. They called their village Neath after the town in Wales from which many of them came.

By working as a day laborer and farmer, Grandfather Thomas raised enough money to go to college. In 1837 he walked one hundred twenty miles to Easton, Pa. (it took him three days), and entered the Preparatory Department of Lafayette College. Here he earned his support and helped build West College, actually quarrying the stones. After six years at Lafayette, Thomas Thomas was graduated with the class of 1843, the oldest man in the class. He then entered Princeton Theological Seminary, where he spent two years. Upon his return to Bradford County he married Mary Evans, a member of the original Neath colony, and spent the rest of his hard-working life preaching at various country churches in the area.

The Mattoons, Norman's mother's people, had settled in America earlier than the Thomases. The family name was derived from an original French Huguenot emigré who came to the United States by way of England to escape the persecution of Protestants in France. Grandfather Stephen Mattoon grew up in Jefferson County, N.Y. Like Thomas Thomas he was attracted to the ministry, and by teaching earned his way first through Union College in Schenectady and then through Princeton Theological Seminary. After his marriage to Mary Lowrie, Stephen Mattoon and his wife went as pioneer missionaries of the Presbyterian Church to Siam in 1847, and served the church there for almost twenty years. He learned Siamese and became a good friend of King Mongkut, who insisted that Mattoon be the person to translate for him in negotiations on a new treaty with the British. When consular relations with the United States were set up, Stephen Mattoon was appointed the first consul, but he remained in that post only until a permanent consul could be named. Mission work was his first love.

In 1851 King Mongkut invited Mary Mattoon and two other American women to come into the forbidden area of the palace to teach the women of his household. Shortly afterward Mary Mattoon urged King Mongkut to employ a full-time teacher who could also teach some of the young princes as well as the wives. This suggestion eventually led to the arrival in Siam of Anna Leonowens, later to be immortalized in the best-selling *Anna and the King of Siam.*

The Mattoons, despite their good relations with the King of Siam, were by no means blind to conditions in that country. In a speech to the American residents of Bangkok on July 4, 1865, Stephen Mattoon said:

"But how shall I speak of liberty here, where the very atmosphere is heavy laden with oppression; where the master is only less a slave than he who crouches and crawls at his feet and is chained and scourged at that master's pleasure. . . . You can now appreciate the liberties of our own country, by contrast with the oppression of this."

Mattoon mourned Lincoln, whom he called a "special gift of Providence to his country at this time of great peril," but stressed the stability of our democratic form of government which continued without interruption even after Lincoln's assassination. He was hopeful that, with slavery extinguished, "there will be no longer any necessity to seek new fields for its extension, and we shall be less likely to be drawn into foreign wars." Foreshadowing his grandson's approach, Stephen Mattoon urged aggressive and propagandist efforts "to see the day when everywhere . . . free thought, free speech, and a free press shall be enjoyed—when argument shall be met only by argument, moral force by moral force, and truth shall be left free to make its way unshackled."

In 1866, after he had finished translating the Bible into Siamese, Grandfather Mattoon returned to the States and became pastor of the Presbyterian Church in Ballston Spa, N.Y., a town near Saratoga. However, the life of a minister in a small town soon proved too tame for him. In 1870 his educational and missionary zeal triumphed over his pastoral interests, and Stephen Mattoon became the first regular president of a Presbyterian college for Negroes in Charlotte, N.C., then named Biddle College, but now called Johnson C. Smith University. At this time, right after the

Civil War, there were few schools for white children, let alone Negroes, and the college had to begin its educational efforts for Negroes at a very elementary level.

Emma Mattoon, Norman's mother, was a girl of about twelve when the family moved to Charlotte. She was to remember vividly that the other white girls in the area ostracized her and her sister because their father, a Northerner, taught "niggers." Fortunately with the passage of time the situation changed greatly for the better.

Emma was sent to Peace Institute in Raleigh (now Peace Junior College) to prepare for college. At Elmira College, where she became a student, she first met Welling Evan Thomas, a young Presbyterian minister on a visit to his sister Mary. A friendship developed, but after graduation, Emma went back to teach at Peace Institute. Welling pursued her and the couple married in 1881, returning to the bridegroom's pastorate at Eden, Ohio.

In 1884, a few months before the birth of their first son, Norman, the young couple moved to Marion, Ohio, a bustling town of almost ten thousand which was to become known as the home of that ill-starred president of the United States, Warren Gamaliel Harding. The Presbyterian parsonage where Norman Thomas was born on November 20, 1884, was a substantial, red-brick, two story house next to the church on Prospect Street. There were fine old maples, a tempting grape arbor, but water for the family's needs had to be carried from a pump and there was no plumbing in the house. Rain water collected in a cistern for washing. The family kept warm with a "base burner" into which hard coal was poured, and with fireplaces which burned lumps of soft coal. Saturday night baths in wooden tubs were the rule for the Thomases as well as for their neighbors.

Later a new church was begun on another site and the family moved to a rented house on Oak Street. Although the house was almost on top of the railroad tracks and had no gas or electricity, it did have a bath tub, indoor toilet and a furnace, cause for great rejoicing. And watching the long freight trains with cars bearing names of distant railroads gave Norman a more interesting and romantic sense of geography than he would have received from any textbook. He also liked to study the maps of the Erie Railroad System because they showed Marion, in bold black letters, as a junction point.

While Norman's boyhood contained much happiness, it was far from blissful. Marion was oppressively hot in summer, bone-piercingly cold in winter. When Norman was only a few months old, his two-year-old sister died of what was then called "membranous croup," a form of diphtheria. Norman himself, who weighed four pounds at birth, was sickly much of the time. He was to suffer from croup and chronic colds throughout childhood, and he once overheard some women telling his mother they doubted that she could "raise" him. The family concern for his health, which often isolated him from other boys and girls, was undoubtedly responsible for the awkwardness Norman felt as he was growing up. An intense, blue-eyed boy with a large head and spindly arms and legs, he was shy with children his own age, and with older people he tried to disguise that shyness by over-talking.

When Norman was about four years old, his mother took him to Charlotte, N.C., to attend his grandfather's funeral. Certain striking images were to linger in his mind for years: cabins with cotton fields coming almost to the doors; the oppressive heat; and colored people everywhere. He had seen very few Negroes in Ohio. Aside from this visit, Norman's early life and memories were centered around the typical Northern town of Marion, where the main attraction was an ugly court house, without a patch of green to soften its lines. He remembers that several streets were lined with trees and that there were no slums, but soft coal smoke and conventional Victorian architecture made the town far from beautiful.

According to the public school system in Ohio, all six-year-olds went to school morning and afternoon, with no exceptions for ill health. Therefore, Norman's parents started him in a little private school taught in her own home by one of Welling Thomas' parishioners. Norman attended only in the mornings and, when sick, could be kept home without falling behind the class. Under Evelyn Gailey's expert tutelage, in two years of irregular attendance in the mornings, Norman learned enough to enter the public school's fourth grade.

In one respect Miss Gailey and Norman's parents were bound

by tradition. Although naturally left-handed, Norman had to learn to write with his right hand. His father even tried to make him throw a ball with his right hand. Aware that present-day educators and psychologists believe that such insistence on right-handedness can cause psychic disorder, Thomas wryly doubts that it was responsible for his development as a socialist, but admits that it probably added to his lifelong lack of manual skill and dexterity.

Not until he entered the seventh grade did Norman really begin to enjoy school and the schoolyard and its games. Lessons came easily and he had little studying to do at home.

From his Welsh ancestors, Norman came honestly by his love of singing which, in his family, had to be confined to hymns. He took flute lessons from a young lawyer who played in Welling Thomas' church, and with his brother Ralph, who played the piano, found much pleasure in music.

In an unpublished autobiography which Norman Thomas later wrote for his children, he speaks of his parents and his early family life:

"I don't think strangers who did not see mother through eyes of filial affection would have called her beautiful but her charm and force of character made her stand out in any group. Father was a little taller than mother—about five feet, ten inches, I think. From my earliest recollection his dark hair was streaked with gray. He was clean shaven except for a rather light mustache—but heavy enough to warrant lady parishioners giving him hand-painted mustache cups, popular in those days. He dressed very neatly and nearly always in the style considered appropriate to a (non-Episcopalian) Protestant preacher. A frock coat was a sort of uniform. He lived for his family and his profession. He was a diligent pastor and preacher, a sincerely orthodox Presbyterian who frowned on playing cards, marbles for keeps, dancing and theatre going. He was sure that all drinking was immoral and thought that smoking wasn't much better. We children weren't allowed to study our school lessons on Sunday (but we could read books out of a curiously assorted Sunday School library) and as soon as we were old enough we were kept busy going to Sunday School, Church—usually twice—and something called 'Junior Christian

Endeavor.' "

Reading was one of Norman's greatest enjoyments. In addition
to a large and very dull theological library, his father had a sizable
collection of other books, particularly histories. There were also
many magazines—*Youth's Companion*, occasionally *St. Nicholas*,
the *Nation*, *The Independent*, and various church papers. At the
public library young Norman read rapidly and indiscriminately:
Scott, Dickens, Gibbon's *Decline and Fall of the Roman Empire*,
and Motley's *Rise of the Dutch Republic*, as well as various American, British, and French histories. He rather shocked older people in town by reading Bryce's *American Commonwealth* at an
early age.

By Marion standards the Thomas family was quite well off. Of
the six children Norman was the oldest, with three brothers, Ralph,
Evan, and Arthur, and then—after a gap—two sisters, Agnes and
Emma. Preacher Thomas received $1,200 a year and house rent.
Norman's mother had a small income from inheritance and from
her own savings as a school teacher. The family tithed conscien-
tiously, but always had enough left over to be free from cold and
hunger, and, as Thomas puts it, to have a little of life's cake as
well as bread. From time to time the family had a "hired girl," but
even then Emma Thomas, an excellent cook, prepared the meals.
Norman was especially partial to her baked apples and applesauce.
Because of the size of the family, the Thomas boys helped with
the canning, were called upon for carpet beating during spring
housecleaning, and washed dishes. Thomas would sheepishly pull
down the curtains when engaged in the latter task.

Like most of their neighbors, the Thomas children had to be
frugal. The boys earned whatever spending money they had, and
gave most of it to church and Sunday School. Ralph and Norman
both kept chickens, and for a while a cow which Norman milked.
His younger brothers were smart enough, Thomas recalls, to avoid
the job by claiming that their milking hurt the cow. There was
a small barn in the back yard of the parsonage and good pasture
nearby, at the edge of town. Summers, when the boys were older,
they earned money at neighboring fruit farms by picking berries
and cherries (they received a cent a quart for strawberries), and
sometimes they worked on shares. The sharecroppers then sold

27

their fruit to their mother or to other customers. Mowing lawns was another source of income, and during a period of affluence Norman was paid a steady thirty-five cents a week to distribute books on Saturday mornings to the members of a book club.

For several months, when one of the regular newsboys was sick, Norman served as a carrier for Warren Harding's *Marion Daily Star*. It was a salaried job, paying a little over a dollar per week, which he thought good pay. (Adult workers then averaged around $400 a year and the magistrate's familiar sentence, "ten dollars or ten days," conformed to economic realities.) The *Star* was an afternoon paper—there was no Sunday edition—and the boys walked their routes, delivering each paper at the door, or placing it on the stoop or porch. Norman collected ten cents a week from each of his patrons.

Thomas remembers that Harding sat in the office and shook hands with visitors or walked around town with a Great Dane, while his wife managed the newspaper. Evidently no one had yet told Harding that he looked like the American ideal of a states-man, so he lounged in comfort in his office, a shirt-sleeved citizen appropriately dressed to withstand the heat of a Marion summer.

Norman was waiting for his supply of papers when news came of Harding's first nomination for an important office, as a state senator. At the time the news caused little excitement. "But," Thomas later said, "we and our fathers would have roared with laughter if we had been told that Harding had begun his march to the White House."

Politically young Norman loyally followed his father in the Republican cause, although in 1896 he was greatly impressed by William Jennings Bryan's voice and figure when Bryan spoke from the courthouse steps to an enormous crowd. That year the boys had a fine time collecting campaign buttons, a relatively new election device.

For recreation the boys enjoyed the activities common to all country boys, fishing and camping, but Norman did not care for hunting. On one occasion he shot a bird, but felt sorry immediately that he had done so. He loved walking in the woods, especially with a dog and sometimes with other people, but the actual killing of game repelled him, primarily on aesthetic grounds rather than

28

because of any particular moral scruples.

Every two or three years the Thomas family went to visit Grandfather Thomas in Bradford County, Pa. It was quite an expedition on slow trains, but finally they would alight at the little Wyalusing station and pile into an old horse-drawn stage which ran up the creek valley. In the earlier years their destination was Stevensville, some eight miles away, where Grandfather Thomas Thomas (Thomas "Dwyaith" or Thomas "Twice," the Welsh would call him) lived in his white frame house. Behind the house was Grandfather's famous vegetable garden with Grandmother's gay hollyhocks against a stone wall. Beyond, a hill rose sharply with pasture lots and thick woods.

When he was well along in his eighties, Grandfather Thomas, who until then had been preaching in two or three churches on Sundays, riding or driving between them rain or shine, retired to Wyalusing, and the reunions of the Thomas clan were held in a sizable house there. As the number of grandchildren grew, it was impossible to accommodate them all, and friendly neighbors offered rooms to the relatives. Blanche, Grandfather's old white mare, and Uncle Lewis Cook's younger horse, Sam, hitched to various ancient vehicles, provided the transportation to bring the family together.

At high school Norman enjoyed his studies. He was by all odds the best-read student in the class and breezed through his recitations with a brilliance still remarked upon by his former classmates. Several claim that in history, Latin, and debates, Norman only had to read the material once and then could handle it perfectly —a claim Thomas regards as a pleasant legend rather than fact. He did love to debate, however, and was president of one of the school's literary societies. By this time his general health had improved and no longer interfered with his activities, although in junior year he suffered a bad attack of scarlet fever, followed by ear trouble which has lasted all his life.

There were no organized school games or athletics, but Norman enjoyed playing basketball, then a new sport. As the tallest boy in the class, he was a natural for center. He was also a champion high kicker in the gym and for a time had a standing broadjump record. During the winters, Norman and several other boys formed the

"Tiger Athletic Club," devoted principally to boxing. Once a week they would meet at a member's home, or in the hayloft of a local doctor's barn, where the boys would box strenuously and clumsily and, sometimes, fence even more inexpertly. After these sessions it was customary for the hostess mother to feed the club.

Young Thomas also served as manager for various kinds of entertainments at school, not dances of course, for dancing was still considered dubious. He once put on a show proclaiming the wonders of popular science, and joined groups of other young people on hayrides and bobsled rides. He had singularly few girl friends during his high school years, however, possibly due to his shyness.

In his senior year, 1901, Norman was elected class president and started his career as a dissenter by leading what could be called his first civil-liberties fight. It is ironic that Thomas, who would almost rather speak than eat, made his first public protest against having to speak.

For some years it had been the custom at high-school commencements for every member of the graduating class to get up and speak before the audience of adoring friends and relatives. However, the thirty-two girls and eleven boys of the graduating class of 1901 (the largest class in years) decided to rebel against these starched and squeaky performances and held a meeting to petition the Board of Education for an outside speaker. Superintendent Arthur Powell, who was not popular either with the students or the teachers, promptly banned further meetings in the school building, whereupon the issue became a holy crusade. The students met outside the school grounds, appointed committees, and campaigned for support from their parents and from members of the school board. They won. The board selected a lawyer from Cincinnati to be the official commencement speaker. The victory soured; the speaker went on for two hours and was extremely boring.

In the summer of 1901, after Norman's graduation, the Thomas clan foregathered for one of their reunions at Wyalusing. It was the last, and indeed the only, summer when Grandfather Thomas had all of his nineteen grandchildren and five children around him. Thomas fondly recalls the family excursions and picnics in the woods and by boat along the river. Of his grandfather he says: "With the years the benediction of peace and sure confidence settled about his snow-white head. He, a man of few words, of simple devotion to a stern Calvinistic creed, was 'father' to a whole countryside. . . . However far his grandchildren have wandered physically and spiritually, I do not think we shall forget family prayers about his chair nor shall we think of them as perfunctory superstition or an insincere rite. As we sat quietly around him, with his large-type Bible in his lap—one of his few concessions to advancing age—dimly at least we understood from him the sources of a light which gave meaning, yes and glory, to the humdrum task, and all the vicissitudes of the year, a light which bathed, in beauty greater than the sun's, the fields, the shining river, the wooded hills, the cottage and the cherished garden in which this Preacher of the Word lived out his days."

Such was the environment of Norman Thomas' youth. Later, in reviewing his life as the son and grandson of ministers, he was to note with amusement: "What a setup for the modern psychologically minded biographer or novelist! A study in revolt born of reaction from Presbyterian orthodoxy, and the Victorian brand of Puritanism in a Middletown setting! The only trouble is that isn't what happened. I both loved and respected my parents. I was a very loyal Marionite who can still recall the pangs I felt when we all sang 'God be with you till we meet again' on my father's last Sunday in the church that he had built. . . .

"Today I cannot accept my father's religious creed nor altogether his moral code. We children probably lost something because as my sister once said, 'In those days only morals counted.' The moral code was too narrow, for example, in its Sabbatarianism; it had both its blind spots and its over-emphasis. Yet, even so, I challenge any Freudian to show that it led to as much nervous disorder, instability, or more unhappiness than the current laxity of standards. I am so old-fashioned as to be glad that I lived in a home, a time and an environment in which sin, yes and moral vices, were realities to be forgiven and cured but not condoned."

Still there were evidences that Welling Thomas did not adhere unquestioningly to the Calvinist creed. Young Norman noted on several occasions that while his father believed literally in Hell, he was unwilling to say that anybody he knew was going there. And a book marker sent by Reverend Thomas in 1900 to the members of his congregation as a "New Year and New Century Greeting" carried the message:

> We are living, we are dwelling,
> In a grand and awful time,
> In an age on ages telling;
> To be living is sublime.

Such thoughts were hardly representative of fundamental Calvinism, but exemplified the belief held by most Americans in a basic rationality of life and its essential goodness. America was a country of life and hope. The past had been good; the future would be better. Thomas realized later that the years of his youth were also years "of the robber barons, of an aggressive and 'soulless' capitalism, of the long day for workers, of an individualism which made miserable provision for the unfortunate. Freedom was limited by color—especially in the South; by bitter poverty; and by the economic exploitation of the acquisitive society." But he recalls his own youthful conviction that "all the great victories essential to the onward march of man had already been won; what was left was but to press onward toward that far-off divine event to which the whole creation moves."

Thomas' environment and heritage foreshadowed his strong social conscience and a streak of progressivism, but not yet were there indications that America's "Mister Socialist" was in the making.

TWO

Bucknell and Princeton

৶৯ IN THE SUMMER of 1901, following Norman's graduation from high school, his father decided it was time to go to another church and town. He accepted a call to the First Presbyterian Church in Lewisburg, Pa., a sleepy town beautifully situated in a fertile valley where the Buffalo Creek flows into the west branch of the Susquehanna River. Most of the older houses in Lewisburg were built in Pennsylvania style, flush with the old brick sidewalks. Unlike Marion, lawns and gardens were behind the houses.

Had the Thomas family remained in Marion, Norman would have attended Wooster College, a substantial Ohio Presbyterian college from which Welling Thomas had received a Doctor of Divinity degree. But Bucknell University in Lewisburg was a comparable institution, and the fact that it was Baptist rather than Presbyterian in background hardly seemed sufficient reason for the family to strain its resources to send Norman away from home. It was reasoned that he could always find odd jobs to do in Lewisburg, and again the family cow was Norman's responsibility.

In the fall of 1901, Norman entered the freshman class at Bucknell. He took a class in Greek at the Academy attached to the college while also carrying freshman Greek in college as part of the general freshman course, added some lessons in flute and on the cello and sometimes played in what he describes as an indifferent college band. But for the most part Norman did not enjoy life at Bucknell. At the time, the university's standards were low, its cultural atmosphere almost nonexistent and most of the extracurricular activities poor. However, he probably would have stayed at Bucknell, and perhaps even learned to like it, had not his

Uncle Frank Welles offered him $400 a year to enable him to go to Princeton. This offer came as the answer to a dream. Norman knew about Princeton because his father had gone to Princeton Theological Seminary; also, a cousin was in the class of 1901 at the University, and a Marion friend in the class of 1902. Moreover, he had been given a book of Princeton stories by Jesse Lynch Williams which had made his interest stronger than ever.

Norman realized that $400 wouldn't cover all the costs of even a frugal year at Princeton, but there was a chance for a partial scholarship and he could earn some money in his spare time. Besides, if necessary, the family was prepared to help financially. Actually, they never had to. Norman earned all that he needed by writing syllabi for less energetic students, tutoring a little, doing odd jobs, winning prizes, and working during the summers.

Since freshman year at Bucknell was not equivalent to one year at Princeton, Norman had first to decide whether to repeat freshman year at Princeton or try to enter as a sophomore. His pride induced him to try the latter. He was unaware of how unprepared he was, and also was anxious to make way for the education of the younger children in the family, as well as to save time if he decided to enter a profession.

Norman spent most of the summer of 1902 preparing for Princeton; one of the Bucknell professors helped him to learn German. He reported at Princeton in the fall, and persuaded the authorities to give him sophomore class examinations. With some misgivings they allowed him to enter the sophomore class, but he was told he would have to take conditional exams later in both mathematics and German, for which the sophomore requirements were far beyond what Norman had studied at Bucknell or during the summer.

A combination of pride, fear, loneliness, and the impending threat of conditional exams caused Thomas to work at fever pitch that first semester at Princeton. At the end of the term, he had not only satisfied the conditional requirements but got first group in every sophomore subject. Having established this precedent, he went on to win first group in all subjects for the rest of his stay at Princeton. Modestly Thomas claims that he was not as brilliant as such a record might imply, but suggests that the average in

some classes might have been low. He adds that he did not necessarily prefer a Phi Beta Kappa key to a varsity letter, but simply
couldn't get the letter.

Following his earlier interest in public speaking, Norman spoke
often at Whig Hall, which still operated along historic secret society lines, and was a member of three varsity debating teams. A
mutual love of debating drew Thomas to Raymond B. Fosdick,
who was soon to win acclaim in many areas of public service. They
had discussions on theology and many other subjects. At the time,
Ray's theology was more radical than Norman's and it never occurred to him then that a time might come when Norman's thinking would be further to the left on any subject. Fosdick tried,
without much success, to interest Thomas in Frank Norris' two
socially-conscious novels, *The Octopus* and *The Pit*. (Later, the
noted historian W. E. Woodward, in the Socialist Party's 1928
campaign handbook, *The Intelligent Voter's Guide*, implied that
when Thomas was at Princeton he questioned the "smug complacency" of the time. According to Woodward, Thomas even
"wondered" whether, after all, there might not be some connection between the endowments which were constantly making it
possible to add some new dormitory or class-room to the college
community, and "those great and powerful capitalists who were
denying decent wages to coal miners and casual laborers." Such
speculation did come, but at a later date.)

Each year it was customary for a member of Whig Hall who
won in a debate on a subject related to French politics to receive
a gold medal, "valued at $150," and known as the "Baron de Cou-
bertin" award. Ray Fosdick and Thomas decided to sign up for
the debate. As it turned out, the two young men were the only
ones to enter their names. As usual the debate subject was announced the day before the event, in order to insure spontaneity.

After the debate was over, Professor Jerry Ormond delivered
a devastating statement which neither Thomas nor Fosdick ever
forgot: "Before announcing the name of the gentleman who has
won the competition, the judges wish me to say that in their deliberate opinion it was the worst debate they have ever listened to."
He then awarded the medal to Fosdick.

When the inscribed medal finally reached Ray, he rushed to a goldsmith in New York and found that the award was worth not one hundred fifty dollars, but seventy-five cents. Fosdick protested that the medal was gold. "No, it isn't," the goldsmith replied. "It's an alloy with a thin gold wash." Fosdick always insisted that some of Norman Thomas' "sparkle and irrepressible gaiety" was due to the inextinguishable merriment which the memory of this event brought him.

Thomas himself remembers with amusement the occasion of another public experience involving himself and Fosdick. Both young men gave five-minute extemporaneous talks at Whig Hall after the Wright brothers had made their first flight at Kitty Hawk. Both agreed that the feat was an interesting stunt but felt it had no practical significance.

Choir, Glee Club, and the Triangle Club orchestra (where Norman played the flute) gave him considerable pleasure. He also took singing lessons which were of real value years later in managing his voice on days when he had a heavy speaking schedule.

Thomas was active in the Philadelphian Society, the University Branch of the Young Men's Christian Association. In his junior and senior years he lived with two roommates on the ground floor of Old Reunion, and their rooms were a popular hangout for many Princetonians. He did not expect to be elected to a club, since he was no athlete and had little money. While he thought the upperclass club system open to some criticism and perhaps conducive to snobbery he nevertheless had friends among members of the Colonial Club and so was both surprised and pleased when the Club asked him to join as part-time manager late in his senior year. The job called for very little work, was kind to his purse, and Thomas was to remark later that it gave him confidence that his eventual espousal of unpopular causes was not a result of some personal incapacity for social success.

During his college years, Thomas was a great admirer of Woodrow Wilson, and still considers him the speaker he most liked to hear. Wilson was popular as a professor, continuing to teach even after he was burdened with the president's administrative responsibility, and Thomas took every course with him that he could.

When Wilson was installed as president of Princeton in 1902, Thomas says he almost literally sat at his feet, since Wilson spoke from a raised platform.

Shortly after Wilson became president, he began to raise the scholastic standards and to change Princeton's reputation as "the best country club for boys in America." He tightened up examinations with the result that more students flunked. Although there was a certain amount of grumbling, Wilson's early moves were heartily supported. He was to lose popularity later by his efforts to replace the college social clubs with his quadrangle plan, which would have made the existence of fraternities, with their resulting cliques, superfluous. Thomas was among those who approved of the plan, but it did not go through.

Apparently Wilson, despite his intellectual stature, was sorely hurt by personal criticism and little inclined to forgive. Thomas was to gain curious evidence of this years later when he was introduced to Mrs. Jessie Wilson Sayre, the youngest of the President's daughters, at a wedding reception. Mrs. Sayre looked at him, then said coldly, "Mr. Thomas and I have met." Rapidly Thomas began to consider all his political sins as they would appear to a daughter of Wilson; by this time his socialist and pacifist views were well known. Mrs. Sayre continued: "What class were you at Princeton?" "1905," he said. "I thought so," she replied. "That was the class that was so cruel to Father."

Only with some difficulty was Thomas able to recollect the incident to which she referred. The summer before Norman's senior year, Mr. Wilson had had a high iron picket fence put around the president's house, an old-fashioned, rambling but attractive Victorian residence. The students considered the fence an eyesore and decided to make it that year's target for the senior parade which satirized life at Princeton. Garbed in black, the marching seniors carried signs reading "Picket Lane, formerly McCosh Walk" and "Drawbridge to the Right." One student rented a young pig which they carried with them in a boy's cart. The townsfolk and faculty were highly amused by this childish prank, but Wilson called in some of the class officers and expressed his displeasure. Nothing was done about the fence until the summer after graduation when it was moved a little ways back to a more appropriate location and hidden by shrubs. Most of the class forgot the incident, but the Wilson family evidently could not blot out the memory of the "cruel" college prank that had so hurt their father. Thomas wondered what he had once said to his daughter to have her place so great a stress, after many years, on such an insignificant event. Here was a man who later reached one of the highest pinnacles attainable to a human being, and who then suffered the humiliating defeat of the League of Nations.

As has been mentioned, Thomas worked during summer vacations to provide for his education. One summer he sold aluminum kitchen ware from door to door on eastern Long Island. No born salesman, he disliked ringing door bells, but he made a little money. Another summer, Ralph and Norman worked in Lewisburg's one good-sized factory, which made inexpensive chairs. The hours were long, the pay low, the chairs shoddy, and of course there was no union. Yet Norman found this insight into a typical worker's factory life a useful experience.

Although Thomas was graduated with very high standing, he felt that he did not receive a first rate education at Princeton. He learned no foreign language well. While he got a first group in the history of philosophy, and was deeply interested in the problems with which it dealt, he insists that he scarcely understood what it was all about. Although he liked history, Thomas remained critical of the dullness and superficiality of certain courses in English and American history, which added little to what he had already learned in high school.

On the other hand, he enjoyed his good courses in English with Wilson's brother-in-law, Stockton Axson, and Henry Van Dyke, and economics as it was soundly taught by Winthrop Daniels along classical *laissez-faire* lines. He also attended a course on socialism taught by Walter Wykoff, one of the first of the "human interest" sociologists, who took to the road with casual laborers during the depression of the '90s, and set down his experiences in colorful style in a book called *The Workers*. The course called for reforms of capitalism and emphasized what he thought was wrong with socialism. It impressed Thomas, and at one point after graduation he toyed with the idea of writing a book exposing the errors of socialism. It helped interest him in both econom-

38

ics and politics. He considered himself more or less a progressive Republican.

The years at Princeton were happy ones for Thomas, and opened the door to friendships and opportunities that shaped his future life. He fondly remembers the protracted bull sessions, walks around the triangle, beer parties in Keg Hollow (Thomas didn't drink but he didn't mind being with others who did), long spring evenings of senior singing, good athletic teams and spacious playing fields. But as senior year was ending, he was faced with the question of what life work he was going to undertake.

While Thomas had been more or less destined for the ministry by his parents, they had never put direct pressure upon him. And although he felt a strong sense of duty to enter some form of missionary work at home or abroad, he experienced no mystical sense of call. He was reluctant to go to a theological seminary, and considered teaching for a year or two in order to save money while thinking over what his next step should be. There was also the possibility of a job in a successful lawyer's office in New York if he studied law. By this time Thomas was keenly interested in political life but not in the drudgery of wardheeling. He envied the British system where Gladstone and other Englishmen could be groomed for political careers, and felt that law might be the nearest thing to it. He didn't admire the profession as much as he did medicine or engineering, but thought he was more likely to succeed at law.

While he was still uncertain about his future, Thomas met the Rev. H. Roswell Bates, a clergyman who urged him to come for a year to work at the Spring Street Presbyterian Church and Neighborhood Center in New York. Thomas' friend Tom Carter, Princeton 1904, was working there and expected to stay a second year. After visiting Spring Street, Thomas decided to go there and in the fall started at the munificent sum of $500 a year, plus his room. His experiences at Spring Street were to make him forget the law as a profession.

THREE

First Years in New York

꿗 For THOMAS, his first job meant a plunge into an entirely
different world from the small-town life he had known. While
New York had a certain fascination for him, he was slow in learn-
ing to like it. It was, he says, like vice—"first seen, then endured,
then embraced." He still recalls his surprise one night when he
was returning from New Jersey on a ferry and discovered the
affection he felt for the city of lights that lay ahead, even though
he was aware that the radiance concealed much that was sordid
and ugly. This was the first time he thought of the tumultuous
metropolis as home, and home New York or its vicinity has been
for nearly three score years.

In 1905, the parish of the Spring Street Presbyterian Church
was by no means a social worker's paradise. While it contained
some blocks of old-fashioned family dwellings, most of them
housing more than one family, there were also many blocks of
abominable slums. Rear tenements, outside toilets, and cold water
flats abounded in the neighborhood. Thomas frequently visited the
small rooms, crowded with big families. Sitting gingerly on a
broken wooden chair, he would see rats scurry, and cockroaches
and bedbugs moving along the grimy, broken plaster of the walls.
Often the mother of the family was sick, lying on a filthy bed
around which dirty toddlers played. Nursing service was almost
nonexistent—there was only one nurse attached to the Spring
Street Neighborhood House. Thomas was naively appalled to
find that the Health and Tenement Departments, controlled by
corrupt politicians, were slow to compel slum landlords to abide
by even the inadequate laws of the times.

40

On one particularly dramatic Sunday night a frightened child came running to the Neighborhood Center for help: "Come quick! Papa's killing Mamma!" Thomas climbed three flights of a tenement stairway and, although scared green, managed to persuade the drunken longshoreman to put down the baling-hook with which he was about to perforate his wife. On other occasions Thomas would call in the heads of some of the local gangs to try to arrange some sort of armistice—the first of his many arbitration efforts.

Strong liquor was the chief escape in this poverty-stricken district with a large sprinkling of hard-drinking, hard-living Irish teamsters and dock workers. Drunken quarrels were the main source of release for frustration and apathy. The neighborhood had none of the abounding vigor or the tremendous intellectual and social interest that characterized the equally poverty-stricken Jewish east side. This, of course, made the settlement workers' task much harder but at the same time more necessary.

Adding to the difficulty was the lack of equipment at Spring Street, especially for boys' club work—there was no gym, and leaders for the work were inexperienced. Spring Street was primarily a church with an evangelical emphasis, which the settlement work was expected to supplement. Pastor Bates was remarkably effective in rebuilding a slowly dying Presbyterian church and interesting its respectable members in remolding the neighborhood. He had just acquired an old tenement adjoining the church at the time Norman joined the staff, and this was renovated to provide sleeping quarters and club rooms. Tom Carter was the other full-time worker, and by early winter he and Thomas had brought together a group of residents who took breakfast and dinner at the house, worked at other jobs during the day, and gave some time as volunteers for club and Sunday School work. Board on a semi-cooperative basis was cheap.

Mr. Bates had genuine compassion for the poor and a strong religious zeal which made him not only a force for good in his parish but also in the colleges where he told his story. Foppish in manner, he was yet a man of tremendous energy who would work at dynamic speed for several days and then collapse. He expected his staff to work as hard as he did, but without the breakdowns, and for some reason, in his bad times Bates relied mainly on Norman.

In his first year at Spring Street, Thomas did a little of everything appropriate to church and settlement work, from running clubs and singing in the choir to family visiting. He did a good deal of speaking, some of it at open air street meetings. Before his first open air meeting, his knees shook with fright—not from fear of violence, but fear of having to speak. All that day he hoped for rain, or possibly an earthquake. However, neither phenomenon occurred, and Thomas survived the speech as well.

He organized a men's club, but not a very active one, which had little interest in politics. In fact, even though William Randolph Hearst was running for mayor that year, 1905, on a radical platform, Tammany Hall was good enough for most people in the district. There was in the club a lone single taxer, who also read the *Weekly People*, journal of Daniel De Leon's Socialist Labor Party. He introduced Norman to that paper, which later was to make Thomas the perpetual target of some of its most venomous shafts. At this time, however, Norman was still primarily a Teddy Roosevelt progressive, and actively non-socialist.

Because Mr. Bates was in ill health and Tom Carter was leaving to study at Auburn Seminary, Thomas agreed to stay at Spring Street a second year. The work seemed interesting and important enough for him to postpone for a year the theological course on which he had finally decided.

As the fall of 1907 approached, Norman was preparing to enter either Auburn Theological Seminary, Auburn, N.Y., where Mr. Bates had matriculated, or Union Theological Seminary in New York. But Mr. Bates was again sick, and felt that a world tour would cure his ills, while giving him an opportunity to inspect missions. He secured an ordained minister to carry on at Spring Street, and persuaded Tom Carter, who had finished his first year at Auburn, and Ted Savage, who had been with Thomas at Spring Street, to go along on the world trip. Without Norman's knowledge, Bates also went to Uncle Frank Welles and arranged for him to finance his nephew's participation on the same tour. Thus it was that Thomas embarked on his first trip abroad

They sailed from Seattle in July and visited Japan, Korea, China, the Philippines, Siam, Burma, India, and Egypt. Carter remained for the rest of the year in China, Bates and Savage returned home from Egypt, but Thomas stayed on to tour Europe, reaching home in March, 1908.

Through Bates' friendship with missionaries, the party saw more of the Asian countries than most tourists. They traveled overland in Southern China by mule and boat to Hwai Yuen in Anweh province and back again to Hangkow with some of the remarkable men who made the Hwai Yuen mission a center of medical work and relief from famine. Thomas still remembers trying to ride a Chinese donkey with the uncomfortable Chinese saddle. Everyone in the party became saddlesore and when one of the donkeys went lame, each member politely offered to walk and let the others ride. Part of the time, Bates suffered attacks of sickness, and a sedan chair and carriers were hired for him.

Shanghai was then controlled by white foreigners, and Thomas was appalled to read the signs in Shanghai parks: "Dogs and Chinese not allowed." He found that he liked the Chinese people very much. While he also enjoyed Japan, his sympathies were with the Korean people, innocent pawn of the Russo-Japanese war.

In India, Thomas liked most of the missionaries he visited, and at the time he was so conservative that he was inclined to agree with them that British rule, on the whole, was necessary and beneficial. However, he was repelled when, on a Calcutta street car, he saw a British civilian strike a native conductor across the shoulders simply because the seat where he wanted to sit was dusty. Even though the blow was light, Thomas began to understand that men could more easily forgive injuries than insults born of arrogance.

When Thomas returned to America, awaiting him were two interesting offers: one as assistant to Dr. Dulles of the First Presbyterian Church of Auburn, who also taught homiletics at Auburn Theological Seminary. Dr. Dulles was the father of John Foster and Allen Dulles. The other was as assistant to the Rev. James M. Farr at Christ Church, situated in New York City on

West 36th Street, in a drab tenement district. Either job would have enabled Thomas to finance his seminary course easily, but he chose the latter, and also began his studies at Union Theological Seminary.

Although Union Theological Seminary was too liberal and heterodox for his orthodox Presbyterian parents, Norman was drawn to it by the men he knew there. The teaching at Union Theological Seminary, Thomas felt, was better, on the average, than that at Princeton, and certain of his philosophical problems seemed to be answered. He lived happily in the dormitory of the old Seminary building at 700 Park Avenue.

Thomas soon made his mark at the seminary. On one occasion there was a seminar on "Mysticism," which George L. Bradlee attended with an old college chum, the Rev. C. H. Holbrook, then studying at Union. One student read a paper; its critic, a tall, slender young man, sat at the end of the long table. When the paper was finished the professor called for the critic's report. "His first words," wrote Bradlee later, "made me prick up my ears. Swiftly and incisively this youth dissected the paper which had been read, and, with apparently nice discrimination, pointed out the strength and weakness in the argument. Appreciative, keen and forceful, the tall student's way of putting his case was the only thing that I carried away with me."

Bradlee spoke of his impressions to his friend, who replied, "Yes, that was Norman Thomas. He's just about the brightest, keenest man we have here!"

Thomas liked the work offered at Christ Church through his good friend William Sloane Coffin, whose religious and civic interests were many. Coffin was a trustee of the Spring Street Neighborhood House and Sunday School superintendent at Christ Church. The latter was in some sense a mission of—and largely supported by—the fashionable Brick Church, then located at Fifth Avenue and 37th Street.

Christ Church, Norman found, differed a good deal from Spring Street in that it was admirably equipped and competently staffed. While Mr. Farr inspired no such devotion as Roswell Bates, he was reasonably competent both as a preacher and parish head. A Princeton man with good social connections, Farr was conventionally and cautiously liberal, easy to work with, uninspiring and uninspired, yet well liked. The church had both the strength and the limitations of any well-financed institutional church or settlement in a poor district, yet was more self-governing than most "missions" of rich churches. While the parish district was less poor and miserable than the worst blocks in the Spring Street parish, it was similar to that parish in its lack of intellectual and social ferment. It touched but did not include the district called "Hell's Kitchen."

In the summers Thomas lived at Christ Church, where groups of students from various colleges congregated. Here his life-long friendship with Sidney Lovett of Yale began. During this period Thomas was so far from being a radical and was so anti-Tammany that he volunteered to speak for the Republicans in the 1909 mayoralty campaign, for which he was duly thanked by the president of the Republican County Committee, Herbert Parsens.

Of greatest importance to Thomas, at Christ Church he met Frances Violet Stewart, who was to become his wife. Violet came from an aristocratic banking family; her grandfather, an ardent Presbyterian and Princetonian, had worked in the Treasury Department during the Civil War and later was instrumental in organizing the United States Trust Company, the first in the nation. Her sister Mary taught young children at the Christ Church Sunday School, and Violet herself organized at the church the first class for the home treatment of tuberculosis in New York. Having been unable to convince her family to allow her to become a full-time nurse, she raised money for the class and did the visiting nursing. Since hospitals were unable to treat all tubercular patients, Violet felt it was important to help keep their homes sanitary and build their morale.

In the traditional courting fashion of the time, the young couple toured the surrounding countryside on walks and canoe trips. It was in a canoe near Princeton on a beautiful day in June, 1909, that Norman suddenly realized he loved Violet. But still he could not find the courage to propose. Months passed, and then in February of 1910 Norman went to the old Presbyterian Hospital for a minor operation, and was told he would be hospitalized for three

or four days. Something went wrong and he developed first phle-
bitis and then a bad infection. Violet, who knew many of the doctors and nurses, arranged for him to be moved to an empty room
at the end of the ward until he was able to accept her mother's
invitation to recuperate at the Stewart home. (Incidentally, Norman claims he fell in love with Violet's mother and her gracious
hospitality even before he did with Violet.)

Although Thomas never intended to propose from a sick bed,
the moment seemed propitious and he shamelessly played upon
Violet's emotions. He told her that he refused to go to her mother's
house unless they were engaged. Just after his proposal, a nurse
marched in to take Norman's temperature, and all conversation
was held in abeyance. The temperature was, the nurse said, "satisfactory" and she left the room. Whereupon the proposal was
accepted.

While Thomas was in the hospital the pastor of Brick Presbyterian Church, Dr. Richards, who with his family had been among
Thomas' dearest friends, died suddenly. Dr. Henry Van Dyke,
who had been the minister of the church for many years before
going to Princeton, agreed to fill the pulpit, at least for some
months. Since he planned to continue his work in Princeton, he
badly needed an associate, and urged Thomas to accept the post.
Norman, who had attended Dr. Van Dyke's classes at Princeton,
doubted that he wanted the Brick-Church type of ministry for a
life work but thought the experience would be valuable. And the
salary would make marriage both possible and appropriate even
before he finished seminary—a matter much on his mind even
though he was not yet engaged when Dr. Van Dyke called.
Thomas accepted the invitation with the proviso that he could,
during the summer, supervise at Christ Church a college group
for which he felt responsible.

While still weak from his illness, and working hard to make up
lost time at the seminary, Thomas assumed his duties at the Brick
Church. He suffered agonies of stage fright on the first few Sundays, even though Dr. Van Dyke was reassurring. The morning
services in which Norman participated were dignified and beautiful, and soon things went smoothly.

Dr. Van Dyke was a good preacher, a minor poet and lecturer

in English literature. His Christmas story, *The Other Wise Man,* won considerable fame. He was well liked at Brick Church and there was much talk about his returning as permanent pastor, but during the discussions his feelings were hurt in some manner. He sharply curtailed his activities for the church, refused to preach the Palm Sunday sermon, and told Norman he would have to act as substitute. This gave Thomas both a heavier preaching schedule and new opportunities to be heard.

At this time Thomas was not a Socialist but was beginning to approach socialism. He was appalled by the deplorable slum conditions in both the Spring Street and Christ Church parishes. And the "uprising of the 20,000," the famous strike of young Jewish and Italian girls against the evils of the sweatshop system, made him sympathetic with labor.

Norman worked with vigor on his Palm Sunday sermon. The church was packed and he tried very hard to preach the social gospel. He frequently directed his gaze at a prominent pew holder whom he considered, in the language of Teddy Roosevelt, a "malefactor of great wealth." The service ended and Thomas was surprised that there were no repercussions. Several elderly ladies encouraged him by saying, "Keep on, young man, you're improving." Some weeks later, Norman heard that the "malefactor" had gone to the church committee which was looking for a pastor and said: "Brethren, you are making slow progress. Why not take a likely young man like Thomas and bring him up? He preached a good sermon Palm Sunday."

During the months that followed, Thomas listened to many guest ministers proclaiming generalities, which, if taken seriously and applied, would have been far more revolutionary than anything he later heard on Union Square or read in Marx. He became very skeptical of clergymen who told him how much they "got across" without their congregations knowing it. He learned that one can easily come out against sin and corruption, and for righteousness and peace—but that one has to be specific to be understood.

Norman and Violet were married September 1, 1910, by Henry Sloane Coffin in the Madison Avenue Church to which Violet belonged. Norman's parents were unable to attend because his father was taken suddenly ill with a mild case of typhoid fever and his mother had to nurse him. But the parents insisted that the wedding should not be postponed and Thomas' brothers were among the ushers. At the wedding a Hearst reporter called Violet "The Angel of Hell's Kitchen." During that summer she and Norman had organized children's gardens on vacant lots in Hell's Kitchen, and these were going very well.

The bridal couple went on a short honeymoon trip, canoeing on the waters near Princeton and riding on a "bicycle built for two," with Norman supplying most of the motive power. They then settled in an apartment in a small West 42nd Street tenement. They rented the basement and ground floor and persuaded the landlord to put in a bathroom. This he did, and painted roses on the tub as a wedding present. The couple spent a happy and comfortable year on West 42 Street, although on Saturdays they were frequently visited by repentant drunks who came "to take the pledge," having mistaken the Thomas apartment for the priest's residence which was on the other side of a big Catholic Church.

Since Dr. Van Dyke spent most of his time at Princeton, the Brick Church was eager for Thomas to be fully ordained. Usually ordination comes at the end of senior year of seminary but there was no difficulty about pushing it forward a year. Ordination required an examination before the presbytery, a rather large body composed of clergymen and representative ruling elders from each church. The Presbyterian Church was then in the midst of a theological controversy which involved not only the infallibility of the Bible (especially the New Testament), but also the whole Calvinistic theology, which had been considerably softened even among the orthodox. In 1903 the church had revised its principal theological standard, the Westminster Confession of Faith, to repudiate fatalistic misinterpretations and to emphasize God's love for all mankind. Yet some felt that the liberal wing was dangerously adrift from the old moorings.

Principal spokesman and examiner for the orthodox group in the presbytery was the Reverend John Fox, whose questions to Thomas dealt with the historicity of the Virgin birth and a literal resurrection of the body of Christ rather than with more philosophical matters. Thomas, having been well schooled at Union in the arts of interpreting and verbally reconciling opposing theories was able to satisfy the big majority of the presbytery that his doubts did not affect his fundamental faith. After a long examination he was accepted without much difficulty. Norman then believed in basic Christianity and had strong ties to the Presbyterian church.

The verbal duel with Dr. Fox resulted in some surprising newspaper coverage, shook the confidence of some of Norman's friends among the orthodox elders of Christ Church, but had no repercussions in the Brick Church. Norman's later political and economic heresies were to cause some distress to the elders of Brick Church and embarrass them at that bulwark of respectability, but in the winter of 1910–11, his mild theological deviations were well enough received. Hurt most by the controversy was Norman's father, who wrote the Rev. George Alexander, Moderator of the New York Presbytery, protesting about publicity to the charges of heresy against his son without the defense being heard. "Norman does not deny either the resurrection of Christ or the authority of the Scriptures in matters of faith and practice," wrote his father. "Yet the protest gives the impression that he denied both, or refused to affirm them. . . . These sensational rumors are exceedingly painful to me, who am conservative in my views and anxious that my son be not made to appear more liberal than the facts warrant." To Norman's delight, his father willingly took an impressive part in the ordination ceremonies.

In the spring of 1911, Thomas had to decide what to do after finishing seminary. He probably could have remained at the Brick Church, but felt that it was not the sort of ministry in which he could be most useful. Besides the church had just selected a new pastor, William P. Merrill, and Norman thought Merrill ought to be free to choose his own assistant.

At this moment, the Rev. William P. Shriver of the Presbyterian Board of Home Missions proposed that Norman head an exciting new project. The Board, in cooperation with the Presbytery's Home Missions Committee, planned to federate a number of churches and social agencies in immigrant districts into the American Parish. Thomas was asked to be the pastor of the old and run-down East Harlem Presbyterian Church, which had so few members that it was almost ready to shut its doors, and be director of the larger parish work, as a kind of chairman of a board of pastors and workers. This plan gave Norman the opportunity he had wanted—to get into immigrant work in the poorer parts of the city. The idea appealed also to Violet.

There followed seven crowded but happy years, when Norman and Violet were in contact with almost all phases of the lives of city workers. At a rather low rental, they found a house at 221 East 116th Street between Second and Third Avenues, and across the street from the East Harlem Church. This was home, office, and headquarters for many meetings. While Tommy (Norman Jr.) was born before the family moved in, four other children were born while the Thomases lived on 116th Street. Bill, Polly, Frances, and Becky are all natives of East Harlem, which then boasted the highest homicide rate in New York. Gangs of all sorts flourished and crimes of blackmail and violence were common.

South of 116th Street, the district was solidly Italian, with occasional enclaves of the older populations. To the north, there was a mixed population with very strong Hungarian and Slovak colonies. West of Third Avenue was mostly Jewish.

The Parish centers of work ranged from East 106th Street in Manhattan to East 153rd Street in the Bronx. In the latter location was the Church of the Holy Trinity (Italian), whose building was just being completed when Thomas came to the Parish. The old East Harlem Church housed not only an English-speaking congregation, but a Magyar Church, an Italian branch, and a Swedish Sunday School. The Church of the Ascension (Italian) on East 106th Street, which Norman helped build, and the Friendship Neighborhood House on Pleasant Avenue, a roomy old house with an old-fashioned yard, completed the Parish inventory. Among the remarkable people who were active in the settlement and Sunday School work were Virginia Murray, Sidney Lovett, Leonard Covello, John W. Darr and Norman's brother Evan.

One of the settlement workers induced a gang of Italian teenagers to form a club at the settlement house. The gang leader was horrified when his godfather subsequently joined the police force. But after he'd been in the club for awhile, he said, to the social worker's astonishment, "You know, I believe in prayer."

"Well," the social worker replied, "that's nice. Tell me about it."

"The night before last Christmas," said the leader, "our gang was over on First Avenue. And we stuck up a guy and he was a poor man, a worker. We took his pay envelope. Then he cried, 'Oh boys, have a heart. I want to buy something for my children for Christmas and now I haven't got anything.' So we gave him back the pay envelope. And he folded his hands and said, 'May God bless you boys.' And you know what! God blessed us. We went over to Mount Morris Park and we stuck up a guy and he had a hundred dollars!"

Thomas enjoyed keeping his miniature League of Nations on an even keel and watching its steady though not spectacular growth. The work was so hectic that there was little time for reading or reflection. He also became secretary of the local school board and took his duties there very seriously. An occasional visit to the theater was a great event. One winter, Norman joined an informal tennis club which used a nearby armory.

At about the same time, William Sloane Coffin bought a farm in New Jersey which he made available for a summer camp, first to Christ Church and then to the American Parish. At Oak Ridge Camp in the early days, equipment was very rough and simple —camping was almost like pioneering. But, because of unusual leadership, the camp was always a success.

One summer, Sidney Lovett was in charge. There was a terrible infantile paralysis epidemic in New York City, and it was an up-hill struggle for Thomas and Lovett to persuade the local country people that Oak Ridge Camp should be kept open. Toward the end of the summer, greatly relieved that nothing had gone wrong, Thomas went to see Lovett about some camp administration matters. While at Oak Ridge, one of the campers, against orders, climbed a tree, fell out and broke his leg. It was necessary to take him to a hospital. Thomas and Lovett knew the neighbors were so fearful of polio that, if they thought the boy had contracted the disease, they would have forced the camp's closing. So the boy was loaded onto a camp cot and put in an open farm wagon, where everybody could see him. A sign on the wagon indicated that he had fallen out of a tree and broken his leg. The parade was successful. The camp stayed open.

It was during this period that Thomas had a disillusioning experience with the labor movement. There was a wire mill in East Harlem, near the East River, called the Washburn Wire Mills, which was notorious for exploiting the linguistic differences between immigrants. Slovaks were played off against Hungarians—and both against Italians. There was no union in the mill and the workers had very low wages and miserable working conditions. A spontaneous strike finally erupted. Thomas got in touch with the strike leaders, foreigners who knew little English, and arranged for a meeting in the Parish Neighborhood House. In his innocence, Norman thought that the American Federation of Labor would be delighted to get into the picture. He went down to the city AFL headquarters and with difficulty persuaded AFL organizer William Collins to speak.

The strikers came out in droves to attend the meeting. Collins made a perfunctory address and took no steps to organize the workers into a union. After the workers filed out, he turned to Thomas and blithely said:

"Well, that's over. My wife says she can tell what kind of Wops or Dagoes I've been talking to from the smell of my clothes when I come home. You know, the I.W.W. and the priests have it right; you have to crack a whip over these Hunkies."

Seeing poverty, filth and vice at first hand tremendously moved young Norman. He registered Bull Moose Progressive in 1912, yet it was becoming apparent to him that life was far different from the theories taught at Princeton. So different, indeed, that in a class letter he wrote: "With all my love for Princeton I sometimes think, unjustly of course, that my education really began when I left there and that not the smallest part of it has been the life here in this district. It is a sort of school which sets hard lessons and asks some difficult questions. What is our democracy worth? How shall we make it apply to our social, industrial and political problems? Are we preparing well for national safety in peace or war when so many of our workers cannot even under favorable conditions make the proper living wage? I wish more

Princeton men were students in this school—but that is preaching, which is against the rules in a class letter."

Yet the contact with the dirt and clamor of slum life did not unduly depress Norman. In that same letter, he wrote: "Looking back on the ten years since we left Princeton I almost marvel to think how happy they have been, happier I am inclined to think than I dreamed of the night we sang 'here's to you my jovial friend' out on the campus in the dark."

FOUR

From War to Socialism

⳩ WHEN WORLD WAR I broke out in 1914, Thomas was, like most Americans, bewildered and horrified, pro-Ally in sympathy but certain that America should remain neutral. For generations, the Thomas clan had been "Old Testament Christians" who approved of "good" wars for "holy" causes. Thomas dimly recalled a sermon by his father pledging support to President Cleveland's ultimatum on Venezuela to Britain, even if it should mean war. His father had backed the Spanish War in 1898 and looked upon American troops as servants of the Lord in subduing the Philippines. Norman's view in 1914 was that large scale war was horrible and peace good, but he was convinced that the progress of the world was toward peace.

The first consequence of the War in the East Harlem district was unemployment. In a year, as war trade zoomed, there would be a great war boom, but at this time the slump was extreme. And, as Thomas wrote in his Princeton class letter, "When business conditions are poor, our people, very many of whom never earn enough properly to support their families, are the first to suffer." New York was completely unprepared to deal with unemployment. A citizen's committee was set up, under Judge Gary, the head of U.S. Steel, which gave jobless workers a little food, practically no money, and occasional work rolling bandages. Upon Violet's initiative, the American Parish and Union Settlement on East 104th Street organized workrooms where the unemployed could make baskets and similar items. Work could be provided for 450 men and women at 50 cents a day, and it was heartbreaking for Thomas to have to turn away hundreds of others who ap-

54

plied. As he watched some of the broken jobless fumbling at their jobs in the workrooms, he thought, "Even when jobs pick up, these people will be hopeless, they're unemployable." But he was surprised to find that when the war boom got rolling, the "unemployables" found jobs in a hurry. This was but one more incident in his role as a minister and social worker which led him to believe that "our various reform efforts were like bailing out the tub while we kept the faucet running."

When President Wilson, in August, 1914, issued a neutrality proclamation and appealed to the American people to observe the letter and spirit of neutrality, most applauded his warning that: "Every man who really loves America will act and speak in the true spirit of neutrality." By the end of the year, however, both Britain and Germany violated the rights of Americans as neutrals. And when the *Lusitania*, a British ship carrying both munitions and passengers, was torpedoed by a German submarine in May, 1915, with 114 Americans drowning, Wilson protested vehemently. Thomas, too, was angered by the German torpedoing but was anxious for America to remain neutral.

On Sunday morning, November 14, 1915, Norman's father was stricken with apoplexy and died two days later. Lying on his desk was a sermon, which was read to the congregation on the Sunday following their pastor's death. This last sermon by the Rev. Welling E. Thomas departed from his earlier views and contained much food for thought:

"We have boasted that the deadly explosiveness of modern guns and explosives was a guarantee of peace. Some of the nations have even justified the maintenance of vast armies and navies on the same plea, that preparation for war is the surest preservative of peace. We have thought that airships and undersea craft would make war so frightful that all sensible people would shun it and would settle their disputes by diplomacy . . .

"Can it be that this war in Europe is going to undo in great measure what centuries of Christian effort have accomplished?"

His father's last sermon was much in tune with Norman's thinking, which was that Christians must support the philosophy and ethics of Jesus. Little by little, he came to the conviction that

Christianity and war were in complete opposition. God, he felt, was not the "God and Father of our Lord Jesus Christ" if His servants could only serve Him and the cause of righteousness by the "diabolical" means of war. Along with the growth of this belief, but independent of it, came his gradual acceptance of the socialist charge that the war was imperialist on both sides and that the Allied side held no overwhelming margin of virtue. One book which strongly impressed him along this line was H. N. Brailsford's *War of Steel and Gold*.

During this same period, Norman was also moving closer to accepting the Socialist critique of capitalism in general. The development of his thinking was based not so much upon reading Socialist literature or hearing Socialist speakers but mainly because life itself was continuously confronting him with examples of grotesque inequalities, conspicuous waste, gross exploitation and unnecessary poverty.

Insofar as any one man influenced Norman towards socialism, it was Dr. Walter Rauschenbusch, a Christian Socialist minister. Norman had only a slight personal acquaintance with him, but was much moved, emotionally and intellectually, by Rauschenbusch's books, *Christianity and the Social Crisis* and *Christianizing the Social Order*. Thomas was also deeply indebted in the years when he worked at the American Parish to Rauschenbusch's *Prayers of the Social Awakening*. He read the above books at a time when pressure of administrative and pastoral work left him very little leisure for reading, which, added to the excellence of the books, made them influential in his thinking. Yet, while books and men contributed to his education, the process by which Thomas was led to the Socialist Party was long and slow and the major influence was his painful reflection on the origin and nature of World War I.

Living in New York, Thomas was familiar with what Socialists were doing and thinking. He read, and was favorably impressed by, Morris Hillquit's debate with Monsignor John A. Ryan. But he had never voted for Eugene V. Debs for president, although he had split his ticket and voted for some Socialist candidates whom he considered the best choices for their particular posts. He knew comparatively little about the Socialist movement, and had not lived in any districts where the Socialists were strong. He went to a few Socialist meetings but they didn't appeal to him, with one exception—the time he heard Keir Hardie, the founder of the British Labor Party. Thomas liked the old Scot very much, but not enough to become a Socialist.

In 1916, his brother Evan was in Britain with the Young Men's Christian Association, visiting German prisoner-of-war camps. Viewing from afar Wilson's pledge that he "kept us out of war," Evan wrote Norman in June:

"Every day I hope more than ever for Wilson's re-election. He is hated here by the majority, though not by all by any means. He is accused of all sorts of weakness and duplicity; but in my mind he is the greatest man in public life in the world, and the greatest president America has had since Lincoln."

Norman was by no means so enthusiastic about Wilson. Nevertheless, with some doubts, he voted for Wilson in 1916 as a little more likely than Charles Evans Hughes to keep us out of war. By the end of the year he had joined the Fellowship of Reconciliation, a Christian pacifist group. "I was a long while coming to it," Norman wrote a college friend, Howard A. Walter, "but finally became convinced that as far as I could see, war and Christianity are incompatible; that you cannot conquer war by war; cast out Satan by Satan; or do the enormous evil of war that good may come. It seems to me that the validity of Christ's method of dealing with life's problems almost stands or falls with this test and that if we would honestly try His way God would guide us to unimagined solutions of our problems."

Thomas also joined the American Union Against Militarism and was added to its executive committee several months before America entered the war. Lillian Wald, head of Henry Street Settlement House, and the organizer of home nursing in America, served as chairman, while Crystal Eastman, Max's sister, was the executive secretary.

The Union was an able and powerful group of men and women which had already stirred up opposition to the policy of both Taft and Wilson of sending American marines to serve as "bill-collectors" for private American companies in Latin America.

Thomas was proud to work in the Union with such outstanding

people as Jane Addams of Hull House, Rabbi Stephen S. Wise of the Free Synagogue, youthful Rabbi Judah L. Magnes of New York's fashionable Temple Emanu-El (who later became chancellor of the Hebrew University of Jerusalem), Max Eastman (then a left-wing Socialist), Quaker Hollingsworth Wood, and Roger N. Baldwin, then a social worker. With a curious mixture of reluctance and elation, Norman did considerable speaking for the Union in and around New York and some lobbying in Washington.

Even in those early days, Thomas was a passionate speaker whose intense convictions drew forth strong responses from his audiences. After a talk in February 1917 at Wesleyan University's Y.M.C.A., its president, Stevens, who had been in the U. S. Army for six years, was much impressed by Norman's remarks. At a meeting the next day of the entire college, where officials praised Stevens as an officer of the army who had consented to drill the students and give blackboard talks, Stevens upset the meeting by saying, "Fellows, after last night's Y.M.C.A. talk, I am an out-and-out pacifist and I can't take this job."

"During World War I," wrote publisher Henry C. Alsberg to Thomas many years later, "I have a very vivid recollection of you talking from the tail of an auto, at the corner of 96th Street and Broadway, against our entry into the war. And when somebody asked you whether you would buy Liberty Bonds, instead of dodging, as some very courageous radicals and anti-war people did, among them Morris Hillquit, you frankly said you wouldn't. The crowd was composed of run-of-the-mill people, among them some newly-drafted doughboys. At first they were hostile, but your calm reasonableness and utter frankness had them eating out of your oratorical hand in the shake of a lamb's tail."

Sidney Lovett was present at a debate where Thomas first seemed to realize his extraordinary power to rouse and sway people, and to feel that perhaps he had a wider mission than directing the American Parish. Thomas had conducted his regular Sunday service and then rushed to a public school to debate a well-known speaker; the subject was whether or not the United States should enter World War I. He arrived when his opponent, who wore a dinner jacket, was concluding with a few remarks.

Thomas, Lovett noted, picked up those remarks and slew the speaker with his own words. When the debate was over, many people, including old Italian immigrant mothers who could hardly understand a word Thomas said, swarmed around to shake his hand.

Thomas spoke at many street corner meetings against preparedness, often picking corners across the street from rallies supporting preparedness. It was the custom for street meetings to end at ten o'clock at night. One evening, the pro-war rally had lost almost all its listeners to Thomas, who argued that the end did not justify the means—that preparing for war brought war and that only the organizing of good will could bring about peace. Lovett recalls that a war supporter went to the policeman on the corner and insisted, "It's ten o'clock and you have to stop that man Thomas' meeting." Replied the policeman, "Not on your life. I'm not going to stop him. He's talking sense."

Soon after America declared war, the American Union Against Militarism faded away. First, however, one of its sub-committees, under the inspiration of Roger Baldwin and with Hollingsworth Wood and Thomas as members, set up the National Civil Liberties Bureau, which in 1920 became the American Civil Liberties Union.

Thomas was not then aware of how drastically the war would change his work and life. Whether, if war had not intervened, he would have become a Socialist or left the work of the church is a moot question. Yet, in later years, Norman thought that the daily confrontation with slum poverty, exploitation, inequality and waste would eventually have brought him to non-Marxian socialism as a more logical and adequate answer than any brand of progressivism. As for the church, it was the war which caused his thinking to go far beyond the bonds of conformity to a well-intentioned but conventional creed. He was forced to face basic questions which he could not put off, consciously or unconsciously, by pleading the importance of the engrossing but routine job he had in hand.

During the first months of 1917, while he maintained his parish activities, his heart was in the struggle to keep America out of the war (he always felt that that imperialist war might better have

59

been settled by a negotiated peace right after the first battle of the Marne in 1914 rather than by the vindictive Versailles Treaty); after America declared war on April sixth, Thomas' aim was to protect civil liberties, including the rights of conscientious objectors, and to work for an early and enduring peace.

Not only war but the tragic contrasts of contemporary civilization horrified Thomas. In a William Penn Lecture on "The Christian Patriot" in Philadelphia a month after America entered the war, Thomas challenged the argument that America was in a war to make the world safe for democracy, and noted that no referendum of the people preceded our entrance into war and adoption of conscription. Moreover, he said, no adequate exemption existed for conscientious objectors, an espionage bill had been introduced which would deny absolutely fundamental rights of information and discussion, and a determined effort was being waged in various states to break down all the laws safeguarding conditions of labor.

Calling the religion of Jesus "profoundly revolutionary," Thomas urged his listeners to struggle for peace and freedom as devotion to God's cause.

Most of his friends and classmates disagreed heartily with his viewpoint and the arguments waxed hot and heavy. When Alfred Carton wrote Thomas that "I'm for my country right or wrong and am ready and willing to do anything my chosen representatives may legally require" and added, "if I were a German, I should feel the same way about the German government," this did not much concern Thomas. But he was deeply grieved when an old pacifist friend, Ralph Harlow, wrote, "Sad as it makes me feel, I must make confession that I have come to feel that rather than let Germany have her way, rather than let the Turk hold sway over helpless women and children, it is better to go forth to war."

"Do you think," Norman retorted, "Americans in general with their shameful record for race riots are purely disinterested redressers of the crimes to Belgium and Armenia? Do you find now that we are in war that there is a real passion for conquering imperialistic tendencies and the exploitation of the weak anywhere else except within the territory of the German power? . . . Your position may be the only practical one but what have you to say for a religion which leaves its followers with only a choice between evils? Does it sound like the faith that will overcome the world?"

Meanwhile, at the Socialist Party national convention in St. Louis, the delegates voted overwhelmingly for a militant anti-war resolution written by Morris Hillquit and C. E. Ruthenberg. It condemned the war as one neither to destroy militarism nor to promote democracy, on the grounds that neither aim could be achieved by force of arms.

When Hillquit, the author of this resolution, ran for Mayor of New York in 1917 on the Socialist ticket and an anti-war platform, Thomas decided it was time for him to help. Hillquit, who had come to this country from Russia at the age of sixteen, was a brilliant lawyer who had been active in organizing the needle trades workers on the East Side. He was the most prominent American Socialist theoretician and espoused a municipal program which among other things called for public housing projects, something badly needed in Thomas' parish.

"The hope for the future," Thomas wrote to Hillquit in offering his support, "lies in a new social and economic order which demands the abolition of the capitalistic system. War itself is only the most horrible and dramatic of the many evil fruits of our present organized system of exploitation and the philosophy of life which exalts competition instead of cooperation . . . I am especially concerned because in this war for democracy, autocracy is growing so fast. I do not believe that democracy is a garment that can be taken off and put in moth balls for future use or that you can secure democratic ends by Prussian methods of which the latest example is the legislation which makes the Postmaster General judge of what the American people shall read. A vote for you is to protest against this sort of tyranny."

To his surprise and delight, Thomas was invited to join a committee for independents for Hillquit. The committee included Dudley Field Malone, a Tammany sachem; another clergyman, Allen McCurdy (a good friend of Thomas'); Rabbi Judah L. Magnes; J. A. H. Hopkins; and Amos Pinchot, who was then radically inclined. Thomas took a very active part in the campaign, speaking night after night about bread, peace and freedom at a time when the war fever was at its frenzied height. He was not arrested, but soon became accustomed to police inquiries and the hostile presence of representatives of the law, in and out of uniform, at meetings. Some meetings were broken up. Several of the independents, including Thomas, spoke to an enormous audience at Madison Square Garden. There were no loud speakers then, and to speak to so large an audience meant a good deal of voice strain. But Thomas enjoyed the campaign and became personally friendly with Hillquit.

When his mother became fearful that his support of Hillquit would hinder his church work, Thomas replied:

"As for the church, I believe I am doing her the highest service by proving or trying to prove that she is catholic enough to make room for social radicals. The strife between radicalism and conservatism is the battle of the future. . . . For myself I believe that the Christian ethics are impossible in the present order of society and that every Christian must desire a new social order based on cooperation rather than competition. . . . This is the hope of the Socialist Party. I will grant that it is far from perfect . . . it has more idealism though than any party I know of.

"Whether the church will tolerate me or not is for it to say. I hope it will. If it does not it will injure herself far more than it will injure me and I say this without conceit because her attitude toward me will be symbolic of her outlook for the future. I am perfectly aware that the stand I am taking is costing me many friendships; every possible chance of getting another church if I should leave here; and perhaps, though I think not, my present position. I can only say that if it costs me more than I fear, it is to my mind the only way for I could not maintain my self-respect and do differently nor could I serve the Kingdom of God as effectively."

On Election Day, the Tammany candidate, John F. Hylan, won easily. But Hillquit received the largest vote any Socialist candidate for that office had polled before, and ran only a few thousand votes behind John P. Mitchel, the Fusion candidate. With 145,332 votes, he ran nearly a hundred thousand votes ahead of the regular Republican candidate, William F. Bennett. In addition,

18 Socialists were elected: seven city aldermen, ten state assembly-men and a municipal judge.

This remarkable vote was won despite powerful opposition to Hillquit. Teddy Roosevelt campaigned against him as a "Hun . . . inside our gates." Charles Evans Hughes called Hillquit "un-patriotic" and "treasonable." Even the famed liberal lawyer, Clar-ence Darrow, upon the advice of President Wilson, campaigned against the Socialist candidate.

By the end of 1917, Thomas had become a part-time secretary of the Fellowship of Reconciliation (F.O.R.) and also editor of *The World Tomorrow*, a pacifist magazine whose first issue appeared in January 1918. And early in 1918, Thomas resigned from his parish to work full-time for the F.O.R.

There have been many published reports that Thomas was forced out of his church, but that was not quite what happened. A more subtle process took place. The work of the parish was supported very substantially by the Home Missions Committee of the New York Presbytery, and Thomas raised considerable other sums himself. These were the funds that were threatened by Nor-man's stand, not only on the war but on socialism.

The man who had been his chief backer, Dr. William Adams Brown, chairman of the Home Missions Committee and a former teacher of Norman's at Union Seminary, sent for Thomas when he announced that he would support Hillquit for mayor. "Now you know," said Brown, "I'm not going to interfere with free speech, but do you have to do this? Sometimes the way to keep free speech is not to use it. It's bad enough for you to be a pacifist, but now you're going to speak for that Socialist, Hillquit. Do you think that's fair to the church?" When Thomas answered, "Yes, I think it's fair. And, what's more, it's no good having free speech unless you use it in this manner," Brown told him how difficult his stand was making the financial situation for the Parish, that money was falling off because Thomas was "contaminating" the people of his parish in the eyes of potential contributors, and hinted at, without actually demanding, Norman's resignation.

Thomas was aware that many contributors did feel that way.

One patriotic merchant who formerly contributed many dolls and toys wrote Norman that he would give none for the children on this Christmas of 1917, not with an anti-patriot like Thomas in the parish. If the parish had been self-supporting, Thomas would not have resigned voluntarily, nor, in his opinion, would the church have demanded it. Indeed, many of his parishioners were friendly to his views. But the pressure of respectable church folk with money made it obvious that social work for the poor people in the parish would suffer. Therefore, a few weeks after the mayoralty election, Thomas told Dr. Brown—to the latter's delight—that he would resign.

Dr. Brown and the committee then overlooked the danger of Norman's "contaminating" the poor and begged him to stay on until April 15, 1918, when a successor could replace him. Norman's sense of humor once more came to his aid. In a letter to the Rev. William P. Shriver, secretary of the Home Missions Committee, he noted:

"While I am glad to do what I can to help the work in the Parish that I love, your own understanding of the situation will make it clear that I cannot possibly become a sort of unsalaried secret director of things here. To do so is not fair to my own work or to my successor. I do not suppose that that is contemplated but there is always a danger. . . . I confess to finding a certain amusement in the situation. It looks as if several members of the Committee care more for appearances than realities. They are highly relieved that I am not to be publicly connected with the work yet willing to have my advice, counsel and companionship on the committee in charge."

A curious footnote occurred twenty years later, when Thomas again met Dr. Brown. In the course of conversation, Dr. Brown said, "Oh Norman, Norman, why did you ever leave?" Apparently he had forgotten his role in seeking Norman's resignation. Thomas did not remind him.

FIVE

Safe for Democracy?

ᴥ§ FEELING THAT SURGERY was the best solution, Thomas cut off many of his former activities, to the great relief of all concerned. He resigned as a member of the graduate governing board of Princeton's Philadelphian Society, as secretary of the local school board, and as the instructor in a course on immigration which he had started at Columbia University's Teacher's College.

This gave Thomas more time and freedom to work at his new causes, but the breaking of old ties and friendships caused him considerable emotional shock and strain as the direction of his whole life underwent a drastic change. For, while his conversion to pacifism and socialism was not the result of any sudden "vision on the Road to Damascus," but rather the result of a long and gradual process of reevaluating his basic assumptions, the completion of the process brought an abrupt end to his old way of life. What lessened the strain was the closeness of new friendships with fellow non-conformists, and the confident hope that mankind would inevitably emerge from war's darkness into a better world. Above all, there was the love and loyalty of Violet, who helped soften for Norman the transition from a conventionally respectable life to one where he was regarded by a large segment of society as subversive and a potential criminal.

Actually, it was Violet who bore the greater burden of the change. Accustomed to the easy and full social life of a popular minister's wife, she was subjected to snubs and ostracism by former friends. She turned inward, involved herself more and more with Norman's work and the children. Norman's conversion to pacifism and socialism met with the stern disapproval of Violet's conserva-

tive grandfather, and there were rumors—later proved unfounded
—that she might be written out of his will.

At the Fellowship of Reconciliation Thomas doubled in brass
as F.O.R. executive secretary and editor of *The World Tomorrow*.
His associates were warmed by his radiant Christian faith—every
Friday afternoon the staff and volunteers would troop over to the
Thomas home on 17th Street for a prayer session followed by
tea—and by his fantastic capacity for work. When new books
on economic, social, political and theological subjects arrived,
Thomas would grab them, read each in about an hour and then
rapidly dictate reviews. On some occasions, he would answer
telephone calls and dictate to his secretary at the same time.

Clemenceau once said, "He who is not a Socialist by the age of
twenty-one has no heart; but if he is a Socialist after thirty he has
no head." Norman Thomas was the living refutation of Clemenceau's epigram. He did not become a Socialist until the mature
age of thirty-three, a happy husband and father of five children.
And even his worst enemies have been forced to concede both
his brilliance and great love of humanity.

During the Hillquit mayoralty campaign, Thomas had not yet
been ready to join the Socialist Party. For that matter, the Party
preferred to have him as an "independent" at the time. But in
October, 1918, he wrote to the party office to apply for membership, because "I think these are days when radicals ought to stand
up and be counted." Apparently his suspicion of orthodoxy in
theology pertained to socialism too, for he wrote:

"Perhaps to certain members of the party my socialism would
not be of the most orthodox variety. As you know, I have a profound fear of the undue exaltation of the State and a profound
faith that the new world we desire must depend upon freedom and
fellowship rather than upon any sort of coercion whatsoever. I
am interested in political parties only to the extent in which they
may be serviceable in advancing certain ideals and in winning
liberty for men and women. My accepting of the socialist platform
is on the basis of general principles rather than of details. If I were
a farmer and lived in certain states of the middle west, it is quite
likely that I should be a member of the Nonpartisan League and
I regret that provision of the party constitution which would

automatically expel me. Though I am a staunch pacifist, I should not have voted for the preamble of the St. Louis platform . . . If this statement is satisfactory I shall look forward to the fellowship of the party as a real privilege."

Even before he joined the Party, Thomas was doing an increasing amount of speaking for the Fellowship of Reconciliation, the American Union Against Militarism and its Civil Liberties Bureau, the Socialist Party and the new People's Council of America for Democracy and Peace. Life became very exciting. Government agents swarmed at these meetings, haunted Norman's office at the F.O.R., and tapped his telephone line. They were, he insists, less intelligent and far less courteous than J. Edgar Hoover's current F.B.I. men. What is more, they were at least partly responsible for Thomas' bad habit of speaking very rapidly, since he found out that they could never make an intelligible record of a speech delivered at some speed.

It is difficult for Americans today to reconstruct the atmosphere of those times. The Espionage Act granted the federal government the power to censor newspapers and ban them from the mails; obstructing the draft or enlistments, or attempting to do so, was made punishable by fine up to $10,000 and twenty years' imprisonment. To this must be added hysterical mob action and violations of civil liberties by city and state governments. The kind of mentality that renamed sauerkraut "liberty cabbage," that sang a song called "I'd Like to See the Kaiser with a Lily in His Hand," that deleted the study of the German language from school curriculums, resulted in a very dangerous environment for both Socialists and pacifists.

Postmaster General Albert S. Burleson used the Espionage Act to revoke the second-class mailing privileges of many Socialist papers and went so far as to refuse to deliver even first-class mail to the Socialist daily, the *Milwaukee Leader*. President Woodrow Wilson strongly supported Burleson's censorship, describing the latter as "inclined to be most conservative in the exercise of these great and dangerous powers." For three months straight, in the summer of 1918, the Post Office Department excluded *The World Tomorrow* from the mails for absurd reasons. Twice Thomas succeeded in inducing the Department to lift its ban. But the third issue, according to Solicitor-General William H. Lamar, a slow-spoken Southern politico, was too extreme to be tolerated. Various government agents had complained about an article called "The Search—a Parable" by John Haynes Holmes. In it, Holmes sought for Hate but did not find it in the trenches, or in the military hospitals, or at army headquarters, but at a well-appointed table where were seated "an old, old man, a childless matron, and a curate." The argument that Hate dwells chiefly among noncombatants was considered subversive. Even worse, said Lamar, was Thomas' article, "The Acid Test of Our Democracy," which protested American military intervention against Soviet Russia in Archangel and in Siberia. (While the article contained some illusions about the Bolshevik revolution—"She [Russia] is striving to secure economic democracy as a basis for the development of mankind"—Thomas was nevertheless foresighted enough to write in September, 1918: "The glorious end of the abolition of class privilege and the establishment of a fellowship of free men does not justify—indeed it cannot be secured by—a proletarian dictatorship which denies suffrage and freedom of discussion to a middle class minority . . . If, for example, *The World Tomorrow* were published in Russia it might be suppressed . . . Even if in prison, we should doubt the power of foreign intervention to correct the mistakes of the Bolsheviki just as we should doubt the power of foreign intervention to right some of the terrible social injustices of America.")

Lamar told Thomas and Nevin Sayre, secretary of the Fellowship Press, which published *The World Tomorrow*, that as far as he was concerned, the magazine should remain banned. But he suggested that they visit Burleson, the Postmaster General. As already mentioned at the beginning of this book, Burleson expressed considerable resentment against both Thomas and *The World Tomorrow*. He finally offered to drop proceedings against the current issue of the magazine if Thomas would promise to "behave" in the future. Thomas, of course, indignantly rejected the suggestion, whereupon Burleson said, "Good day, gentlemen," and turned to the papers on his desk.

Disconsolately, Thomas and Sayre tried to decide what to do

next. They had spent the whole day in Washington with no success. Nevin Sayre was, however, the brother-in-law of President Wilson's youngest daughter, and had been entertaining her and her children at Martha's Vineyard, Mass. Thomas urged Sayre to try to see the President. With a good deal of foreboding, since Wilson was reputedly not easy to talk to, Nevin agreed.

Luck was with him. When he went to the White House at 6 p.m. and told the guard he would like to see President Wilson, the President not only received him but also asked him to stay for supper and give him news of his daughter and grandchildren. After supper and the family briefing was through, the President asked, "What brings you on this hot summer day to Washington?" Sayre told Wilson of his connection with *The World Tomorrow* and of its troubles. The President listened silently until Sayre was finished, and then said, "Let me see it," whereupon he looked over the articles. Then he told Sayre, "Well, I don't think this is seditious and I'll tell the Post Office and Justice departments so, and say that Thomas shouldn't be sent to jail. But you go and tell Norman Thomas that an English historian once said, 'There is such a thing as an indecent display of private opinions in public'!" The next day, Wilson told Burleson to release not only *The World Tomorrow* but also *The Nation*, which Burleson had banned for an article criticizing Samuel Gompers, president of the American Federation of Labor.

Thomas' own closest call came when police under the leadership of a so-called patriot, Archibald Stevenson, a dollar-a-year man for the Department of Justice, raided the offices of the Civil Liberties Bureau and confiscated all its papers. Roger Baldwin phoned John Haynes Holmes at his summer home in Maine to come to town because word had been received that the Attorney General was preparing indictments against the officers of the Bureau. Roger wired Norman, who was in Kansas with his mother, and they agreed to get George Gordon Battle, an outstanding lawyer who was also prominent in Tammany, to handle the Civil Liberties Bureau case.

The story of how the Bureau was saved had its humorous, as well as serious, side. Thomas, at the request of his associates in the Bureau, went to Washington to see Assistant Attorney General Alfred Bettman. "I can't see," said Thomas, "what protection civil liberties will have in America if the Civil Liberties Bureau itself is to be prosecuted." "It's not my business," said the Assistant Attorney General, "to discuss that. But, Mr. Thomas, I think you and your colleagues are pretty safe. You can go back and tell your friends that. And I'll tell you why. We haven't had very good luck prosecuting the editors of *The Masses*. They were acquitted. And when we prosecuted Scott Nearing and the Rand School, for publishing his book, the jury acquitted Scott and convicted the Rand School. Scott would have had to go to prison —all the Rand School got was a small fine. What we've found out is this: in New York City it's very hard to convict any of you folks who can make a good speech to the jury. And you've got John Haynes Holmes and Roger Baldwin and yourself—there would be too many speeches. We're not taking the chance."

Roger Baldwin, who ran the Civil Liberties Bureau, was a conscientious objector, and when his number came up in the draft he refused service and was sentenced. For a long time the government kept him at the Tombs and out of the Federal penitentiary because Archibald Stevenson and his dollar-a-year amateurs had hopelessly mixed up the Bureau's files, and Baldwin was needed to straighten them out. Roger became very popular with the Tombs jailers. At Christmas they sent him a carton of cigarettes inscribed "to the only criminal we ever loved." He was allowed to phone Thomas and others from the Tombs and once was allowed to see the recording of his phone conversations. It contained marginal notes: "We think they said this on purpose. We think they knew the lines were tapped." They were right. Thomas and Baldwin both assumed the lines were tapped.

Finally Roger got the files in order and had to begin to serve his prison term in Newark, where the warden was a good Irishman. The F.B.I.'s chief detective asked Roger if he would like to see some friends before going to the Newark jail. The answer was yes, and it came about that Violet and Norman invited Roger and the F.B.I. man to lunch with the two Thomas boys, Norman, Jr. (Tommy) and Bill. The two boys were entranced to see their friend Roger and this very amiable policeman, who pleased them by throwing back his coat and showing them how many kinds of weapons he was carrying in various holsters and in various places of concealment. It was an extremely successful lunch.

When the detective left, he shook hands with Violet, thanked her for a fine lunch and pleasant visit, and said: "If I can ever do anything for you, just let me know." Said Violet to Norman: "I feel the same as if he had been an undertaker, considering the kind of business he is in."

In other parts of the nation, convicting Socialist orators and writers was much easier than in New York. The most important case of all dealt with the speech Eugene V. Debs, famous Socialist leader, gave before the Ohio State Convention of the Socialist Party at Canton in June, 1918. Debs had repeated the speech on numerous occasions, but that afternoon in Canton the air was electric with tension. The U.S. Attorney for northern Ohio, E. S. Wertz, had stenographers taking down in shorthand Deb's charge that: "The master class has always declared the war; the subject class has always fought the battles. The master class has had all to gain and nothing to lose, while the subject class has had nothing to gain and all to lose—especially their lives." Debs was tried, found guilty of violating the Espionage and Sedition Act and sentenced to ten years' imprisonment.

When Wilson first heard that Debs was arrested, he said, according to Claude Bowers, "I never meant *my* law to be used like that." (Wilson himself had proposed the Espionage Act.) But the next day a great many irate telegrams and letters of protest poured in to the White House. Wilson then hardened his heart and resolved that Debs must serve his full term.

While Thomas escaped indictment or jail for his activities in the Civil Liberties Bureau and *The World Tomorrow,* he found life very hectic indeed. For one thing, his family was sorely divided on the war. His brothers Ralph and Arthur went into the army while Evan, who had praised the "anti-war" Wilson as "the greatest president America has had since Lincoln," became a conscientious objector. In March, 1918, Ralph wrote Norman from Camp Upton: "We'll soon be off and this is my last message in this country. There's a general feeling of relief and almost a gala atmosphere . . . I am sorry we don't agree on this, the biggest

71

affair of our lives, but you know I respect your courage of conviction and idealism . . ."

Evan Thomas had hated war since childhood. He disliked war books and could not understand why some people thought Napoleon a great man. The deceit of war repelled him even more than the killing and the thought of being completely under orders in the armed services he found intolerable. He had come to this decision while in Britain visiting German prison camps, and gave up his work there to return in the fall of 1917. He made his home with Norman and Violet. He registered in New York and was called to Camp Upton by the draft in the spring, where he refused military service.

A letter to President Wilson from Emma Thomas in October, 1918, illustrates some facets of her heartbreaking dilemma:

"Dear Mr. President:
"My only excuse for troubling you with this letter is my profound faith that amid all your perplexing world problems, you constantly have at heart the welfare of even individuals in your own country.
"During the years from 1902 to 1915, four *tall* Thomas boys [Emma Thomas always liked to say she had 25 feet of boys] took their academic courses at Princeton University. I am the widowed mother of those boys. Judging by their admiration for you and their quotations from your teachings and writings, your influence over them was as strong as that of any teacher in their lives—yet in this time of decision for thinking men, two of them have taken the line of war service for their country and two have felt that so inherently evil a thing as war is not the Christian method of bringing righteousness, and that conscription of men's lives by the State is a thing to be opposed even to the extent of refusing to serve under military orders . . .
"When he (Evan) refused to fight I hoped he would accept substitute farm work, but he refused because always when offered it, he was assured that he would still be in the army ranks working under military orders and could be sent anywhere.
"At the Upton barracks he worked and induced others to work at cleaning and caring for their quarters and when in July they were taken to Fort Leavenworth for examination by the Board of Inquiry, Evan helped the officers by making lists and schedules of work for the C.O.'s who were willing to work at preparing food—building their mess hall, etc., and himself worked with the plumber . . . Suddenly they were taken to Fort Riley and

ordered to begin work there. Again Evan tried to help, but new officers were giving orders and meting out punishment as to regular soldiers . . . Discontent and confusion brought revolt and they were sent to an open field, given supplies and told to care for themselves. . . .

"August was a hot month of discomfort for them all in the open field tent colony . . . and there was a so-called hunger strike . . . When I heard Evan was in that strike I hurried to him and stayed near him and some twelve of his companion C.O.'s for ten days . . . My ten days' study of that group of C.O.'s convinced me that each one was well worth saving to the State . . . (they) had never used their influence against the draft except by their example. . . .

"Soon after I left Fort Riley, the men were returned to their tents, and Evan reported better conditions, but two weeks ago I ceased hearing from him and was informed by relatives of other men that he was put in a solitary cell in the guard house and later about fifty of the C.O.'s were confined also—one or two in solitary cells . . .

"In my woman's way and from a mother's heart, I wonder why these extremists might not be interned in a civilian camp officered by themselves or by civilians—or be allowed to choose their own 'essential work' under government observation . . . I would plead for some definite mode of treatment, and if it must be imprisonment that it be given in as merciful a way as possible, not with the solitary cell and loss of communication by letter with outside friends."

Earlier, in August, Norman Thomas accompanied his mother to Fort Riley, and wrote Roger Baldwin his reaction to the hunger strike:

"We found Evan in the base hospital where he was taken Tuesday . . . At first Capt. Henry, medical officer at the hospital to whom Evan was turned over, cursed him forward and backward and up and down—said he'd land him in a strait jacket. As a beginning at 11 p.m. he ordered Evan roused and scrubbed by orderlies with the stiffest brushes of the kitchen variety they could find. This over, Evan settled down at 12 (midnight), the Captain ordered him forcibly fed, whereupon Evan apologized for the trouble he was causing! . . . Captain Henry is now friendly and decent to him . . .

"I still by no means agree that Evan hit upon the right method but there is something (to his fond brother at least) quite mag-

73

nificent about his spirit, his calm, his interest in affairs, and the friendship he has won from men who on principle abhor what he's doing. . . ."

While Evan was hunger striking, word came that Ralph had been very badly wounded—the first dispatch indicated almost fatally—over in France. Arthur, the youngest brother, saw his best friend killed in air training in Texas and Norman was expecting to be arrested for his part in *The World Tomorrow*. It was a worrisome time, particularly for his mother. Soon however, Ralph wrote that his wounds were less serious than originally feared and that he was convalescing happily in beautiful Paris. In a letter to his mother sent Nov. 6, 1918, Ralph wrote:

"I feel ashamed of myself to be having a good time in Paris and classed as a young tin hero because through no fault of mine a boche shell dropped beside me. Much as I may disagree with him, I must say Evan has what in college we called guts."

Some weeks after the hunger strike ended, Evan was sent to Camp Funston and court-martialed on the charge of violating an Article of War, in that he refused to obey the order of an officer to eat, thereby rendering himself unfit to serve as a soldier! He was found guilty and sentenced to life imprisonment. Major General Leonard Wood "in his mercy," as Norman put it, reduced the sentence to twenty-five years.

Evan was sent to Fort Leavenworth early in October and at first went to work there. Soon however he found that a group of Molokans, a Russian pacifist sect which had migrated here during President Grant's administration on the assurance that the United States never conscripted people, had been sent to Fort Leavenworth. They refused to work under military orders, considering this a violation of their religion. They were confined in solitary cells, manacled nine hours a day, and abused by the guards. They had no influential friends to plead their cause or communicate with the outside world.

Evan, outraged at the treatment of the Molokans, refused to work any longer, in order to bring the barbarism of the prison system to the attention of the outside world. He, and several others who soon joined him, were put in solitary confinement from November 2nd until the end of December, long after the

Armistice was signed.

A prisoner who continued to work "undergrounded" a letter from Evan to Norman, so that weeks after World War I ended, the American people learned that men whose only offense was loyalty to conscience were confined in dark cells day and night, forbidden to read, write or talk. They were fed on bread and water every alternate two weeks, manacled nine hours a day, in standing posture, to the bars of the cell, and compelled to sleep on the cement floor.

Norman's mother went to see Secretary of War, Newton Baker, about this treatment of the C.O.'s. He told her it simply wasn't true.

SIX

Civil Liberties
Under Fire

✑ THOMAS FOUND IT DIFFICULT to understand why Wilson acted as he did on civil liberties, especially after he announced his Fourteen Points as America's war aims. Socialists everywhere hailed the Fourteen Points. Debs, for instance, wrote that they were "thoroughly democratic and deserve the unqualified approval of everyone believing in the rule of the people, socialists included."

German onslaughts against Russia after the revolution, plus the Wilson peace program, modified Socialist views on the war. The New York Socialist aldermen, elected in 1917 on an antiwar platform, supported the third Liberty Loan drive in April, 1918. Socialist Congressman Meyer London spoke at war-bond rallies in New York. In a letter to Lillian Wald on March 1, 1918, Thomas, who then had not joined the Socialist Party, wrote:

"Frankly my own feeling with regard to the war is undergoing something of a change. On religious grounds I am still obliged to think that war is a hideously unsatisfactory method of righteousness but the Russian situation and the progressive abandonment of imperialistic aims by the Allies under pressure from the President and British Labor remove the reproach of hypocrisy from us. Meanwhile the German people seem to be more completely under the dominance of their cynical Junker class than I had thought. Things change so fast that one is at a loss what to think. I wish Mr. Wilson could have taken the liberal stand he now has last summer."

Thomas was on a committee which met with the President's adviser, Colonel House, and Thomas warned that the President was piling up difficulties for himself by putting left wing and pacifist critics in jail while allowing reactionary Republicans to flourish openly. All Colonel House replied was, "Trust the President. He'll win." When the committee asked House about the secret treaties (which Oswald Garrison Villard had published in the *New York Evening Post*), they received the same sort of answer—although Wilson was later to deny that he knew about them. And when the Republicans won a majority in both houses of Congress just a few days before the Armistice was signed, it seemed to Thomas proof of the validity of his warnings to Colonel House.

While Armistice Day brought Thomas exultant joy over the end of bloodshed, and the expectation that war repressions would cease, he still feared the growth of reaction. In an editorial in the December 1918 issue of *The World Tomorrow*, he asked:

"If Mr. Wilson had not deliberately approved the legalized tyranny of the Espionage Act, and the autocratic and reckless administration of that Act by the Post Office Department and the Department of Justice, would he have found himself at election time lacking the support of radical opinion, which he so sorely needed to counterbalance the virulent reactionary criticism which could not be suppressed because it came from quarters too powerful for Mr. Postmaster Burleson and Mr. Attorney General Gregory to attack?

"If Mr. Wilson's liberal friends had been able to see that sometimes you can better support a man by being ahead of him than being behind him, might not he and they now both be in an infinitely stronger position to fight for the principles he has at various times so nobly enunciated?"

Thomas optimistically had assumed that despite its record of war hate and hysteria, the church would swing to support of humane policies with the war's end. He was cruelly disillusioned. Much to his surprise, sorrow and shame, he got no help from the Federal Council of Churches to his plea that it call for an end to the shocking mistreatment of conscientious objectors at Fort

Leavenworth, if not for their release. He scarcely got an audience for his recital of grossly cruel disciplinary practices.

Perhaps Thomas was naive to be surprised. After all, a questionnaire sent to progressive churchmen in the early months of the war had brought back such replies as, "The real conscientious objector is unbalanced. True Christian churchmen are dying for Christ" and "Strike till the last armed foe expires." Many C.O.'s reported that their most bitter and intolerant enemies in the army were chaplains and Y.M.C.A. secretaries. When Evan Thomas was hunger striking at Fort Riley, the post chaplain told him that Wilson, Lansing, Pershing, and Joffre were Presbyterians whom the Lord was using as once he used Moses and Aaron. One Y.M.C.A. physical director, A. E. Marriott of Camp Sevier, wrote a manual entitled "Hand-to-Hand Fighting." The author listed the chief points of attack with appropriate comment. Thus: "Eyes. Never miss an opportunity to destroy the eyes of the enemy. In all head holds, use the fingers on the eyes. They are the most delicate points in the body and easy to reach. The eye can easily be removed with the finger."

Rebuffed continually when he tried to protest the treatment of C.O.'s, Thomas finally approached Don Seitz, general manager of *The New York World*, whose family had been Mennonites. Norman convinced him that something was wrong, and Seitz sent one of his best reporters to Leavenworth. The reporter verified what Thomas had charged and wrote a series of articles attacking the practice of manacling. Once again, Nevin Sayre went to see President Wilson—this time to appeal to him for abandonment of this brutal practice. Wilson, about to leave the next day for peace treaty negotiations in France, was in high good spirits. "They needed us to win the war," exulted the President, "and we'll bring back a good peace treaty." As to Sayre's immediate request, Wilson expressed shock and surprise that such conditions existed and immediately ordered Secretary of War Baker to eliminate the practice.

Moreover, within a few weeks, the government set up a Board of Inquiry at Fort Leavenworth, as a result of which one hundred thirteen C.O.'s, who would have been willing to do farm work if furloughed, were released on January 27, 1919, on the ground that their sentences were contrary to the War Department's instructions. In addition, the War Department soon found other grounds for setting aside or shortening sentences. Among those discharged was Norman's brother, Evan.

But the release of some of the C.O.'s did not mean a complete return of sanity in the nation. As a matter of fact, the end of the war intensified anti-radical hysteria. In March, 1919, A. Mitchell Palmer became U.S. Attorney General. Palmer, a Quaker, who had refused appointment as Secretary of War, proved to be much worse than his predecessor in his assault on civil liberties. After a bomb exploded, blowing off a part of a porch of his house, he went wild, and rounded up scores of alien radicals. (When their sentences were completed, they were deported on the *Buford* in December, 1919. So many leftists were on the ship that it was dubbed by the press the "Soviet Ark.")

On May 1, 1919, when the Socialist daily, *The New York Call*, held a house warming in its new building at 112 Fourth Avenue, the tone of the speeches, the jubilation of the people, the offerings of flowers and cake reminded Thomas of the festive celebrations in any American small town when the church debt was paid off. But late in the afternoon a mob of a hundred men in uniform broke into the building, beat up the staff and kicked them downstairs into the pouring rain. Several were seriously injured and one girl became blind as a result of shock. The same mob then raided the Rand School, a socialist adult education institution. That evening larger mobs tried to break up a May Day concert of the Amalgamated Clothing Workers in Madison Square Garden.

Two months later, on the night of July 10th, police in Paterson, N.J., broke up a membership meeting of the Amalgamated Textile Workers, arrested Norman's brother Evan, who was now the union's executive secretary, and the meeting's chairman, Henry Berger, and took all the union's papers from the union offices without a search warrant. The police explained that they did not need warrants in Paterson.

Politicians and business leaders were advocating ruthless, repressive action against unions, Socialists and other radicals. Senator George E. Chamberlain, at a dinner in New York, proclaimed: "As for the Bolsheviki, we have a way of dealing with them out west; we string them up."

Not to be outdone, the *Wall Street Journal* wrote in an editorial:

"We have a flabby public opinion which would wring its hands in anguish if we took the labor leader by the scruff of his neck, backed him up against a wall and filled him with lead. Countries which consider themselves every bit as civilized as we are, do not hesitate about such matters for a moment."

The arguments for amnesty for all political prisoners received support on September 5, 1919, when President Wilson, at the St. Louis Coliseum, enlightened the world as follows:

"The real reason that the war that we have just finished took place was that Germany was afraid that her commercial rivals were going to get the better of her, and the reason why some nations went into the war against Germany was that they thought that Germany would get the commercial advantage of them . . .

"Is there any man here or woman—let me say is there any child—who does not know that the seed of war in the modern world is industrial and commercial rivalry? . . . This was a commercial and industrial war."

The same Archibald Stevenson who had, during the war, threatened Thomas and other officials of the Civil Liberties Bureau with jail sentences ("more in sorrow than in anger," he kept assuring Norman) persuaded a publicity-hungry New York State Senator named Lusk to set up an investigating committee with Stevenson as the investigator. Stevenson had already appeared before a Congressional committee with the first of the "blacklists," a strangely-assorted collection of names of eminent Americans, beginning with Jane Addams and ending with Lillian Wald. All of these, he said, were conspiring to overthrow the government.

Stevenson devised the brilliant idea of ousting the elected New York Socialist assemblymen on the ground that they were disloyal. A trial was held, which had in it many of the elements of high comedy. Counsel for the prosecution constantly popped up to read from Marx's "Communist Manifesto," which their stenographer constantly set down as reading, "You have nothing to lose but your change." Over and over again the Democratic prosecutor charged the Socialist legislators with being the agents of the arch-conspirators, "Trotine and Lensky."

Thomas was called as an expert to testify on the relation between socialism and religion, since, of course, his comrades had been tagged with the atheist and "free love" label. This task was easy, since from its early days the Party had held that "religion was a matter of the private conscience" and had included many devout believers in its ranks. At the ouster proceedings, Thomas proved himself an expert on another subject—socialism and the family. When Seymour Stedman, Socialist defense counsel, asked Norman: "You are a married man?" Thomas replied, "I am." "Family?" asked Stedman. "Five children," said Norman, "and proud of it."

The New York State Bar Association appointed a committee composed of Charles Evans Hughes, Ogden Mills and Joseph Proskauer to plead for the seating of the duly elected assemblymen, but not even such a distinguished trio was able to persuade the assembly. The elected Socialists were illegally expelled.

The Socialist Party, as well as the labor movement, suffered severely not only from post-war repressions, but from many internal wounds, which were to have a more permanent detrimental effect. The Bolshevik revolution in Russia led in America, as throughout the world, to splits in the Socialist movement into Socialist and Communist parties.

Thomas disliked the factional fights between the left wing and the old guard that began soon after the Armistice. His sympathies were with the Russian Revolution. In fact, when no hall could be hired, he and Violet opened their new home on East 17th Street (where their sixth child, Evan, was born) to a meeting for the Bolshevist Government's representatives, Martens and Nuorteva. The crowd in the big living room also contained half a dozen secret service men.

Despite his sympathies, Thomas was opposed to dictatorship and to Lenin's demand for absolute control of all parties affiliated with his Third International. On the other hand he didn't like the tactics the right wing used within the Party to fight the left wing—he felt the right wing sometimes used undemocratic

81

methods against those who condemned democracy. But when he swung against the right wing, the bombast used by the left-wingers, led in his branch by Jay Lovestone, who later became national secretary of the Communist Party, again moved Thomas the other way. Most of all, the everlasting discussions, the endless chewing of the same bitter cud of controversy, bored and irritated him. So, while Thomas did much speaking for the Socialist Party at various meetings, he was only tolerably diligent in attending meetings of his Party branch.

As the country swung back toward "normalcy," both Democratic and Republican presidential nominees in 1920 were conservatives—Harding for the G.O.P. and James M. Cox for the Democrats. Thomas variously termed it a Cox and Box or Tweedledee and Tweedledum campaign. Young Franklin D. Roosevelt, then Assistant Secretary of the Navy, did some lively campaigning but said little of significance. He did admit, in fact even boasted, that he wrote Haiti's constitution when American marines occupied that island.

When Gene Debs campaigned for President on the Socialist ticket from his jail cell in Atlanta, Thomas spoke frequently at meetings. Many Congressmen and Senators joined in the campaign for Debs' release, now that the war was over. Newsreels of Debs, dressed in prison uniform, accepting the Socialist nomination, brought applause in New York theaters, much to the dismay of a *New York Times* editorial.

In the campaign Debs polled his largest vote, 915,302, but this was only about 3.5 per cent of the total vote cast, considerably below the nearly 6 per cent he had received in 1912. The total vote was unprecedentedly large because it was the first time women had been allowed to vote in all states.

On January 31, 1921, Attorney General Palmer recommended to Wilson that Debs' sentence be commuted on Lincoln's Birthday because Debs was 65 and in poor health. When he received the recommendation, Wilson wrote across it the single word: "Denied."

After Harding won the presidency, Thomas was on two committees to see him about releasing Debs. The second time, only

Oswald Garrison Villard was with Norman, and Harding talked very frankly. He had a pile of pardon papers stacked on his desk, perhaps to impress his visitors. Harding pointed to them and said, "Norman, you see that? Nothing gives me more concern than justice in these pardons." Then Harding made the astonishing admission that he saw no reason for keeping Debs in jail any more, or for that matter, many of the others whom the Palmer raids had put in prison. Said he to Norman (who, after all, was a home town boy): "Norman, do you remember old Fritz so-and-so in Marion?" "Yes," Thomas replied. Fritz was an old-fashioned German, good natured and portly; he had never learned to speak much English but everyone liked him.

"Well," said Harding, "I just pardoned a man who must have been just like him down in Kentucky. As far as I could make out, he was only in jail because his wife had died and his daughter-in-law had to keep him. She got tired of keeping him and so she said he talked disloyally. I just let him out."

Then the conversation got back again to Debs. Finally, Harding said to Thomas and Villard words to this effect: "You check and come back and show me that there are as many people in the country who would be glad for me to let Debs out as there are who want him to stay in, and I'll let him out." He later decided that public opinion would react favorably toward affirmative action, for on December 23, 1921, the White House announced that Eugene Debs and twenty-three other political prisoners would be released on Christmas Day.

Thomas had also been active in the cause of Irish freedom, partly he admits, under the spell of a fascinating and persuasive advocate, Dr. William J. M. A. Maloney, but mostly out of deep conviction that the Irish had a good case and that both justice and world peace required a fair settlement of an ancient feud. He had addressed many Irish-American rallies and roused them to applaud a demand for release of Gene Debs by making proper comparisons with the Black and Tan outrages.

Opposition to racial discrimination was, in addition, an active part of Thomas' philosophy. How far we have progressed since those days is indicated by this editorial note he wrote in 1921: "Northern industrial centers may seem by comparison desirable

83

to the Southern Negroes who emigrate to them. But they are a very poor sort of earthly paradise as *The World Tomorrow* can testify. This thought has been brought home to the magazine from an experience of its own. We are obliged to move to new offices at 108 Lexington Avenue, and the reason is this: the owners of the building in which we have shared offices with the Fellowship of Reconciliation demanded of us signature of a lease forbidding the employment of any Negro. We should have refused such a demand on principle, but in addition we are proud of the fact that one of the most faithful of our office staff is a Negro woman. That her race should be discriminated against in more than one office building in New York City is a practical denial of the fundamental principles of brotherhood and Christianity."

Thomas also found time to speak at various organizing and strike meetings for unions and to participate in free speech tests. The mayors of certain towns in New York and Connecticut had denied permits for street meetings to Socialists and other radicals. In Mt. Vernon, New York, where a particularly stringent ordinance had been enacted, the American Civil Liberties Union (the name adopted by the National Civil Liberties Bureau in 1920) sent word to Mt. Vernon's mayor that Rose Schneidermann of the Women's Trade Union League, Dr. John Haynes Holmes of Community Church, and Norman Thomas would speak at an open air meeting in his town on a certain evening. At the appointed time, Holmes ascended the rickety wooden platform, announced the purpose of the meeting and started to read the Constitution of the United States. Before he could complete the opening words, "We the people," he was placed under arrest and carted off to the station house. Thomas promptly took his place and started to read the New York State Constitution, when he was pulled down and taken to the police station to bear Holmes company. Miss Schneidermann received the same treatment. They were released on bail and the next morning found guilty by the local judge. A higher court soon reversed this judgment and the streets of Mt. Vernon were made free to the speakers of all parties.

SEVEN

Family Worries
and New Careers

ᴥᔰ By 1920 there were six children in the family, and the Thomases had moved to East 17th Street. Although Violet had a weak heart, her courage, resourcefulness, and competence enabled her to manage her growing household in a way that was easily compatible with Norman's outside activities. As on 116th Street, the home was made the center for much of Thomas' work for civil liberties and against colonialism and economic exploitation.

Then, in the latter months of 1920, Thomas' emotions, time and energy became desperately involved in a long, complicated fight for the health of his family. Tommy (Norman, Jr.) was stricken by a streptococcic infection in his ear. In those days, of course, there were no sulfa drugs or penicillin, and it was an agonizing time for the family. Finally, following a mastoid operation, Tommy developed spinal meningitis and died. Thomas was sorely grieved by the loss of his oldest son. Tommy had been a precocious youngster and was very interested in socialism. Billy, then eight, tried to console his father by telling him, "Now I'll be a Socialist for you."

It was discovered that everyone in the family except Norman had also been hit by the infection. For years, Violet and the five other children were to suffer from recurrences of the infection, which took the form of various illnesses. Violet's heart trouble was intensified, and was to plague her for the rest of her life.

These family concerns greatly curtailed the time Thomas could be away from home and caused him to reduce as much as possible his evening engagements. From the end of 1920 to the end of 1923 the situation was so acute that Thomas declined offers to run for local offices on the Socialist ticket on the ground that he did not want to run unless he could campaign actively, which, under the circumstances, was impossible. Dr. Maloney, with whom Thomas had been engaged in the campaign for Irish independence, felt that the strep infections might be caused by the city air, so the family moved to Westchester, where they stayed for a little more than a year.

During this time, with Norman commuting daily to the city, Violet was very unhappy. She had little desire to socialize with other women in the neighborhood, possibly because of fear of rejection—a sensitivity that she was to feel long after it was necessary. Moreover, she wanted to return to the city to be near her regular doctors. And above all, she wanted to share Thomas' working day and be with him as much as possible. When Norman and Violet returned to New York, they bought a house at 206 E. 18th Street, where they lived until 1939. They still felt the children should have the benefits of a country atmosphere, and spent the summers away from the city—at Ridgefield, Conn., in 1921 and 1922; at Woods Hole, Mass. in 1923; and on Long Island from then on.

Life for the Thomas children was pleasant enough despite repeated illnesses. The new family home was big enough to provide a private office where Thomas conducted much of his business. Sundays would frequently be excursion days, when the whole family would go to the Statue of Liberty, the Zoo or some museum. Thomas read children's stories to the youngsters on nights when he was home, and made up a long, continued story about Johnny Jones, which he would relate when any of the children were sick. Violet would chime in with poetry—Keats, Shelley and Shakespeare, which she recited from memory, but always, Norman teased her, without any change in expression.

In 1922, Norman's brother Evan again came to live with the family, and was to stay with them except for short intervals until

1946. When the Thomas children learned that their uncle had been in jail as a conscientious objector, they felt what he had done was wholly admirable. Many of the people who came to their home, the friends of their parents and uncle, were liberals, pacifists and Socialists, who viewed being jailed for one's principles as a sign of heroism, and so the young Thomases did not see arrest as a disgrace. Their reaction was the same when their father was arrested in free speech campaigns.

The youngsters were particularly elated when famous personalities came to their home. Such visits made them feel that the Thomas family was of considerable importance, and mitigated the effects of occasional snubs the children received from conservative neighbors. In 1924, after General Plutarco Elias Calles had been elected President of Mexico, he came to the Thomas house for dinner. Prior to his arrival, Mexican secret service men arrived and were horrified because the French doors to the back yard could not be locked. Mrs. Thomas made light of their distress. "There's nothing out there but back-yard cats, so why worry?"

The children were curious about the dinner party and kept sneaking downstairs to see what was going on. As one daughter put it: "Mother, who had a great tendency to exaggerate, talked to Calles through an interpreter. Everytime he mentioned what a large family he had, she would try to top him with a few more children. She ended up with a much larger family than we actually had. And when we were brought in later to shake hands with President Calles, we discovered that she had given the impression that several of her children spoke Spanish quite well, when actually only Bill had had as much as a year of Spanish in school. As Calles was introduced to each child, he would ask if this was one of those who spoke Spanish. It was quite an ordeal."

On another occasion, when Bertrand Russell was visiting, Norman was busy with a delegation in his office. To pass the time, Violet asked Lord Russell, who had just published an important book about child care, if he could answer some questions about her problems with her children. "How old are they?" asked Russell. Given their ages, he promptly replied, "Well, since they're older than two, it's too late to recommend anything."

In 1923, discovering that the children tended to reinfect each other, Violet decided to minimize the danger of illness by sending them away to boarding schools. To Violet and Norman, who loved their children dearly, this was a heartbreaking—but necessary—compromise. Billy went in 1923 to Gilman School in Baltimore; Polly was sent in 1925 to Edgewood, a progressive boarding school in Greenwich, Conn., and Frances, Becky and Evan went to the same school in 1926.

All of the children had the conviction that their father was a very great man, but they soon discovered that the sentiment was not universally shared. At Edgewood, Polly was shocked when a student revealed her fear that the daughter of the notorious radical, Norman Thomas, might put a bomb under her chair. Frances had a similar experience. A schoolmate had invited her to come home for lunch, and a date was set. Later the girl apologetically told Frances that her grandmother, with whom she lived, refused to have a child of that Socialist in her home. So secure was Frances in her feelings about her father that her reaction to the snub was, "The nuttiest thing I ever heard of."

Among people who knew Thomas, however, even where his views were unpopular, he was still admired as a person. In 1925, Bill went with his father to the latter's Twentieth Anniversary Reunion at Princeton. By then he had often heard that his father's pacifism and socialism were "not quite respectable." So he was amazed when one of his father's classmates, a colonel in military uniform, greeted Norman very cordially, saying, "We're still friends, Tommy, aren't we, even if we don't agree on everything." Bill was heartened to discover how popular his father was among classmates who disagreed with him so strongly.

The children understood that they were thoroughly loved, and that going to boarding school was because of health needs. All understood, that is, but Evan, who was only six when he first left for boarding school. He hated leaving home and has remained convinced that it was a mistake. He knew perfectly well that he was loved, but there was a tremendous difference between being at a school where he was completely cut off from his mother, and coming home for vacation, where his wish was his mother's command. For four or five years, after Christmas vacation, Evan would make himself cough and try to induce a cold or bronchitis. On one occasion, he managed to stay home for two weeks after vacation ended. Finally his father came to him and said, "Now look, do you want to lead a normal life, or don't you?" So Evan said, "I do," and went back to school the next day.

In a vague sort of way, Thomas had expected to return to the pulpit as an active minister when the war ended, but his experiences with the clergy had disillusioned him. In addition, he was becoming increasingly interested in economic and political problems, which was fortunate, since for several years after the war, he was almost black-listed by the church.

Meanwhile certain philosophical and theological doubts were arising in his mind. Towards the end of 1921 he decided that it would be wise to hand over leadership of the Fellowship of Reconciliation and *The World Tomorrow* to men whose Christian orientation was stronger than his. He accepted Oswald Garrison Villard's invitation to become an associate editor of *The Nation* and stayed there a year, liking both the work and the association. However, it gradually became obvious that the magazine was overstaffed for its size and income. Both Villard and Thomas were relieved when the League for Industrial Democracy (LID) invited the latter to become its co-executive director, with Harry W. Laidler. Thomas accepted, remaining a contributing editor of *The Nation* until after Villard sold it.

The League had been started in 1905 as the Intercollegiate Socialist Society to promote "an intelligent interest in socialism among college men and women, graduate and undergraduate, through the formation of study clubs in the colleges and universities, and the encouraging of all legitimate endeavors to awaken an interest in socialism among the educated men and women of this country." Signers of the call to its initial meeting in New York included Thomas Wentworth Higginson, Charlotte Perkins Gilman, Clarence S. Darrow, William English Walling, J. G. Phelps Stokes, Jack London and Upton Sinclair.

Upton Sinclair, then only 26 years old, told how he had failed to learn about labor and the fundamental social problems of the day in college, and declared, "I decided that since the professors

would not educate the students, it was up to the students to educate the professors."

Jack London was elected president, Upton Sinclair and J. G.
Phelps Stokes vice-presidents and Owen R. Lovejoy, treasurer.
Harry Laidler, still an undergraduate at Conn. Wesleyan, short,
slim and bright-eyed, was elected to the executive committee to
represent the undergraduates.

League chapters were formed on many campuses. In 1910 Dr.
Laidler became Secretary and Organizer of the I.S.S. That same
year, a petition of 300 Harvard students for a course on socialism
bore fruit. Among the members of that Harvard chapter were
Heywood Broun, Nicholas Kelley, Lee Simonson and Kenneth
R. Macgowan. Their president, Walter Lippmann, proudly declared, "The only evil we really fear is blind ignorance . . . In
a general way our object was to make reactionaries, standpatters;
standpatters, conservative liberals; conservative liberals and liberals, Socialists."

With World War I, many colleges were virtually turned into
Reserve Officers Training Corps (R.O.T.C.) encampments where
the majority of students gave their primary thought to preparedness for military service. Under these conditions, many college
chapters failed to continue their activities, and lecture and organizing work declined. About the time of America's entry into
the war, Thomas joined the I.S.S. and became fairly active in it.
Harry Laidler recalls that when he heard Thomas speak at that
first meeting, he decided, "There's a man who'll go far. We
should keep in touch with him."

In 1921, the I.S.S. was reorganized as the League for Industrial
Democracy and placed on a somewhat broader basis. While
strengthening its work in the colleges, it devoted increasing attention to the general public and, while educating for a far-flung
system based on production for use, gave attention to the immediate problems before the labor movement on the economic,
cooperative, political and cultural fronts. Robert Morss Lovett
became the League's first president and Charles P. Steinmetz,
America's electrical wizard, its vice-president.

In 1922 the League received a good deal of money from the
Garland Fund to try an expanded program of work in the col-

leges, which were slowly opening doors closed during the war. That year, Charles Garland, a young liberal Harvard graduate, had inherited over a million dollars from his father, a Wall Street broker. A sincere idealist, Garland insisted on giving the money to Roger Baldwin to use for liberal and radical causes. Baldwin refused to be the sole trustee, but helped set up a committee for the American Fund for Public Service, which Garland endowed with over $900,000.

By the fall of 1926, to jump ahead a bit, the Garland Fund had spent hundreds of thousands of dollars on behalf of radical causes, and the *New York Times* and *Herald Tribune* both reported with a tone of conservative satisfaction that the funds had been completely spent. However, the stock market boom was to give the lie to the press. Capital for the Garland Fund was invested in common stock of New York's First National Bank, and by the spring of 1929 the supposedly depleted fund had grown to nearly $2,000,000, more than twice what it had been before any money had been spent. Capitalist Wall Street speculation made money for the Garland Fund faster than the radicals could spend it.

When Thomas joined Harry Laidler in the fall of 1922 as LID co-director, a remarkable team was created. As Thomas strode across a college campus with Harry, whose head scarcely reached Norman's elbow, trotting along beside him, the physical contrast was amusing. But intellectually the two men made an excellent match, with Harry stressing research and publication while Norman concentrated on activities.

Thomas had been at his LID post for less than a year when he was invited to assume a challenging new job, serving as editor-in-chief of the daily *New York Leader*. For years the Socialist Party, with much sacrifice, had published the daily *New York Call*. Under the skillful editorial guidance of editor Charles Ervin, it weathered the storms of World War I. But it had never had enough financial backing or advertising to make it a strong paper. Now the *Call* was about $50,000 in the hole and was near bankruptcy. Evans Clark, a Princeton economist who was then active in Socialist affairs, conceived the idea of transforming the *Call* into the daily *Leader*, under a board of directors representing supporting unions and the Socialist Party. The Party, the Call Association (which was legally independent of the Party) and a number of progressive unions endorsed the new plan. Considerable funds—but not enough—were raised from certain unions and the Garland Fund.

Morris Hillquit, who spoke for the Socialist Party and represented the *Call* interests on the board, persuaded Thomas to accept as editor-in-chief. Since Thomas had no daily newspaper experience, Heber Blankenhorn, trained in the *New York Sun* tradition of accuracy tinged with mellow humor, was named managing editor; and Evans Clark, later a *New York Times* editorial writer, was induced to become business manager.

On October 1, 1923, the *New York Leader* started publication with an unusually fine staff. The city editor was Herbert Gaston, who later became editor of the *Sunday World* and eventually an assistant Secretary of the Treasury. Cartoonist Edmund Duffy later went to the *Baltimore Sun,* where he twice won Pulitzer prizes (he ended his working life as chief cartoonist for the *Saturday Evening Post*). Ed Sullivan, the sports editor, is today known to millions of televiewers as well as newspaper readers. Howard Brubaker, later with the *New Yorker,* was a columnist, as was McAlister Coleman, who had previously worked for the *New York Sun.* Eddie Levinson, a labor reporter, later became a publicity man and an important factor in building up the United Auto Workers. Paul Sifton, playwright and crack reporter, fresh from covering the Herrin riots for the United Press, was also there; together with Anita Block, later of the Theatre Guild, who wrote dramatic criticism. Bill Feigenbaum, a one-man encyclopedia of socialism, and cartoonist Ryan Walker helped round out the group.

This crew had a fine time for a few weeks and put out a good paper—in many ways an exciting one. To the bewilderment of many old-time labor editors, the daily *Leader* did not confine itself to detailed accounts of local union meetings, lengthy treatises on union policies or adulation of union officers. When the World Series was on, sports news took over the front pages. The paper covered exciting murders, not so gruesomely as some of the tabloids, but as something significant in the social scheme. As a matter of fact all news, even sports news, had to have social significance.

Take this excerpt from Ed Sullivan's column: "Yesterday's near riot in Columbus, Georgia, precipitated by the Mike McTigue-Young Stribling championship go, can be traced directly to the Ku Klux Klan. McTigue, an Irish Catholic, managed by Joe Jacobs, a Jew, had as much chance of getting an even break in Georgia as the well-known snowball has of enduring the scorching blasts of Dante's Inferno."

News headlines ranged from "Berlin Menaced By New Military Plot; Government Totters; Dictator In View" to "Debs Returns to Jail for a Day to Swap Stories with Tom Mooney" and "Poison Killed Mrs. Webb, Expert Finds." One Thomas editorial, "Does Europe Matter?," commented on an editorial in *Wallace's Farmer* (owned by Henry Wallace's father, who was Harding's Secretary of Agriculture, but edited by Henry) which said: "We are producing surplus wheat, hogs and corn sufficient to feed 20,000,000 people abroad. This might be a fine thing, but unfortunately these 20,000,000 people are unable to give us in exchange for our surplus anything which is of value to us. The only way out seems to be to reduce our surplus for export, not only of wheat but also of corn and hogs."

Of course, if Thomas had remembered this editorial, he might not have been so surprised and shocked a decade later when Henry Wallace adopted this very plan to deal with the country's farm crisis.

One problem of writing a paper to build mass circulation was illustrated by the following story. The *Leader* was located nearer than any other newspaper to the Fourteenth Street horse players, and many staff members insisted that carrying racing news was important to boost circulation. The staff would get these race results by telephone. On the day when Thomas was writing the above editorial about surplus grain shipments, he came to Paul Sifton to get certain facts. Paul was on the phone taking racing news. When Norman interrupted with his question, Paul acidly replied, "I'm trying to get the right spelling for the horse that won the last race. How can I waste time on unimportant things like surplus grain shipments?"

During a wildcat pressmen's strike which closed all the other papers, the *Leader* circulation boomed. The rise in circulation, coupled with ads tied to the old rate base, sent the deficit up beyond all expectations. Then, when the strike ended, the readers went back to their old papers. And advertising remained poor. When Thomas was bearing down on the dairy ring in his editorials, one advertising solicitor, a Socialist who was critical of Norman for his Socialist unorthodoxy, wired Thomas to go slow because he thought he could sign up an important dairy. The editorial blasts continued, and the lack of advertising also continued.

Suddenly, the bubble burst. The *Leader* had been in existence for about six weeks. Thomas, Heber Blankenhorn and Evans Clark were in the Fourth Avenue subway, leaving 14th Street on the way to 23rd Street, where they were to meet with the *Leader*'s Board of Directors. When the subway doors closed at 14th Street, Evans Clark leaned over to the other two as they swayed, clinging to the straps, and announced, "I haven't had a chance to tell you before, but we're broke." This was the first Thomas and Blankenhorn knew that the initial fund, intended to last six months, had been completely dissipated in the first six weeks.

The three went into an immediate huddle but were unable to work out a plausible program for continuing publication. Thomas' pride that he had always kept solvent the organizations for which he had executive responsibility came to an abrupt end. His was the unwelcome chore of breaking the sad news to a board of directors which had previously been assured that everything was going well.

Thomas blamed himself for accepting easy reassurances from Clark at their frequent conferences without closer inspection. Clark, who achieved much in many fields, was unfortunately inexperienced in the highly technical field of business publication. Moreover, while the amount set up to launch the paper ($110,000 was subscribed of a $500,000 capitalization), seemed large to impecunious Socialists, it was wholly inadequate for the kind of paper the unions wanted and the editors encouraged them to expect.

Despite all this, the paper might have continued except for a sharp division in the ranks of the progressive unions which made their leaders welcome so good an excuse for winding up this venture in independent journalism. At this time the unions, particularly the needle trades unions, still had fairly substantial treasuries and their members had money in their pockets. But, by the fall of 1923, the communists were waging an all-out drive to capture the progressive unions. The fight was at its most bitter in the International Ladies Garment Workers Union. While the entire *Leader* staff was anti-communist or non-communist, all felt that their main concern must be with straight reporting—thus communists were not always damned. Even on the Board of Directors, viewpoints varied. Sidney Hillman and the Amalgamated Clothing Workers had one approach, the ILGWU spokesmen, another. The tactics of the conflict with the communists made a free labor press, editorially labor's champion but objective in reporting, an impossibility. At every meeting of the board, Thomas had trouble protecting the staff from members of the board, but did, however, have Morris Hillquit's full cooperation. None of the board ever criticized any general editorials on issues of public policy. Nor did either the board or rank and file readers ask for more news on labor problems at home or abroad. (There were dozens of requests for racing charts.)

At the board meeting, when it was suggested that the unions contribute more money and that a matching sum be sought from the Garland Fund, with practically one accord the union leaders said, "Oh no, we've got to liquidate." As one board member said, "It's too much of a strain to read the damn paper through to see what's wrong with it this time." The paper closed, and expert union accountants wound up its affairs in orderly fashion. An ironic footnote to the whole venture was that as the staff walked down the stairs for the last time, a sign painter was putting gold leaf on the door announcing that this was the office of the *New York Leader*. McAlister Coleman pleaded with the painter to stop wasting this expensive gold leaf and asked for a bit of it as a souvenir. The painter looked at Coleman as if he were crazy and continued until he had completed the sign.

Thomas' spirits were at low ebb. He was relieved to find that the rest of the staff found good jobs quickly but he was uncertain what to do himself. Here he was almost forty, father of a large family, well trained for the ministry, which he felt he could no longer honestly follow. He disliked the kind of young minister and rabbi he then ran across who seemed to say, "Of course we don't really believe in all this religious dogma, but this is a good service to render." And Thomas felt he had been a failure in meeting the great opportunities which had come to him. He envied doctors and engineers, who earned their living by doing things rather than by lecturing and imparting ideas. They had, he thought, objective standards of value and accomplishment.

While he felt very depressed, Thomas realized that he was far more fortunate than most men in similar circumstances because he could earn some income by writing and speaking, and because Violet, unfailingly sympathetic, had by this time inherited some money (never more than $10,000 a year) from a trust fund through her grandfather. In addition, when her health permitted, Violet undertook various jobs—working as a part-time nurse in a doctor's office, running a tea room, and raising and selling cocker spaniels. That latter business was never directly profitable but it enabled Thomas to keep the house on Long Island at a time when the health of the children was precarious. In the case of the Thomas family, inherited money proved to be a great boon since sickness imposed heavy and continuing expenses. (It never influenced, however, Thomas' stand in support of graduated income and inheritance taxes.)

EIGHT

Back to Normalcy

ᴇᴔ Aꜰᴛᴇʀ ᴄᴏɴsɪᴅᴇʀᴀʙʟᴇ mental anguish over the loss of the *Leader,* Thomas decided to accept the invitation of the League for Industrial Democracy to return to the unfilled post he had left. The nation was now in the midst of its "golden decade." Prosperity was here to stay. Gold was the symbol of the decade. Small boys received gold watches on graduating from school, little girls were given gold pieces as birthday presents. The Stotesburys, a noted Philadelphia banking family, boasted gold fixtures in their bathrooms ("You don't have to polish them, you know").

Unhappily, the fruits of prosperity were being divided most inequitably. While the number of families with an income of over $1 million per year rose from 65 in 1919 to 513 in 1929, 12 million families, more than 42 per cent of the population, had incomes under $1500, and the jobless constituted ten to thirteen per cent of the labor force.

There had been a brief economic collapse in 1921, and with economic recovery industry was determined to prevent organized labor from recapturing the heights it had attained during the war, when union membership went up to five million. A tremendous drive for the open shop started. Employers forced yellow-dog contracts upon employees, planted labor spies in unions, exchanged blacklists of undesirable union members and—where trouble developed despite all these precautions—used strong-arm guards and imported strikebreakers. At the peak of 1929 prosperity, total union membership was 3,443,000—less than it had been in any year since 1917.

The uneven prosperity, the open-shop drives, and the Teapot

97

Dome scandals which destroyed the Harding administration left many Americans unmoved. The 1920s remained the "era of wonderful nonsense." Speakeasies, bootleggers and gangsterism flourished, and newspaper sensationalism focused public attention upon million dollar prize fights, long distance marathons and bathing beauty contests. In his postscript to the 1927 edition of *Is Conscience a Crime?* Thomas wryly noted that "once more the voice of those who proclaim the duty of civil disobedience is heard in the land" but that the Volstead Act rather than conscription was at stake.

In the feverish search for "normalcy," however, the postwar anti-radical hysteria was lessening. It was again possible to gain a hearing in colleges, churches and other areas. Thomas, for instance, had been blacklisted at Princeton until 1924. Teachers' colleges, under political control, were particularly fearful of allowing socialists to speak. Nevertheless, by offering good people and hammering away, the LID progressively broke the boycott. Paul Blanshard, a young minister who had been dispossessed by the war, was appointed the League's field secretary. He joined Norman in carrying the message of industrial democracy to student and civic groups in hundreds of colleges and cities throughout the nation. By the end of the twenties, there were more than a hundred student chapters.

As early as the 1921 Socialist convention, Morris Hillquit introduced a resolution calling for a Socialist survey of radical and labor forces in the nation which might be interested in political cooperation with the Socialists. In 1922, a Conference for Progressive Political Action was formed by representatives of the railroad labor brotherhoods, the Farmer-Labor Party, the Non-Partisan League and the Committee of Forty-Eight (Roosevelt Republicans who had followed their leader out of the GOP in 1912 but who refused to follow him back into the Republican fold in 1916).

In February, 1924, the conference of the CPPA in St. Louis decided to run a slate of candidates in the 1924 elections and, to the delight of the Socialists, adopted a resolution welcoming the electoral victory of the British Labor Party. But the Socialists were unable to persuade their coalition partners to form a third party. Senator Robert M. La Follette, the unanimous choice for President, accepted the nomination at the July 4th nominating convention in Cleveland in a message read by his eldest son, Robert, Jr. He stressed that he ran as an independent, not as the candidate of a new political party. But he predicted that the election would bring about a new party.

The Communist Party, which at this time operated under the name American Workers Party, had captured the Federated Farmer-Labor Party and tried to endorse La Follette. That seasoned old veteran had no intention of being seduced by communists in sheep's clothing. Since their support was like the support a gallows gives to a hanging man, he insisted that "all progressives should refuse to participate in any movement which makes common cause with any communist organization."

Only the Socialist Party, of all the groups in the La Follette coalition, had the framework of a national organization. Spurred on by Hillquit and Victor Berger, the Party adopted tactics which required unselfish cooperation and genuine sacrifice, yet ones which were almost inevitable in a country based on a presidential rather than a parliamentary governmental system. It put its main strength in the national La Follette campaign, turning over to it almost all its manpower, finances and press resources. The powerful *Jewish Daily Forward* gave the La Follette drive virtually all its contributions. Thomas, sensing the dangers to the Party in this situation, nevertheless heartily supported Hillquit's position and served actively on the National Campaign Committee for La Follette.

At the same time, the coalition put up no state ticket in New York and agreed to support none officially. The Socialist Party therefore held a state convention at Finnish Hall in New York City to nominate its state ticket.

There is an old Chinese proverb: If you save a man's life, you are responsible for his welfare as long as you live. Thomas must have thought of this often through the years. Although he was not a delegate to the 1924 Socialist state convention, that body, with the strong approval of Morris Hillquit, offered Thomas its nomination for Governor. By accepting the nomination offered over the telephone, Thomas acquired, as he later put it, "a responsibility for the Socialist Party as a party" which he has never felt able honorably to drop.

Since the family's health was now somewhat improved, Thomas felt that he could arrange time to campaign. He accepted the nomination because he thought it would enable him to help create a farmer-labor party in which the Socialist Party would be the intellectual ferment, much as the Independent Labor Party functioned in relation to Britain's mass Labor Party.

The La Follette campaign did not run smoothly. Many veteran Socialists, who had bitter experiences in the past with well-meaning but impractical liberals, resisted the new harness. Old line labor leaders also looked suspiciously upon the alliance. While the executive council of the American Federation of Labor broke its historic non-endorsement policy and voted to support La Follette, it gave little more than lip service to the campaign. The brunt of campaigning was left to the Socialist leaders and rank and filers (Jimmy Higginses, they were called), and those few practical liberals like Arthur Garfield Hays, Walter Frank and Morris Ernst.

But an even more difficult situation existed in New York State. Al Smith as Governor had made a creditable record for friendship to labor, efficiency and devotion to civil liberties. Many Socialist unionists hoped for Smith's reelection, even though they also felt that the Party should run its own ticket. This attitude was particularly strong in the ILGWU, for which Hillquit had long been both attorney and braintruster.

The distinguished attorney, Joseph Proskauer, Smith's close friend and organizer of independent support for him, came to see Thomas to urge him to withdraw from the race, or at least—in view of the union situation—make only a token campaign. Hillquit and the Party committees backed Norman's rejection of this proposal and insisted that Thomas speak at La Follette's mass meeting in Madison Square Garden.

In New York, Thomas worked hard, backed by good running mates, including labor lawyers Charles Solomon for Lt. Governor and Louis Waldman for Attorney General; and Frank Crosswaith, a Negro union organizer and a powerful orator, for Secretary of State. Publicity work by Eddie Levinson and McAlister Coleman

100

was excellent but the Party's campaign work was incredibly bad, much worse than in later years, including those when Socialist voting strength was far less. Thomas literally went out looking for meetings in New York. Almost every night he spoke somewhere, from the Battery to the Canadian border, and he got a warm response to his appeal for a farmer-labor party. But the State Committee and the current Party secretary had almost no plans for the gubernatorial campaign. Thomas was sent to meetings for La Follette where he was forbidden by the La Follette Committee to refer to the Socialist state campaign. At one Syracuse meeting, presided over by the president of the local labor council, Thomas made a stirring speech for La Follette and a labor party. When he finished, the presiding officer arose, thanked Brother Thomas for this "fine speech for La Follette" and proceeded to tell the audience that "the same things Brother Thomas said about La Follette applied to Smith for Governor."

In New York City, most of the Socialist Congressional candidates, except William Karlin, were uncooperative. In fact, Fiorello La Guardia, who broke with the Republicans to support La Follette and ran for Congress on the Socialist line, was far more helpful. As Thomas put it, La Guardia's campaign operated "not only to strengthen the Progressive movement in this campaign, but to make the organization of a new party inevitable." Hillquit, because of his absorption in the national campaign and (some Socialists alleged) because of his union tieups, scarcely lifted his persuasive voice for the state ticket.

One feature of the campaign was the refusal of either the Democratic or Republican parties to denounce the Ku Klux Klan, a pusillanimous policy rejected by both La Follette and the Socialist Party. The Klan in the twenties was the most powerful agency in the country for developing anti-foreignism, race hate and religious intolerance. Cynical demagogues had little difficulty in rousing poor and ignorant men into a frenzy over imaginary dangers. When a Klan orator declared to a crowd at North Manchester, Indiana, that for all they knew the Pope might descend upon the town any day, possibly "even be on the northbound train tomorrow," a mob of 1,500 persons marched to the depot to safeguard the town from this impending doom.

As the 1924 presidential race neared its end, AFL support for La Follette became lukewarm. The AFL raised only $25,000 for the campaign fund. The Miners' John L. Lewis and Bill Hutcheson of the Carpenters threw their support to Coolidge while George Berry of the Printing Pressmen was active in the Davis camp.

Yet, when the shouting and tumult of the campaign died, La Follette received 4,826,471 votes—17 per cent of the total. Coolidge won in a landslide but La Follette polled 59 per cent as many votes as did Democrat Davis. Besides carrying Wisconsin (making him the only progressive third party candidate to score in the electoral college since 1912), La Follette ran second in Iowa, Minnesota, North and South Dakota, Montana, Wyoming, Idaho, Nevada, Washington, Oregon and California. In New York, La Follette polled 467,293 votes on both the Socialist and Progressive lines. (He even carried the Bronx.) La Follette received more Socialist than Progressive votes. But Thomas, as the Socialist candidate for Governor, garnered only 99,854 votes, demonstrating forcibly how the Socialist campaigners had concentrated all their energies on La Follette. La Guardia won election to Congress as a Socialist, but soon turned to the Progressive label, and Victor Berger was reelected as a Socialist Congressman in Wisconsin.

Norman Thomas and the Socialist Party were at first elated by the election results. After all, the highest vote any Socialist presidential campaign had rolled up since 1900 was less than a million. It was heartening to find that five million Americans had voted for what the press had described as a political revolution.

This enthusiastic reaction was not shared by the other groups in the coalition. They insisted on instantaneous victory. The AFL said that the 1924 campaign showed that "the launching of third party movements has been proved wasted effort and injurious to the desire to elect candidates with favorable records." In the future, said AFL leaders, labor must continue "to follow its non-partisan policy." At a depressing post-mortem convention in Chicago held February 1925, the Conference for Progressive Political Action fell apart. In the words of Morris Hillquit, the delegates "had come to bury Caesar, not to praise him." First to leave the hall were the railroad brotherhood chiefs and they were soon followed by almost all the other labor men.

While the Socialist Party nationally almost went into hibernation, Thomas returned to his desk at the LID and carried on Socialist activities there. In addition to its student work, the League helped to raise funds for strike relief and carried on extensive research activities.

Despite the La Follette experience and the eternal squabbles with the communists, the Socialist Party in New York City maintained a fairly active organization. In 1925, when Morris Hillquit made it clear that he would not run for Mayor, Thomas accepted the party's nomination for that post. Dapper James J. Walker was the Democratic choice and Frank Waterman, the fountain-pen king, the Republican hopeful. Publisher William Randolph Hearst was also anxious to run and sought, but failed to get, La Guardia's support. Instead, La Guardia endorsed Thomas and campaigned for him in various parts of the city, carefully explaining that he was not a Socialist but an independent and unattached liberal, expecting the creation of a progressive organization of which the Socialists could be a part.

This was the first campaign in which any party systematically campaigned for a definite program of municipally-owned housing to end the shame of New York's filthy, crime-infested slums. Campaign committees were set up which studied many municipal problems and brought in specific proposals. Thomas called for public ownership of subways and buses, but with direct representation on the Board of Transportation by workers in the transit system and the consuming public.

In that year, forums at which all of the candidates would speak were a common occurrence. Once, at Temple Emanu-El on Fifth Avenue, Waterman preceded Thomas with an extremely dull and stupid speech. After Thomas spoke he left to go to another meeting. One of his listeners followed him into the hall, surreptitiously handed him ten dollars and said, "Mr. Thomas, I'm a Republican, not a Socialist. But I'm so ashamed of the performance of my candidate, who discussed no issues, that I want you to take this for your campaign."

Jimmy Walker and Thomas met on many platforms and Jimmy would contrive, wherever possible, to speak after Norman. He would then say in his debonair way: "I enjoy listening to Mr. Thomas. I want you to know that all the things he wants for New York, I want too. But *I* can get them for you."

Walker won in a landslide and Thomas polled only 39,083 votes. Yet the campaign whetted his interest in city affairs and from that time on he began to haunt Board of Estimate meetings and speak up on city problems. Moreover, as he slowly built up a reputation in the city for speaking on the basis of knowledge, not dogma, people in trouble started coming to the LID office to seek his help. Most of them were poor and easily broken. They had been arrested, they knew this about the drug traffic, they knew that such and such a magistrate was crooked. But all were afraid to testify publicly. His experiences during this time made Thomas more tolerant than others later of the failure of most Germans and Russians to act against Hitler and Stalin. As he put it, "The amount of bravery that is available at any given time against any government, even on the part of those who suffer, is very limited most of the time."

In the winter of 1926 another of Thomas' dramatic and successful free speech tests occurred. In Passaic, New Jersey, the owners of the big textile mills announced a 10 per cent wage cut. Ten thousand woolen mill workers, under the leadership of an effective young communist organizer, Albert Weisbord, went out on strike for a 20 per cent increase in wages, a 44-hour week, and union recognition. Mill after mill was struck and every morning long, grim lines of pickets—men, women, children and infants in carriages—slogged through the slush of Passaic streets. When the employers found that their foreign-born employees could not be divided by appeals to religious and national differences, they turned to the police for help. Strikers were beaten, fire hoses threw icy streams of water at them and tear gas bombs were dropped in their midst.

Relief work formed a major part of the struggle, for the strikers were desperately poor. The Emergency Committee for Strikers

Relief, which Thomas, the LID and the American Civil Liberties Union had formed, sent food and clothing. Thomas frequently talked to large meetings of the strikers. With the coming of spring, the operators made desperate efforts to run the looms with imported scabs. Gunmen of detective agencies were called in to "protect" the scabs and intimidate the strikers. Strike headquarters were raided and young Weisbord thrown into jail under $30,000 bail.

After the strike had lasted some twelve weeks, the police decided to ban all strike meetings. Sheriff George Nimmo of Bergen County read the riot act when strikers tried to meet in Garfield, a little industrial town across the river from Passaic. He proceeded to act as if martial law was in existence. Police dispersed crowds even before meetings could start.

Thomas agreed to test the ban. The League for Industrial Democracy rented a vacant lot in Garfield and the American Civil Liberties Union sent observers. Several minutes before Thomas arrived, accompanied by newsmen, the gathering audience was dispersed by police, so his immediate reception committee was a group of some 50 police. But Thomas' appearance brought hundreds of strikers who came from all directions—over hills, from beyond railroad yards, from factories and houses where they had gone to escape threatened police violence. Six-feet-two notwithstanding, Thomas could not be seen by most of the audience, since there was no platform. So he climbed the stump of an old apple tree which had been struck by lightning. He felt much apprehension as he saw many police and special deputy sheriffs, professional strike breakers with sawed-off shot guns, but he opened with:

"This is the first stump speech I've ever made from a stump. We have come here to test our rights as American citiens to hold a peaceful meeting for a legal and legitimate purpose. Yesterday, Thomas Jefferson was born. You may have heard the name. His birthday is being celebrated in Passaic by a shameful desecration of the cause of liberty for which he strove so valiantly.

"I want to urge upon the strikers here that they continue their fine record of peaceful endeavor to win their just demands. You strikers have shown a wonderful spirit of self-control. The violence in this strike is not of your making. You have had nothing to do with violence except to be the victims of it. This has been a legal and orderly strike. Your leader, Albert Weisbord, is in jail. He is being held in $30,000 bail. This excessive bail is a mockery on American justice—"

And that was as far as Thomas got. A police whistle shrilled. Under-sheriff Donaldson shouted to the gun-slinging police and deputies, "Clean 'em out. Lock that bird up." Into the crowd went rifle butts and clubs and off the tree stump came Thomas, to be hustled away to a waiting police car.

Thomas was driven by back roads to the county seat, Hackensack, where he was delivered to insurance agent Louis N. Hargreaves, who doubled in brass as a justice of the peace. Hargreaves had made a name for himself as a bitter enemy of the strikers; he thumbed through his law books trying to find a law under which to hold Thomas. Finally he phoned the prosecutor's office and got his instructions straight. He held Thomas for inciting to riot and fixed bail at $10,000, a sum which Thomas could not provide at that hour.

Meanwhile a hunt for Thomas was taking place throughout the nearby countryside, since the chief of police and the sheriff refused to tell where Thomas had been taken. Friends and reporters were given false clews and feared that Thomas had been kidnapped. Since Violet was ill at home, his friends were worried about breaking the news to her. At least five persons called Violet and asked, "Has Norman come home yet?" "No," she replied, "he went to Bergen County and I think he's in jail." At which each said, "Oh, that's just what I was going to tell you!"

While Norman was in the J.P.'s office, one of the policemen philosophized: "Mr. Thomas, what you was doing was moral all right, but maybe it ain't legal. Some things is moral that ain't legal and some things is legal that ain't moral. And what's a poor cop gonna' do about it?"

Thomas was kept in the county jail overnight. The next afternoon, a farcical hearing was held before the same Justice Hargreaves and the $10,000 bail continued. Thomas was then released. The A.C.L.U. immediately started proceedings before a vice-chancellor to enjoin Sheriff Nimmo and his underlings from any similar acts, citing in evidence Thomas' experience. The injunction was won and ended a dangerous threat to liberty through misuse of riot law. The grand jury found no indictment against Thomas, who brought suit for false arrest against the sheriff. The suit was dropped when the sheriff died. But the upshot of Thomas' fight for free speech was that from then on the strikers were unmolested at their meetings, and, after a long time, the strike was partially successful.

This same year, Thomas had another experience with campaigning. While Judge Jacob Panken ran for Governor, Norman was persuaded to run for the State Senate in the 14th District on the lower East Side. Campaigning there was colorful. Outdoor meetings that lasted far into the night attracted hundreds, even thousands of eager listeners. Both Panken and Thomas got a fair number of votes but not election.

That was the year that Dr. Sirovich, a Democratic candidate for Congressman, made a reputation for himself by using a placard showing himself with a beard on the East Side and without it on the West Side. Bob Wagner, Sr., running successfully for the U.S. Senate, went him one better. Wagner's managers commended him to Protestants because he once taught a Lutheran Sunday School upstate, to Catholics because his wife was a Catholic (this was before he joined the Catholic Church himself), and on the lower East Side, they distributed cards showing a picture of Wagner's father strikingly bearded in the orthodox Hebraic fashion.

In 1926, during the campaign, Gene Debs died, to the deep personal grief of thousands who were never Socialists as well as those who gloried in having been his party comrades. Thomas was asked to speak at his funeral in Terre Haute, where, from the front porch of Debs' home, he said:

"There may have been a cloud over Gene Debs' citizenship in this country, but there is no cloud over his citizenship in the great immortals. His personal greatness was due to the fact that he was a combined prophet and lover of mankind. The secret of his greatness was that he loved people. We cannot say that we love Debs if we go back to the lack of faith and petty compromises. He lives in us, we have kindled our little torches at his great fire—and we must carry on."

Thomas deeply regretted that he knew Debs personally only after his release from the Atlanta prison. "Long years after he died," said Thomas, "men and women would come up to me and say with reverent voices, 'I knew Gene Debs.' He was a truly great man. His parents were Alsatian immigrants to Indiana. (Only a few years ago, I found in talking with the great Dr. Albert Schweitzer that he and Gene Debs were first cousins.)

"In the Socialist Party, which he helped organize in 1900–1, Debs was never the policy-maker. . . . I was often to be embarrassed by old-timers who constantly told me that Debs never did this or that about shaping policies and platforms at conventions.

"After his release from Atlanta, the party exploited him. The national office sought to substitute his personal popularity for a vigorous political program suitable to the postwar years plus a well conceived organizational drive. Debs himself was failing in health. In prison he had been unable to follow closely events in and out of the party. In his enthusiasm for the Russian Revolution, he had once declared, 'I am a Bolshevik from the crown of my head to the soles of my feet.' While, after some inner struggle, he stuck to democratic socialism and his own party, and criticized the communists, Socialist officials were always a little afraid of what he might say impulsively. . . ."

But Debs' death robbed the party of its greatest single asset. Moreover, the whole labor and radical movement was at a low ebb in the days of Coolidge prosperity. Serious economists talked of the golden plateau of permanent prosperity and offered the slogan, "Every man a capitalist."

In 1927 heartbreak came to millions in America and throughout the world as the Sacco-Vanzetti case reached its climax. It was poignantly appropriate that the first speech over radio station WEVD (named after the Socialist leader Eugene Victor Debs) was by Norman Thomas in behalf of Sacco and Vanzetti. As Thomas noted, Debs' last act before his fatal illness was to send a money order to the Sacco-Vanzetti Committee. Nicola Sacco and Bartolomeo Vanzetti, two warm-hearted anarchists, were arrested on May 5, 1920, and soon convicted of having robbed and murdered two men carrying the payroll of Slater & Morill, a South Braintree, Mass., shoe factory. All over the world, millions protested.

At a "death-watch" meeting in Community Church on Monday evening, August 22, 1927, 1,200 New Yorkers awaited news of the last moments of Sacco and Vanzetti. Hundreds of men and women wept as chairman Sam DeWitt announced, a few minutes after midnight, that Sacco and Vanzetti had been executed.

Thomas told the mourners, "Our children and our children's children will remember this night in an anguish of bitterness because tonight there has been killed in the Commonwealth of Massachusetts that faith in human justice which might have moderated the bitterness of social conflict.

"The Federal courts, we are told, are powerless under the law. We bow to the learned judges, yet it is a fact that if Sacco and Vanzetti were a corporation threatened by Massachusetts law with curtailment of their profits, they would automatically and as a matter of course be entitled to a hearing before the Federal courts under the 'due process of law' clause of the fourteenth amendment. So much better do we protect property rights than human rights in America . . ."

It was probably the memory of Sacco and Vanzetti that prevented another case that year from having a similar ending. Shortly after Mussolini came to power, he had encouraged the formation of black shirt groups in Italian districts in New York. On Memorial Day, 1927, a group of black-shirted members of the Bronx branch of the Fascisti League of North America had started to ascend the Third Avenue El to join fellow members in the Memorial Day parade. Suddenly one, Joseph Carisi, shrieked and fell dead, stabbed a dozen times. Another, Nicholas Amoroso, was shot and died before he reached the hospital. Mussolini had demanded retribution and detectives made the rounds of anti-Fascists and netted about a dozen. Three weeks after the murder, well-known anti-Fascists Calogero Greco and Donato Carillo were indicted. Anxious to prevent any miscarriage of justice, American and Italian liberal and radical groups rallied under the leadership of Carlo

109

Tresca, a great-hearted Italian anarchist. Arthur Garfield Hays, Isaac Schorr, Vito Marcantonio and Carolyn Weiss King offered their aid as counsel, but Tresca insisted that Clarence Darrow was also needed to insure victory. Thomas was urged to approach Darrow, and did so by telephone. Darrow said he would have to ask a $10,000 fee. Since the committee was running largely on nickels and dimes from poor anti-Fascists, Thomas hesitated. But Tresca literally shoved Thomas in the back and ordered him to say yes. He did and Darrow took the case. Actually the prosecution case was very weak and perhaps even a lesser lawyer than Darrow might have won. But Darrow's victory was triumphant.

Printing bills and other costs of the Defense Committee had drained the treasury and after the trial Thomas saw little chance of raising Darrow's fee. Heavy was his gloom despite the victory. Again Tresca saved the day. He said, "Tonight we'll go to the victory party at Art Hays'. After Darrow has had a couple of drinks to mellow him, you tell Clarence how things stand. He's proud of the victory and I'm sure he'll forget the fee." Once more, Thomas obeyed, with considerable misgiving. However, Tresca was a good prophet. Darrow generously forgave the debt. As Thomas pointed out years later, Darrow was immensely skeptical about mankind as a whole, but his concern for justice to individual men was even greater.

Meanwhile, the many Thomas efforts to protect civil liberties and aid union organizing drives were making him somewhat better known throughout the land and preparing him for his new role as candidate for President, a role he was to play more often than any man in history.

NINE

Two Chickens in Every Pot

૪ઙ IN 1928, IT WAS CLEAR months before the campaign that there could be no "third party" campaign similar to the 1924 La Follette coalition. The Socialist Party would have to stand on its own. The party's two outstanding leaders, Morris Hillquit and Victor Berger, were not eligible to run for the presidency since they had been born in Europe. Dan Hoan might have been a logical choice but he was too busy as mayor of Milwaukee to risk certain presidential defeat. Two weeks before the Socialist national convention, Thomas attempted to avoid being nominated. He wrote the *New Leader* that "personal and family considerations almost certainly will make it extremely difficult, if not altogether impossible, for me to take the extensive campaign trips which the Socialist presidential candidate must undertake this year. . . . There is another and even more important reason for my stand. . . . I have been earnestly working for the nomination of James H. Maurer. . . . I earnestly hope that the party will insist on his nomination."

Maurer, president of the Pennsylvania Federation of Labor, had been elected Commissioner of Finance in the 1927 Socialist sweep of Reading, Pa. He refused to be available for the presidential nomination but agreed to serve as vice-presidential running mate to Thomas. Aware that he was still largely an unknown quantity so far as the nation was concerned, Thomas acceded to the convention's demand and, as a sort of Hobson's choice, took the presidential nomination.

While Thomas had achieved considerable publicity through his activity in free speech tests and in helping poor and struggling unions to organize, his appeal was vastly different from that of Gene Debs. Debs had come to socialism from the labor movement and had had little formal schooling. Thomas had two college degrees, was a former minister, and made his strongest appeal to intellectuals. Even before his first nomination, Thomas had no illusions about ever being elected President on the Socialist ticket. He believed that the Socialist Party was unlikely ever to become a mass party itself, but was anxious to make it the spearhead of such a mass party.

In the campaign, Thomas was delighted to have Maurer as a running mate. He was a salty personality, of Pennsylvania Dutch background, self-educated (he started to learn to read at the age of 16), shrewd, humorous, courageous and incorruptible. Although a right-wing Socialist, Maurer had been on a union tour to Russia earlier in 1928, and had liked much of what he saw. He hated American communists as destroyers of the labor movement, but felt Russia was doing a good job.

Party machinery for a campaign was virtually nonexistent. The national office in Chicago was in the hands of an incompetent, William H. Henry. To circumvent him, the new national executive committee, chaired by Victor Berger, set up a Socialist Action Committee in New York. Hillquit was its chairman, Algernon Lee its treasurer, and dynamic young G. August Gerber its secretary and campaign manager. Gerber, son of the old socialist war horse Julius Gerber, was a promoter by temperament and was astonishingly successful in getting the party on the ballot in states where Socialist membership was small, apathetic or incompetent. At the start of the campaign, the party was on the ballot automatically in only four states; through petitions and state conventions it got a place on the ballot in all but eleven states. (After 1928, state legislatures one after the other adopted laws making it difficult or impossible for new or minor parties to get on the ballot.)

Many of the active Socialists connected with the *Jewish Daily Forward* and the Workmen's Circle rendered invaluable service

to the campaign. The Workmen's Circle, a fraternal mutual benefit and insurance society organized originally by Jewish socialist
immigrants, was the largest source of active campaign support
throughout the nation. Under the laws governing insurance organizations it was officially nonpartisan but its members in scores
of cities did yeoman work in helping the Party get on the ballot
and in electioneering. Thomas, incidentally, was one of the few
non-Jewish Workmen's Circle members.

In many respects this first Thomas presidential campaign
was his most difficult. Campaigning on such a large scale was a
new experience, he was unfamiliar with much of the country and
with party membership in most states, and Violet was unable to
leave the children during the summer months to travel with her
husband.

In the campaign, Thomas covered all parts of the country and
spoke in all but three states, not only to collect votes but, more
important, to reawaken Socialist interest and start rebuilding the
Party. He traveled in all sorts of vehicles from busses and autos
to airplanes, but mostly in trains, at all hours of the day and night,
sometimes in coaches and sometimes in Pullmans. The problem
of fresh clothing, after long meetings on sweltering nights, was
a constant one. Often, after spending an uncomfortable night in
an upper berth, Thomas would arrive in a strange city in the
early morning, wondering who would meet him; what sort of
press interviews awaited him; and, above all, what kind of meetings
there would be. Thomas soon recovered from his naive notion
that even a minor party presidential nominee would automatically
draw a crowd. What surprised him most was to realize that his
great foe was not open opposition but public indifference.

Newspapers sent reporters to cover most of the meetings and
to interview Thomas. While the reporters were personally fair
to Thomas and friendly, they were amazingly ignorant of Socialist theory. Thomas and his colleagues had to spend an inordinate
amount of time explaining why they could not be grouped as
"Socialists, communists and anarchists."

For the first time in 1928, radio was widely used in a major
political campaign. Censorship was prevalent to a ridiculous degree
in the early days of radio. The first four times Thomas was invited

to speak, he was ruled off at the last moment for some absurd reason such as the fact that he criticized the teaching of history for perpetuating national pride and hate. Station program directors had no great opinion of the mentality of their audiences. "Remember you are going to speak to a million morons" was an instruction Thomas frequently heard.

Thomas and Maurer campaigned in 1928 on the issue that Coolidge prosperity had not conquered poverty, that serious unemployment still existed and that social insurance was needed. While denying that depressions had been conquered for all time, not even Thomas anticipated the complete collapse which was to come in a year.

Socialists have often been criticized for being high-minded impractical idealists, with their heads in the clouds. In view of this charge it is interesting to note the way Thomas dealt with campaign issues in 1928. Republicans called for an even higher protective tariff as prosperity's guardian angel. The Democrats tried to ride both sides of the issue, in order to appeal to everyone. Thomas pulled no punches and showed how high tariffs not only cheated farmers and consumers to benefit businessmen, but also impaired international relations. Contrary to Hoover's protectionist claims, said Thomas, American prosperity was due to our having the "greatest internal free trade market between our states to be found in all the world." But free trade was no cure-all either. Thomas favored lowering the trade barriers cautiously because "having got so far along on the protectionist track the United States cannot jump to another, even if better, track without a wreck." To cushion any economic dislocation brought by a tariff reduction, the Socialist nominee advocated a comprehensive public works program.

Even in that year of "prosperity," Thomas charged, there were still four million unemployed. He urged a federal public works program, plus federal loans to states and municipalities, to put the unemployed to work on public projects "at hours and wages fixed by bona-fide labor unions." He called for shortening the work day and week as technology increased labor productivity, and urged the adoption of a Constitutional amendment prohibiting child labor. The party platform called for federal old age pensions and unemployment insurance, to be financed by increased corporation taxes, inheritance levies and taxes on large individual incomes. Had this program been in force when the stock market crash occurred, the nation might have been spared one of the most searing and painful crises in its history.

In international affairs, the platform, which Thomas was instrumental in writing, called for American initiative for world disarmament, plus cuts in U.S. military and naval appropriations. It urged American entry into the League of Nations to help make that body stronger, more inclusive and democratic. The Socialists advocated cancellation of both the Allied war debts and reparations of the Central Powers if both groups would cut their military expenditures drastically. While arraigning the Soviet Union's "despotic and brutal" totalitarianism, the party urged "the speedy recognition of Russia, not as an expression of approval of the Bolshevik regime," but to help establish "international stability and good will." The platform also insisted on the withdrawal of all American troops from Nicaragua, home rule for Puerto Rico and the Virgin Islands, and independence for the Philippines.

The platform, of course, called for "the collective ownership of natural resources and basic industries and their democratic management for the use and benefit of all instead of the private profit of the privileged few."

One issue that aroused Thomas' ire was religious bigotry. In 1924, the Democratic convention had failed to denounce the Klan by name. In 1928, with Catholic Al Smith as Democratic nominee, religion was the predominant factor in the campaign. Thomas, in an open letter to the nation's Protestant churches, assailed his former clerical colleagues (mostly Republican) for dragging "religious prejudice" into the campaign and using the prohibition issue as a "mask for religious partisanship."

It was the short-term aims of the platform rather than the ultimate goal of a socialized economy that attracted much of the support which Thomas won from intellectuals and liberals. He urged that the power of the federal courts to issue labor injunctions be inhibited, and called for adoption of a Constitutional amendment to abolish "lame duck" Congresses. Both reforms were effected within a few years by the major parties. Thomas also urged that, in order to insure Negro voting equality, congressional representation be reduced for those states that denied the suffrage to Negroes.

Among more than a hundred educators, artists, writers, clergymen and other professionals who joined novelist and historian W. E. Woodward in backing Thomas and Maurer, were such notables as geographer J. Russell Smith of Columbia University; theologian Reinhold Niebuhr of Union Theological Seminary; Robert Morss Lovett and Paul H. Douglas of the University of Chicago; Freda Kirchwey of *The Nation;* Howard Brubaker of the *New Yorker;* Methodist Bishop Paul Jones; Rabbi M. S. Fisher; Rev. John Haynes Holmes of Community Church; and Harold E. Fey of the *Christian Century*.

While Thomas voters were high in quality, they were few in number. As historian David A. Shannon put it, American voters were more concerned with prohibition, Protestantism and prosperity than with exploitation of the poor. Hoover won by a landslide with over 21 million votes; Smith had 15 million; and Thomas 267,000. Nevertheless, it was obvious to the Socialists that their new leader, Norman Thomas, was an attractive personality who commanded a good deal of respect, if not votes, from the American people. And Socialists were happy to note that the campaign had begun to revive party organization in a number of areas.

After the campaign, so many penitent Republican and Democratic voters told Thomas that they wished they had voted for him that he remarked: "Thanks for the flowers, but I wish you hadn't waited for the funeral."

Following the 1928 election campaign, the Socialist Party got a shot in the arm. Its inept national secretary, William H. Henry, resigned early in 1929 and the national executive committee chose an imaginative and capable young Missourian, Clarence O. Senior, to replace him. Senior, 26 years old, a graduate of the University of Kansas, had been editor of the *International Municipal Digest* and went to Cleveland to work with the Adult Education Association. There he was active in workers' education and helped revitalize the Party in Cleveland. With his aid, the Socialists there ran a strong race in the municipal election. When he took office in the national headquarters in Chicago, Party activities, fund raising and organizing started to hum.

The end of the campaign meant no lessening in Thomas' activities. He went back to work, travelling and speaking under League for Industrial Democracy auspices. In towns and cities, in addition to his main lectures, Thomas usually had one or more formal or informal meetings with Socialist Party or Workmen's Circle groups. Banquets were then, as now, inevitable features of socialist and other liberal enterprises. Socialist dinners always started late, which moved Morris Hillquit to confide to Norman that: "I've spent all my life unsuccessfully trying to be late to a Socialist banquet." Thomas once suggested the following epitaph for himself: "Here lies the body of one who died eating his way to Utopia."

In 1929 there was unanimous agreement among New York Socialists that Norman Thomas would have to run for Mayor of New York against Mayor Jimmy Walker. He entered the 1929 mayoralty drive eagerly and with substantial information about gangsterism, slums, crooked police and politics, on which to base his campaign. A strong and active independent committee for Thomas' election was formed under the chairmanship of his old friend John Haynes Holmes.

During the campaign, Thomas referred to a number of magistrates involved in corrupt practices. Every one whom he mentioned by name was later removed, resigned under fire, or was not reappointed. One was Magistrate Vitale, who had the misfortune to be held up at a dinner in his own honor, even though half a dozen of the guests were famous gunmen. "Famous," noted Thomas dryly, "but not so quick on the draw as the gunmen who robbed them that night." New York City's Bar Association joined Thomas in calling for Vitale's removal as a judge when it was revealed that Vitale had accepted a $19,940 "loan" from the enterprising gambler, Arnold Rothstein, and that his bank deposits contained a mysterious and unexplained $100,000.

Among other scandals cited by Thomas were the habitual sale of favors, legal and illegal, by the police, including speakeasy graft; the Equitable Coach Company scandal in which Jimmy Walker signed a contract on August 9, 1927, and sailed for Europe

August 10 with a $10,000 letter of credit arranged by J. Allen Smith of Equitable; the push-cart market scandal; the zoning scandals and workmen's compensation scandals.

One bit of luck helped the campaign immeasurably. When Ramsay MacDonald, Britain's Labor Prime Minister, came to New York, Thomas and Adolph Ochs, publisher of *The New York Times*, met as members of the welcoming committee on the tug bound down the bay to greet MacDonald. By way of conversation, Ochs said, "Well, Mr. Thomas, I see that you're nominated for Mayor by the Socialists. I hope you'll make a campaign that will discuss the issues." "Mr. Ochs," replied Thomas, "I've always discussed issues. But if you'll forgive my saying so, not even *The Times* seems to know it. Last year, when I ran for President, your paper merely reprinted some wisecracks of mine two or three times over but never carried the substance of my remarks." Somewhat taken aback, Ochs said: "Well, I'll speak to my people and see what we can do." He told the men on his paper to give adequate coverage to Thomas, whereupon other papers followed suit. The *Herald Tribune* and the *Telegram* went further. They endorsed Thomas for Mayor.

McAlister Coleman described a typical campaign night:

"It is seven o'clock in the evening and already there are gathering in front of the old-fashioned Thomas house on East 18th Street just beyond the thunder of the Third Avenue Elevated, reporters, the police escort, the ubiquitous and ever-faithful Eddie Levinson, and Joe Viola, who drives a car as Kreisler plays a violin.

"By 7:30 we are off. Immediately there comes to rushing reality the dream of every small New Yorker, namely, to ride on a fire-engine. For with the motorcycle cop ahead, sounding his siren, all speed laws are off as you dodge in and out of elevated pillars, under the noses of suddenly halted trucks, and through red lights at a speed of forty to fifty miles per hour. Of course this is a courtesy extended to all candidates. Nevertheless it gives you a wonderful sense of superiority to be riding in a Socialist auto past indignant Rolls Royces and Packards, waved to one side by the majestic arm of the law ahead. In one night, you go at this headlong pace from a meeting at the tip-end of the Bronx clear down to where cold winds are blowing along Coney Island's boardwalk.

"Arrived at the big school house, little boys shout exultantly,

'Here he comes! 'Ray for Norman Thomas!' A Yipsel (Young
People's Socialist League) cheering squad in the school yard ex-
plodes boisterously as out of the official car strides a smiling six-
footer to be charged at by a mob of youngsters anxious to get as
near their hero as possible. You follow the plunging form of
Thomas up a flight of stairs to an auditorium packed to the eaves.
At the sight of that looming figure in a dark sack suit, men,
women and children jump up, stamping, yelling and clapping.
They keep up the din until Thomas stretches out his hands and
smiling, says: 'It's fine for you to greet me this way, but my boss
here'—pointing at Eddie Levinson—'says that I have only 20 minutes, and the longer you applaud the less time there is for me to
tell you what's on my mind.'

"Instantly there is silence, and people lean forward in their
seats, while Norman in simple, incisive language, talks to them
about their common problems of rent, housing, transit and the
like.

"The charm of this man is nothing soft, it is all sturdiness and
sincerity. All the while he is speaking you say to yourself, 'This
is courage in the flesh.'

"Five more stops and finally, after midnight, a tired crew turns
into East 18th Street, there to be welcomed by the hospitable Mrs.
Thomas with hot tea and coffee. The events of the night are talked
over, and then the party breaks up, remembering that Thomas
must be up by half-past seven to start another day's grind."

At the Edgewood School in Connecticut, the Thomas children found much of the faculty sympathetic to their father. So
much so that when Evan, then nine years old, heard that Walker
was going to be kicked out he assumed his father would soon be
wearing the Mayor's mantle. He was somewhat disappointed, after
Election Day, to find out that this did not happen. The girls, Polly,
Frances and Becky, were older and while they, too, were hopeful
of victory, they were more philosophical in defeat.

In any event, during that campaign summer, all the children
loved to hear their father speak. They even enjoyed the heckling
at street corner meetings. When someone would accuse Thomas
of believing in "free love," the young Thomases would laugh to
think that anyone could accuse *their* father of such immorality.
Polly was particularly fascinated to see her father go from a
street corner meeting to a university group and then to a labor
hall. In each case, he would give a completely different speech,
speaking directly to each audience in terms it could understand

and yet getting across the same main points.

Jimmy Walker was so confident of election that he hardly bothered to campaign, and felt little need to debate his opponents. The Republicans put up fiery Fiorello La Guardia, more or less as a sacrificial lamb. In this campaign, La Guardia had only GOP support. He was sorely disappointed when *The Nation* decided to support Thomas. The liberal weekly expressed its esteem for La Guardia as the best and most liberal Congressman from New York, but added: "With all respect to him, he is not of the same stature as Norman Thomas."

Thomas campaigned as vigorously against his former ally, La Guardia, as he did against Walker. He denounced him as a machine nominee, a "political chameleon," an opportunist and a spoilsman. When he dared La Guardia to prove his progressivism by repudiating his American Fascist admirers, La Guardia remained silent. Republican Admiral Harris asked Thomas to step aside in favor of the Congressman from East Harlem, to which the Socialist retorted: "Politics is going crazy when a Republican organization wants a Socialist to withdraw on the ground that the Republican candidate will give a pale imitation of a Socialist program."

La Guardia, dependent on a Republican machine which was not overly enthusiastic about him but which he feared antagonizing, presented no constructive program. At a meeting in the Greenpoint section of Brooklyn, when Thomas taunted the Major for ignoring all issues but corruption, La Guardia wailed, "It's easy for you, but I got only the nomination from the Republican party."

But the campaign was not all smooth sailing for Thomas. He had to cope with both right and left wing criticism within his own party. Young left-wingers (who called themselves Militants) argued that the stress on municipal reforms was not Marxist and urged a campaign stressing full socialization. The Old Guard (doctrinaire Marxists in theory if not in action) agreed with much of this criticism. Algernon Lee, running for president of the Board of Aldermen, refused to discuss municipal issues and his formal version of Marxism reminded Thomas of orthodox church theology. Yet while Thomas disagreed with the Militants, he sympathized with their zeal and felt only annoyance with the Marxist verbalizing of the Old Guard. Thomas was accused of being a pragmatist without real philosophy. Actually, as a result of his church experience, he was very leery of any dogma, as evidenced as early as 1918 in his letter of application for membership in the Socialist Party. He wanted the Party to put its major emphasis on a working program around which most of the members could unite.

As the campaign progressed, the Citizens' Union, composed of Republicans and Democrats and without a single Socialist member, endorsed Thomas, saying, "If personal merit alone were to decide the contest, Mr. Thomas would win easily." The Citizens' Union action drew praise from *The New York Times*, the *World* and the *Evening Telegram*.

Thomas amassed 175,000 votes—135,000 more than he had polled for the same office in 1925. Walker won with 865,000 and La Guardia came second with 368,000. Each lost 4½ per cent from their party's 1925 vote, while Thomas gained 9 per cent of the total vote.

The 1929 mayoralty election results were encouraging enough for the independent committee backing Thomas to decide to continue the fight against Tammany. Thomas called the group together and suggested that they organize into a City Affairs Committee. Paul Blanshard, who had been field secretary of the League for Industrial Democracy, offered to serve as executive secretary. Thomas and Blanshard then interviewed Wise, John Haynes Holmes, John Lovejoy Elliott, and a number of others, and all agreed to form the City Affairs Committee. Blanshard persuaded several young active Socialists to work for the committee at token salaries—in those days ten dollars was like a life preserver to many people. Among them were Henry Rosner, later to become assistant to the Commissioner of the New York City Welfare Department, and Louis Yavner. Since Thomas was busy in Socialist Party affairs and was traveling a good deal for the LID, he refused to become the active head of the Committee, but worked closely with it. John Haynes Holmes and Stephen Wise served harmoniously as co-chairmen. They all worked hard and systematically and the City Affairs Committee proceeded to do a remarkable job. Under the impact of the depression, the press was turning against Tammany, and the Committee secured publicity easily.

In 1931, Thomas and the City Affairs Committee brought long and detailed charges calling for Mayor Jimmy Walker's removal by Governor Franklin D. Roosevelt. They pointed to the looting of funds during the Walker regime through levies upon private business by political brokers who had zoning laws, franchises or permits to sell, as well as through appointment of incompetent or crooked public officials. Without even a public hearing, Roosevelt dismissed the charges against Walker as "too general." After the Hofstadter Committee was set up by the state legislature with Judge Samuel Seabury as chief investigator, and after a barrage of revelations of graft by the tin-box brigade, headed by Sheriff Tom Farley, Roosevelt belatedly removed Farley.

When John Haynes Holmes and Rabbi Stephen S. Wise called upon Roosevelt to move against Boss John Theofel of Queens County and Sheriff James A. McQuade of Kings County because of their unexplained fortunes and their ludicrous explanation to Judge Seabury regarding huge bank accounts, Roosevelt rebuked Holmes and Wise. "If they would serve their God," said Roosevelt, "as they seek to serve themselves, the people of the city of New York would be the gainers." This showed far more anger than Roosevelt ever displayed against the Tammany thieves who ruled New York.

One reason for Roosevelt's reluctance to move against Tammany was his hope for its support for the Democratic presidential nomination at the 1932 Chicago convention. Not until August 4th, after the nomination had been finally secured, did Roosevelt finally order Walker to answer Judge Seabury's removal charges; and even then, not until the hierarchy of the Roman Catholic Church passed the word that Walker's private peccadilloes were a scandal to church and state. (Years later, old Dr. Thomas Darlington, Grand Sachem of Tammany, confirmed this interpretation to Thomas and added that colorless Surrogate John P. O'Brien had been suggested as Walker's successor because he was a "good-living man.")

TEN

The Crash
and the '32 Campaign

In MAY OF 1929, more than five months before the stock market crash, Thomas urged the Socialist Party national executive committee to call for organization of unemployed workers throughout the nation. The adopted resolution foresaw that the nation had been living for ten years in a fool's paradise, which was now vanishing not only for workers but for farmers and small businessmen as well. Yet it took many months more, for the dramatic plunge of the Wall Street crash to be followed by the grim misery of rapidly growing mass joblessness, before the Socialists took their own resolution seriously and started to carry it out.

After the stock market plunge, business leaders indulged in a veritable spate of optimistic twaddle. "Never before," intoned Bethlehem Steel's board chairman, Charles Schwab, "has American business been as firmly entrenched for prosperity as it is today (Dec. 10, 1929)." In the same month, George E. Roberts, vice-president of the National City Bank of New York, came up with: "Conditions are more favorable for permanent prosperity than they have been in the past year."

Meanwhile, in the bituminous coal fields of the country, Clarence Pickett of the American Friends Service Committee found schools where 85, 90 and even 99 per cent of the children were badly underweight, and, in consequence, drowsy, lethargic and often mentally retarded. "Have you ever heard a hungry child

123

cry?" asked Lillian Wald of the Henry Street Settlement. "Have you seen the uncontrollable trembling of parents who have gone half starved for weeks so that the children may have food?"

Within a few months of the stock market collapse, unemployment had been catapulted into the country's foremost concern. Selling apples and shining shoes became "occupations" for thousands of the unemployed while men arrested for sleeping in New York's subways rejoiced because it brought them free meals.

In 1929, just when the crash occurred, Mary Fox came to the League for Industrial Democracy as executive secretary and brought great drive, imagination and creative thinking to the League's work. Her presence relieved Thomas of many administrative details and freed him for writing books as well as articles, working with unions, attending American Civil Liberties Union and other meetings, and expanding his Socialist Party activities. He continued to be the League's chief policy maker, yet always found time to be accessible to students, unionists, unemployed workers and others seeking guidance or help. Young people were so anxious to work at something meaningful that they took LID jobs just for carfare and lunch money. They hitchhiked all over the country setting up new LID college chapters, while working with unions and the Socialist Party at the same time.

Through the LID office, Thomas strengthened the Emergency Committee for Strikers Relief. When textile workers in North and South Carolina went out on strike in 1929 against $12 a-week-pay for a 12-hour and 20-minute day, intolerable working conditions and feudally-run mill villages, their union, the United Textile Workers of America, had no money in the treasury to support the strikers. Alfred Hoffman, the union's Southern organizer, turned in desperation to Jack Herling, who was in the South for the Emergency Committee at the time. Herling contacted Norman Thomas, who assured him that the Committee would send money for food. Thousands of pounds of flour and salt pork went to feed the strikers in Elizabethton and Greenville, S.C., and Marion, N.C. In a few months, over $10,000 from the Committee brought a "lot of pertaters" to the strikers.

"To be perfectly frank," wrote Hoffman to Thomas, "if it hadn't been for the Emergency Committee, we would just have been going out on strike to starve."

After a nine-weeks strike in Marion, an agreement was reached on the basis of a 55-hour week, no discrimination against union members, and recognition of a workers' grievance committee. As soon as work resumed, discrimination against union members began, workers were evicted from their homes, and new families were brought in to replace them. Union members were even expelled from their churches. Provoked beyond endurance, the night shift workers started a spontaneous strike. When the day shift arrived, most workers stayed out of the plant but some of the new workers fought with the pickets.

Sheriff O. F. Adkins and fully armed deputies, quartered on company property and waiting for something to happen, ordered the strikers to disperse. The sheriff shot off a tear gas cartridge, and as the pickets rushed away, shots rang out. Six strikers were killed and twenty-four wounded, all shot in the back. One of them, a 65-year-old man who had worked at the mill for $11.50 per week, was carried to the operating table, handcuffed, and died soon afterward. When brought to trial, the sheriff and his deputies were acquitted. So farcical was the trial that Josephus Daniels in the Raleigh *News and Observer* cried out in protest in the editorial bearing the caption, "Their Blood Cries From the Ground." Bitterly Thomas noted: "The employer who boasted that he had fooled the workers, the employer who told a newspaper man, 'The sheriff and his men are damn good shots,'—he will eat his Christmas and New Year's dinners in peace and prosperity. His church has never suspended or expelled or even examined him. It was only the workers whose church threw them out. Such is justice in state and church during the industrial struggle."

Thomas and the Socialist Party helped create Unemployed Leagues, some of which functioned as "barter system" mutual aid cooperatives, exchanging the labor of unemployed workers for food, lumber and other commodities from merchants. Under the direction of Karl Borders of Chicago, the League for Industrial Democracy set up the Workers Alliance. For a while, the two unemployed groups operated independently, but soon merged.

125

Meanwhile, the communists organized rival Unemployed Councils, which held militant unemployed parades and demonstrations before city halls, blending calls for relief with cries of "Defend the Soviet Union." The communists viewed immediate demands for unemployed relief only as helping to "politicalize" workers and prepare them for revolution. This approach Thomas spurned. "No men, still less their children," he said, "can live on the bread of Utopia. They hunger now. Cold and hungry children make for no constructive social revolution. They add to the needless weight of the world's woe."

As the depression deepened (by March 1931, unemployment estimates ranged between 7½ and 8 million, jumped to 12 million by 1932 and still inched upward), the Socialist Party made steady if not spectacular growth. With Thomas speaking throughout the country, the Party organized 32 new locals in 1930. Milwaukee Socialists elected nine members to the state assembly and two to the state senate. In Reading, Pa., Socialists elected two members to the state legislature. Louis Waldman, running against Franklin D. Roosevelt of New York, polled more than 120,000 votes. In 1931, almost a hundred new Socialist locals were formed.

Poverty in the city was matched in the country as John Steinbeck eloquently showed in *The Grapes of Wrath*. Following a drought in the Southwest, several hundred tenant farmers, in January 1931, came to the Red Cross in England, Ark., and asked for food. Some of the white and Negro farmers carried rifles. When the Red Cross administrator said that his supply of requisition blanks had been exhausted, the mob marched on the stores and seized their own flour and lard. "Paul Revere just woke up Concord," said Will Roger, "these birds woke up America."

The mines presented another grim picture. By 1931, one third of the West Virginia coal miners were out of work and another third worked only one or two days a week. Aided by contributions from Thomas and northern liberals, and using a group of young volunteer organizers from A. J. Muste's Brookwood Labor College, Frank Keeney, a one-time Socialist and former president of the West Virginia district of the United Mine Workers, organized the West Virginia Mine Workers Union, enrolling some 20,000 members within a few months.

When the union asked the League for Industrial Democracy to help in its educational work, Thomas enthusiastically approved Mary Fox's plan to set up a six-weeks Labor Chautauqua. Classes were held in eight mining camps. Three days after the Chautauqua started, the miners went out on strike. The great problem was to keep them housed and fed during a long struggle, while countering efforts of the communists, who had organized a National Miners Union, to disrupt the strike. (In the summer of 1931, the author graduated from high school into unemployment, and joined the Young People's Socialist League. The first time I heard Norman Thomas was at an open air rally in New York to raise funds, food and clothing for the West Virginia miners. I was extremely moved by Thomas' eloquence and personality. That same rally provided my introduction to communist tactics. First they heckled and then they began fist fights to break up the meeting.)

Thomas worked desperately to secure funds for the strikers, but conditions deteriorated. On the day 106 families at a single camp were evicted from their homes, Mrs. Ethel Clyde, who generously supported the LID's educational work, had just arrived to see what was going on. She saw miners out in the fields with no shelter, and she put up money so that they could return to their homes.

The next night, there was jubilation. After the regular union meeting and Chautauqua performance, a choir of Negro union members improvised new verses to an old hymn, "We Shall Not Be Moved."

> The people of New York has decided—
> We shall not be moved.
>
> Just like a tree that's planted by the water,
> We shall not be moved.
>
> They're fixin' to take our children but
> We shall not be moved.
>
> They're movin' out our furniture but
> We shall not be moved.
>
> Norman Thomas is behind us and
> We shall not be moved.

And so was born the now famous union song, "We Shall Not Be Moved." Alas, neither Mrs. Clyde nor Thomas was able to replenish the coffers of the Emergency Committee for Strikers' Relief indefinitely. Food did not last long enough and the Red Cross cut off assistance to strikers. By mid-August the strike was called off and the union disintegrated.

Marxism, like Christianity, gave rise to many sects and many schools of thought. Within the Socialist Party, the Old Guard, consisting primarily of New York needle trades workers, European born and tied to the *Jewish Daily Forward*, advocated the type of Marxism personified by Germany's Edward Bernstein. They believed strongly in gradualism and amelioration of capitalism. The Militants, many of them young people out of the colleges and embittered by the depression, wanted quick action, opposed gradualism, and endlessly debated "the road to power." In between was a considerable group of Centrists, a loose, amorphous grouping rather than a caucus, which was repelled by the Old Guard's apparently constitutional aversion to activity but was also suspicious of the Marxism of the Militants, which sometimes approached a watered-down Leninism. The Centrists included many municipal Socialists in Milwaukee, Reading and other cities, along with pacifists and Christian Socialists. They were often closest to Thomas' position, but were not closely knit.

One issue which deeply divided many Socialists was the matter of Soviet Russia and American communism. When the Bolshevik revolution first occurred in 1917, most American Socialists were sympathetic. But during the course of years, the seasoned Old Guardists became critical of the communists, while the Militants, new to the radical movement and joining the Socialist Party at a moment when capitalism seemed to be literally breaking down, were far more friendly. Yet even here it is easy to exaggerate—which both sides did. In the New York City Socialist convention in 1930, David Shannon reports, both the Old Guard and the Militants called for United States recognition of the Soviet Union, condemned foreign interference with Russian internal affairs and disapproved of Soviet extermination of minority opinion. However, while the Militants advocated "a definitely friendly attitude

towards Soviet Russia" and dealt only briefly with Soviet totalitarianism, the Old Guard asked merely for "normal diplomatic
and trade relations with Russia" and spoke at length of Soviet
"denial of elementary civil rights" and "governmental terrorism."
Thomas later conceded that he had tended to be too favorably
impressed with Bolshevik achievements in the conquest of unemployment through planning, and had been inclined to blame
Soviet violations of civil liberties on Russia's Czarist inheritance
and on fears of Allied encirclement and opposition. He had also
been influenced by his disillusionment over the betrayal of the
British Labor Government by Ramsay MacDonald and the sad
failure of German Social Democracy, obvious even before Hitler's
rise to power.

Both the Militants and the Centrists, with the active support
of Thomas, were anxious to create an all-inclusive Socialist Party,
welcoming even ex-communists if they accepted general socialist
policies and were not controlled by any outside party or group.
The Old Guard feared such a party would mean loss of their
control over the party machinery. Having seen the communist
split of the party in 1919, a short dozen years earlier, they were
suspicious of newcomers.

During this era, the communists were in the throes of their
"third period," during which they termed Socialists "social fascists"—more dangerous than actual fascists or Nazis. Nevertheless,
they called for "united fronts from below," meaning repudiation
of Norman Thomas and other Socialist leaders by Socialist rank
and filers. A number of Socialists fell for the communist bait.
Some, like J. B. Matthews (later to become the darling of the
country's ultra-rightists as the staff expert for Cong. Martin Dies
and the House Un-American Activities Committee) were basically
pro-communist; some were naive; and others thought they could
use the communists instead of having the communists use them.

As the 1932 convention of the Party approached, many Party
members, including Thomas, thought it was time to replace Hillquit as the Party's national chairman with a more aggressive
spokesman—Daniel Hoan, the honest and capable Socialist mayor
of Milwaukee. Thomas was motivated primarily by Hillquit's
performance in office and the feeling that Hoan's midwestern

connections would help to give a more "American" flavor to the party. In this he was supported by B. Charney Vladeck, of the *Jewish Daily Forward*. It is only fair to add, however, that the Militants were out to "get" Hillquit as the symbol of the Old Guard. In addition, many midwesterners resented New York control of the Party, feeling that New Yorkers were intellectually arrogant and condescending.

At the convention, a resolution on Soviet Russia was introduced by Oscar Ameringer, Paul Blanshard and Newman Jeffrey to give qualified approval to the Soviet experiment. The resolution, adopted by 117 to 64, said that: "The Socialist Party, while not endorsing all policies of the Soviet government, and while emphatically urging the release of political prisoners and the restoration of civil liberties, endorses the efforts being made in Russia to create the economic foundations of a socialist society, and calls on the workers to guard against capitalist attacks on Soviet Russia."

The earlier vote on the Russian resolution encouraged both the Militant-Centrist alliance and Thomas in their plan to elect Hoan national chairman. But in the debate, when Milwaukee delegate William F. Quick made anti-New York remarks which were construed by some as anti-Semitic, and when this was followed by Heywood Broun's plea that the national chairman should be someone unmistakably recognized as "American," Thomas' heart sank. Hillquit, still a brilliant lawyer, attacked the Militants as "well-meaning, immature, effervescent people, who will settle down in time but who for the moment are wild, untamed, and dangerous"; the Centrists as "college men and white collar elements"; and the Milwaukeeans as believers in the "Socialism of steam-heated sidewalks and overhead sewers." Then, in a dramatic climax which assured his re-election, he said, "I apologize for being born abroad, for being a Jew, and for living in New York." Socialists, constitutionally opposed to anti-Semitism and all racism, voted 108 to 81 for Hillquit.

There was no conflict over the presidential nomination, since it was obvious that the Old Guard had available no member with the needed stature. In fact, Louis Waldman, an Old Guard leader, made the principal nominating speech for Thomas.

In spite of convention controversies, Thomas and the Party made a fighting campaign, the Party's most vigorous since 1912, even though it had only one-seventh as many members. The situation was helped by Jimmy Walker's forced resignation as New York Mayor and Hillquit's active race as the Socialist mayoralty nominee. Despite his physical weakness, Hillquit waged a strenuous campaign, so strenuous that it may have contributed to his early death. He attracted a lot of attention and worked very closely with Thomas. In fact Hillquit polled 250,000 votes, the highest mayoralty vote ever for the Party.

Even more exciting than the city campaign was the national campaign, waged with meager financial resources but with the devoted help of many young, ingenious and energetic organizers who took their pay in satisfaction rather than money. Among the forty organizers were Amicus Most, Murray Baron, Paul Porter, Victor Reuther, Hy Fish and Powers Hapgood. My own Socialist Party branch and YPSL circle in Washington Heights carried on twenty-four street corner meetings a week.

Main stress in the campaign was on the immediate demands to ameliorate the tragic effects of the depression and to lead to economic recovery. The platform called for a ten-billion-dollar federal program of public works and unemployment relief plus laws to acquire land, buildings, and equipment to put the unemployed to work producing food, fuel, clothing and homes for their own use. The platform also urged:

The six-hour day and five-day week with no wage reductions.
Free public employment agencies.
Compulsory unemployment insurance, based on contributions by Government and employers.
Old-age pensions for men and women sixty years of age and over.
Health and maternity insurance.
Improved workmen's compensation and accident insurance.
The abolition of child labor.
Government aid to farmers and small home-owners to protect them against mortgage foreclosures and a moratorium on sales for nonpayment of taxes by destitute farmers and un-

employed workers.
Adequate minimum wage laws.

Neither the Democratic nor Republican platforms showed any comparable understanding of the nation's needs in this time of desperation and crisis. The Democrats, in fact, pledged a 25 per cent reduction of federal expenditures plus an annually balanced budget. Perhaps it should not have surprised the nation, when Roosevelt was elected, to find that he was forced to turn to the Socialist platform for the essential features of his New Deal.

In the campaign, Thomas spoke in 38 states, made 214 speeches. Some newspapermen called it an "upper berth" campaign, because Thomas frequently took such a berth to save the party money. Much of the time he traveled in a second-hand auto, accompanied by Violet, who served as secretary and maid-of-all-work. As Thomas drove and dictated, she sat with a portable typewriter on her lap and typed releases to be distributed in the cities where he was to speak. At the meetings Violet would sit in the audience, busily knitting as Thomas spoke, and she was by no means uncritical of her husband. At one meeting, where Thomas was referring to Hoover in very uncomplimentary terms, Violet remarked to Paul Sifton, publicity director for the independent committee, "Norman is being demagogic about Hoover. I'll have to say something to him about this. I don't like him to be demagogic."

In none of his campaigns would Thomas permit a ghost-writer for his speeches, which sometimes made the task of his publicity men more difficult. Frequently he was irritated by the tendency of local Socialists to make long speeches themselves, thus leaving him with very limited time at the end of the meetings for his own speech. Nevertheless, Thomas had already won a reputation as an exciting speaker and drew remarkable crowds at many of his stops. In Philadelphia, according to *The New York Times*, the crowd that turned out for Thomas was the biggest at any campaign gathering. His talk at the "ultra-conservative" insurance city of Hartford brought out one of the largest crowds ever to attend a political rally there. In Indianapolis, 10,000 thronged the auditorium, where only two hundred had been present in 1928. In

New York City, 22,000 packed Madison Square Garden with another 10,000 outside unable to get in.

The League for Independent Political Action, formed in 1929 by Paul Douglas and John Dewey, voted in 1932 to back Thomas. Douglas, while admitting "a genuine liking" for Roosevelt because of his stand on power and state unemployment insurance, hit the Democratic Party as the chief obstacle in the way of a third party of farmers, wage earners and white-collar workers. "Its destruction," Douglas insisted, "would be one of the best things that could happen in our political life." Elmer Davis, the noted journalist, stressed that "I am no more a Marxist than I am a Mohammedan" in announcing his support of Thomas. But, he added, "the Socialist program is the only one that seriously attempts to cure our disease; probably it will not win this fall, but if it commands strong support it may force the other parties to face a few facts and to consider national instead of local interests."

Students flocked in great numbers behind Thomas. In a nationwide campus straw poll, Thomas made an impressive showing, carrying such schools as Columbia, CCNY and Howard University. Thomas-for-President Clubs were organized in 274 colleges throughout the land, and many carried on aggressive campaigning. Yet college students were mostly conservative. In the above-mentioned poll, Hoover led with 29,289 votes; Roosevelt had 18,212; Thomas polled 10,470; and Communist Foster, 715. Oddly enough, none of the candidates carried his own alma mater. The conservative character of the college vote becomes even more marked when compared with the actual popular vote in November, when Roosevelt won over Hoover by more than seven million votes!

The greatest weakness of the Thomas campaign was the lack of support from organized labor and the farmers. While leaders of the needle trades unions and the Hosiery Workers backed Thomas, other union leaders were conspicuous by their absence. This did not mean that the labor movement supported Roosevelt. The Executive Council of the AFL reaffirmed its traditional non-partisan political policy and even denounced both the Democratic and Republican platforms. John L. Lewis of the Miners and Big Bill Hutcheson of the Carpenters both endorsed Hoover. The most important labor leaders to work for Roosevelt were Dan

Tobin of the Teamsters and George L. Berry of the Printing Pressmen, both of whom were running hard to become Secretary of Labor. When a United Mine Workers official complained that the Democratic platform had no plank supporting collective bargaining, Roosevelt called it an oversight and promised to deal with the subject in a campaign speech. He never did.

For Thomas, there were many interesting experiences during the countrywide campaign. In Sioux City, Iowa, near the South Dakota border, he was to speak at a picnic ground. Nearby was a tent encampment of farmers, members of one of the radical farm groups, the Farm Holiday movement. Thomas had been talking to the group for a while when up rushed a photographer. "Sure we'll take pictures with Thomas," said the farmers, "but please wait." They went into one of the tents and brought out spike-studded railroad ties, for use in puncturing the tires of trucks challenging their farm strike. Thomas refused to be photographed with the railroad ties, and noted with humor that while farmers might deliberately choose to appear in a picture with lethal weapons, union members never would.

In Des Moines a large group came to hear Thomas speak. Afterwards, at a house meeting, Henry Wallace was present and was very friendly to Thomas. He gave $25 for the Socialist campaign, even though he was registered as a Republican and later voted for Roosevelt. Thomas was well satisfied with the meeting and heard later that when Hoover arrived at Des Moines, he was given the silent treatment. As Hoover drove to the auditorium, many farmers threw corn in front of his car, so that he rode over crunching corn. This gesture indicated the farmers' contempt for a situation in which corn was selling for 10 cents a bushel. Nobody booed Hoover. A rule of silence was merely enforced, which was much harder to take.

When the Socialist campaign party reached Philadelphia, Thomas and Jim Maurer, his vice-presidential running mate, requested a permit to speak at the Rayburn Plaza. They discovered that the Republican city authorities forbade political meetings at the Plaza while conceding that educational meetings could be held. While the application was still pending, one of Hoover's campaign managers announced that he would speak at Rayburn Plaza. This of course redoubled Thomas' interest. After the Socialist permit was refused, the Party announced that "Professors" Thomas and Maurer would give educational classes in history and economics. Thomas and Maurer arrived at the Plaza to greet a big crowd. Somewhat anticlimactically, the authorities removed the ban against speaking just before the meeting started. The occasion still provided Thomas with a good deal of amusement, and the audience roared as he stressed the "educational" nature of his remarks.

When Iago said, "Who steals my purse steals trash," he might have been referring to the Socialist Party campaign treasury. While the Democratic and Republican parties each spent millions of dollars, the Socialist Party's war chest totalled $25,663.36. And the Independent Committee for Thomas and Maurer collected only $17,302.31. To make the money go farther, Thomas cut his expenses to the bone. A ten-day swing with his wife through New England cost $55.45—lodging and meals $16.20; gas and oil $22.65; repairs and grease $4.85; ferry charges and tolls $6.25; public stenographer $4; and incidentals $1.50.

The dedicated young Socialists running the campaign, led by 29-year-old national secretary Clarence Senior, worked at a feverish pitch. Eight million pieces of campaign literature—four times the output in 1928—poured from Party headquarters. A sprightly campaign paper, *America for All*, edited by Eddie Levinson, reached a circulation of 120,000 by the end of October. By November 1932, there were nearly 1,600 party locals.

Optimism was rife. A *Literary Digest* poll indicated that Thomas would poll a record two million votes. "The coming election," added the *St. Louis Star-Times*, "will undoubtedly show a large increase in the Socialist vote" and the *Christian Science Monitor* predicted that the Socialist vote might be the balance of power in some states. But, as the campaign drew to a close, Thomas sensed that the protest vote against Hoover would go mainly to Roosevelt.

On Monday night before Election Day, with the sense of a hard job well done, Eddie Levinson, Paul Sifton and others of the campaign staff went with Thomas to a cafeteria for coffee. After some desultory conversation, Thomas burst out with: "I want to tell all of you that I'm not going to get a big vote tomorrow. It's going to be a lot smaller than anybody thinks. For instance, at my wonderful meeting in Milwaukee last Saturday, hundreds came up to shake my hand. One young man came up to me with tears in his eyes and said, 'I believe in everything you say and I agree entirely with your principles, but my wife and I can't vote for you. The country can't stand another four years of Hoover.' You can multiply that couple by thousands, if not millions. I can't help but sympathize with the feelings of that young man, but our vote will be small."

Thomas was right. Roosevelt swept in with 22,815,539 votes; Hoover had 15,759,930 and Thomas polled 903,286. True, this was more than three times his 1928 count, but it was nevertheless a sharp blow to Party members.

What was perhaps even more crushing, the labor protest vote went to Roosevelt rather than to Thomas. In Philadelphia, reports Irving Bernstein in *The Lean Years*, Thomas received a proportionately smaller vote in the working-class districts than in the middle-class 42nd ward. In the riverfront wards, where unemployment was heaviest, Thomas polled only 166 of 23,000 votes. The same situation occurred in many other cities.

After the election, a well-known newspaperman, Paul Y. Anderson of the *St. Louis Post-Dispatch*, who had predicted a Roosevelt victory because "the country is wet, broke, and disgusted," insisted that Thomas polled at least two million votes—with more than a million not counted. As he figured it, this was not due primarily to deliberate fraud. Rather it was the failure of the Socialists to have enough poll watchers. After wading through long paper ballots, old party election inspectors would look at minor party figures and say, "Oh, what's the use. They have no chance anyway." And they would write down no figure or a small, arbitrary number.

In addition, deliberate fraud did occur. One example took place on Chicago's South Side. During the campaign Thomas had spoken to a tremendous crowd in the area, there was a good Socialist Party branch and the Party ran up a fairly impressive vote. The Communist Party had no watcher at the polling booth. As the votes were being counted, Jack Sullivan, the Socialist Party watcher, became aware that communist votes were not being recorded, and he complained to the Democratic and Republican voting inspectors. They looked at each other and then one tolerantly explained, as if Sullivan were a slightly backward child, "When you Socialists have no watchers, we do the same to you. But since you're here, we'll split up the communist vote among the three of us."

In any event, whether Thomas received 900,000 or 2,000,000 votes, the highly optimistic independents were deeply chagrined that the vote wasn't higher. Their disappointment made it easier for them to pass into the Democratic camp when Roosevelt gave them any encouragement.

And here was where Thomas' accuracy dropped in assessing what would happen next. Two days after the election he said, "Democratic failure, which is inevitable, will be bound to play into our hands. We must be ready." He had plenty of company in his view of the clouded crystal ball. "Disillusionment in the Roosevelt regime," said Louis Waldman, "will probably set in at an early stage of his administration." And Dan Hoan predicted that, "As Roosevelt fails, as he surely will, as his party will not let him promote real remedies, there will be a swing towards the Socialist Party."

ELEVEN

The Early Thirties

◆§ THE BLACKEST HOURS for the country came in the winter months between Roosevelt's election in November and his inauguration in March. The Federal Government was at a standstill and the lame-duck Congress was at odds with Hoover. Farmers were particularly bitter. Thomas spoke at a meeting arranged by a radical farm organization in Bloomington, Ill. At this meeting, admission was paid in corn and all decorations were made of corn. One farmer told Thomas that he was getting only 10 cents a bushel for his corn, and for that money all he could buy was two corncob pipes.

Although William Green warned a Senate subcommittee in January 1933 that workers were desperate and would resort to "class war" and "the language of force," the cities remained relatively quiet. But out in the country, direct action was becoming more popular. Committees of action to prevent tax sales and mortgage foreclosures flourished. On one occasion, farmers brandished a rope and threatened to hang a lawyer who was about to conduct a foreclosure. At other times, gun-carrying friends of the debtors bought back farms for a few cents at mortgage sales, and restored them to their original owners.

All sorts of quack nostrums and demagogues began to appear. Khaki Shirts, Silver Shirts, Father Coughlin, Huey Long, Minute Men, American Nationalists, Technocracy—all preached salvation minus democracy. The itch to do something, anything, which grew as a reaction to Hoover's standpattism led Al Smith to argue for dictatorial measures because depression was equivalent to war. "In the World War we took our Constitution, wrapped it

138

up and laid it on the shelf and left it there until it was over."

The day before Roosevelt was inaugurated, Thomas spoke at the University of North Carolina to a huge student audience. He and Violet stayed overnight in Chapel Hill as guests of Frank Graham, then president of the University. The next day, as they listened over the radio to the inaugural speech, Graham said to his wife, "Why, Roosevelt is repeating a great many of the things that Norman Thomas told us last night—about no half measures in dealing with the financial crisis, bank closures, unemployment, and the near collapse of our whole economic system."

On Inauguration Day, Thomas was driven early in the morning to Salisbury, a textile town where a strike had just been lost. Along the way, he heard Roosevelt's inaugural speech, was vastly surprised at its tone and thought that it presaged great things for the country.

Less than two weeks later, Thomas and Morris Hillquit met with President Roosevelt in the White House, seeking to persuade him to push for a publicly-owned banking system, adequate hunger relief for the unemployed, and a six-billion dollar program of public works. They protested against Roosevelt's scheme of enlisting a labor army of 200,000 or more of the unemployed, to be paid only $1 to $1.50 a day and board. They argued that high wage levels were needed for any degree of economic recovery, and that his labor army program would be made the pretext to degrade further the standard of living of workers and unemployed. The President listened to Thomas and Hillquit with keen interest and discussed several of their points with them. But he rejected their approach on the banking system, even though it had a great deal of popular support.

Nevertheless, Roosevelt was taking action and his fireside chats brought a feeling of relief, optimism and hope to the American people. At the end of the first week, Will Rogers summed it up well: "The whole country is with him, just so he does something. If he burned down the capitol we would cheer and say 'Well, we at least got a fire started anyhow.'"

During the First Hundred Days, Roosevelt guided fifteen major laws to enactment, including the Emergency Banking Act; establishment of the Civilian Conservation Corps; the Federal Emergency Relief Act; the Agricultural Adjustment Act; the Tennessee Valley Authority Act; and the National Industrial Recovery Act. These and the acts which followed throughout Roosevelt's first term led ex-President Hoover to write in later years that "Students who wish to arrive at the subcurrents around Roosevelt would do well to examine the platform of the Socialist Party of 1932 and observe the uncanny fulfillment of its recommendations by Roosevelt's first administration."

In later years, Thomas conceded that if Roosevelt hadn't been elected, "We would have had very bad times. Maybe we Socialists would have got stronger but I'm afraid the American fascists —of the type of Huey Long or Father Coughlin—or even the communists, would have come into the picture. Roosevelt's New Deal was not the best alternative, but it certainly was a better alternative than had been offered to the problems of our times, and it was offered with an *elan*, a spirit that made things go and which tended to lift up people's hearts. In retrospect, I wouldn't change many of the criticisms I then made. Yet the net result was certainly the salvation of America, and it produced peacefully, after some fashion not calculated I think even by Roosevelt, the welfare state and almost a revolution. By no means, however, was there an instant solution to our problems. In fact, it must be remembered that at no time in the Roosevelt administration did we get full employment until we were in World War II."

During the months before Roosevelt's inaugural, Socialist national secretary Clarence Senior had come up with the idea of organizing local Committees of Correspondence leading to a New Continental Congress in Washington in May, 1933. With Thomas' support (Hillquit and others were dubious), the plan was approved by the Socialist national executive committee. Seeking identification with the traditions of the American Revolution, the Congress even prepared to adopt a New Declaration of Independence. The local Committees did their work well, and almost 4,000 delegates swarmed into Washington by train, bus, truck, auto and by hitch-hiking. Many of the delegates came from unemployed leagues, but there were a considerable number from unions, farm organizations, cooperatives and fraternal groups as well as from the Socialist Party and various liberal bodies. The communists were carefully excluded.

The Congress, chaired by Emil Rieve, president of the American Federation of Full-Fashioned Hosiery Workers, declared independence from "the profit system" which had "enthroned economic and financial kings . . . more powerful, more irresponsible and more dangerous to human rights than the political kings whom the fathers overthrew." The delegates empowered a National Committee of Correspondence and Action "to explore the best methods of economic and independent political action by the producing classes for the achievement of a cooperative commonwealth."

One of the by-products of the Congress was a pioneering blow against Jim Crow. Most of the New York delegates were originally housed in the Cairo Hotel. When it was reported that the hotel had barred Floria Pinkney, a Negro delegate, hundreds of the delegates marched to the hotel in a body, cancelled their reservations and demanded return of the money they had paid in advance. Thomas was their spokesman. When the hotel refused to return the money, Thomas arranged with several lawyer delegates to bring suit, whereupon the hotel acquiesced. Delegates had difficulty finding other hotel rooms because, it was reported, their names were flashed to all hotels in the city. When Thomas discovered that the Tourist Camp, owned by the Government and operated by the War Department's Quartermasters' Bureau, also discriminated against Negroes, he commented: "How can we either protest Hitlerism with good grace or hope to escape similar ills in America when we chronically carry out a more thoroughgoing discrimination against our colored fellow citizens than he has as yet imposed upon the Jews?"

For some time Thomas had been very much worried lest America develop an American fascism, and had annoyed many Militants when he warned that the collapse of capitalism might well mean fascism rather than socialism. One of the fascist groups then in operation was the Khaki Shirts of America, led by a paranoiac opportunist, "General" Art Smith. The group held a meeting in Columbus Hall, Astoria, N.Y., on July 14th, 1933, and Smith claimed that they were getting ready to march on Washington to take over the government. "If anybody thinks we can't do it," he said, "look at Hitler and Mussolini." At the meeting, one of Smith's supporters, Dominic Siani, began praising Mussolini. Fort Vellona, cartoonist and reporter for *La Stampa Libera*, anti-fascist daily, protested and was struck down by Smith. Meanwhile, Anthony Fierro, a pre-medical student at Long Island University, tried to come to Vellona's defense. Suddenly there was a shot, and Fierro's body fell to the floor. A friend, Athos Terzani, stayed by Fierro's side while his life flickered out. When the police arrived, Terzani, in broken English, pointed out Khaki Shirt Frank Moffer as the killer and led the police to a piano, under whose cover was found the pistol with which the fatal shot was fired. Another eyewitness, Michael Palumbo, also named Moffer.

But "General" Smith called Terzani and Palumbo liars and accused Terzani of the murder. Assistant District Attorney Joseph Loscalzo accepted Smith's word, turned Moffer loose and ordered Terzani jailed. Terzani was promptly indicted and might well have been rushed to speedy trial and conviction except for the intervention of Carlo Tresca—the nemesis of American fascism. Tresca formed the Terzani Defense Committee with Thomas as chairman and Arthur Garfield Hays as principal counsel. A united front was formed with the American Civil Liberties Union, the General Defense Committee of the I.W.W., the Socialist Party and the Communists' International Labor Defense.

On July 23rd, Smith boasted before 1,000 persons in Philadelphia that his men "killed one radical and sent 19 others to a hospital in New York." In September he bestowed medals for bravery in action upon eight Khaki Shirts, including Moffer, who took part in the Astoria affair. Then one Khaki Shirt, Samuel Wein, became ill and suffered from an uneasy conscience because of his false testimony before the Grand Jury that indicted Terzani. When John Nicholas Beffel of the Defense Committee visited him in Philadelphia he confessed and asked to see a rabbi to repeat the confession. In New York he told Rabbi Louis Newman that his testimony had been false, but that he was now prepared to state the facts. The Defense Committee paid Wein $3 a day to keep him in New York pending the conclusion of the trial.

When Wein testified that Moffer, rather than Terzani, had killed Fierro, the District Attorney was annoyed. He said:

"Mr. Wein, do you realize you are guilty of perjury?"

"Yes."

"Well, why did you give false testimony?"

"Because, as I told you, Mr. Smith said he was going to shoot all the Jews in America if I didn't."

"Well," said the prosecuting attorney, "you knew he couldn't do that."

"Yes," answered Wein, "but he said he would begin with me."

Queens District Attorney Charles S. Colden thereupon threatened Wein with prosecution for perjury. The Police Department's ballistics expert took elaborate pains to find out what everybody else conceded: that the fatal shot had come from the gun which Terzani pointed out to the police. Yet that same expert had not troubled to take finger prints, or to try to run down the ownership of the gun by its serial number. The jury, deliberating only 32 minutes, found Terzani not guilty. After considerable pressure from Thomas and Tresca, Moffer pleaded guilty to a plea of manslaughter in the first degree and Art Smith was convicted of perjury.

Thomas learned that it had been a sad mistake to include the communists in the united front committee for Terzani's defense. The communists, then in their social-fascist period, preferred a working class martyr to an acquittal. At a mass meeting to raise defense funds, the communist speakers, contrary to solemn agreement, urged picketing the court, which would have antagonized both judge and jury and invited conviction. After Terzani was acquitted, the communists refused to back Thomas and others in bringing pressure for a trial of Art Smith. They broke up the committee because it was not controlled by them and because it might, by convicting Smith, prove that democracy could work.

Shortly after this came another experience with the communists that was to dishearten Thomas further. In February 1934, Austria's Chancellor Dollfuss, with the aid of the clerical fascist armed Heimwehr, made war on Austrian Socialists, using his cannon against the beautiful working-class apartments built by Vienna's Socialist administration. In New York the unions called for a work stoppage and a meeting was scheduled at Madison Square Garden by Socialists and unions as a giant demonstration of solidarity. The day before the Madison Square Garden meeting, the communists held a meeting at the Bronx Coliseum and ordered their followers to march to the Socialist meeting in a body. The time for the march was set earlier in the day than the work stoppage ordered by the unions, so that the communists would be certain to get into the Garden.

Clarence Hathaway, editor of the *Daily Worker*, made sure that his followers would know how to act: "What the Social Democratic leaders do in calling upon the workers to defend democracy is to pave the way for war and fascism. The unity we seek is the unity which recognizes the historic treachery of the Social Democratic leadership."

When the Garden meeting was called to order, the communists started shouting, booing and shrieking. As one of the color guard at the demonstration, I was heartsick over the disgraceful riot. Neither the chairman, nor any union speaker nor Mayor La Guardia was permitted to speak. Only when Frank Crosswaith, a Negro Socialist orator, arose did the communists remain silent. (Their policy of black supremacy did not permit them to boo a Negro even when he termed their behavior in regard to the other speakers swinish and disgusting.) Then Hathaway made his way toward the platform and tried to seize the microphone from the speaker, while the communists screamed in unison: "We want Hathaway! We want Hathaway!" Throughout the hall, communists started attacking Socialists and unionists; furriers' knives, scissors and beer bottles wrapped in newspapers were used as weapons. The meeting had to be adjourned. As Thomas pointed out, the communists had succeeded in demonstrating how they had helped pave the way for Hitler in Germany.

When Henry Wallace became Secretary of Agriculture, Thomas was at first pleased since he regarded him as both "high-minded and competent." While Thomas had traveled in the South during his 1928 and 1932 campaigns and had frequently spoken on agrarian topics, he was not intimately acquainted with the day-to-day problems of sharecroppers and tenant farmers.

Even so, when Wallace used the Agricultural Adjustment Administration (AAA) program to plow under ten million acres of growing cotton and to slaughter six million pigs, Thomas was shocked. "No satirist ever penned such an indictment of a cruel and lunatic society," cried Thomas, "as AAA's author, who destroyed foodstuffs while millions were still on breadlines."

Thomas soon became even more disturbed by the New Deal's agricultural program. In February 1934, at the invitation of H. L. Mitchell, a Socialist who ran a small dry-cleaning store in Tyronza, Ark., Thomas agreed to speak at a meeting in the local high school. Before the meeting, Mitchell took Thomas on a tour of some of the plantations where the latter talked with sharecroppers, plantation owners, local businessmen and others. He was horrified at the plight of the sharecropper and told an overflow audience at the schoolhouse what he had seen and heard. Planters and sharecroppers were at the meeting en masse. The planters writhed in their seats and the sharecroppers rejoiced as Thomas denounced the system of semi-slavery under which they lived. At a luncheon at the home of Clay East, who ran a filling station next to Mitchell's store, Thomas told the local Socialists that what was needed was a union of the sharecroppers. Thomas left Arkansas determined to wake up the American people to the miserable conditions in the fertile but desperately poor delta country. In a letter to Secretary of Agriculture Wallace, Thomas noted that while cash payments for crop reductions had gone to landlords, many sharecropper families had been driven off the land or reduced to becoming casual day laborers. Wallace could not challenge Thomas' description of the plight of the sharecroppers but insisted that their "extremely low standard of living" was not due to AAA. This reply surprised Thomas, but since he had previously been on friendly terms with Wallace he thought that differences could easily be straightened out if he could talk to Wallace. He went to Washington but Wallace refused to see him, foisting him off on one of his assistants. In fact, this was to remain true all during Wallace's tenure as Secretary of Agriculture.

Undaunted, Norman Thomas encouraged Dr. William R. Amberson, Professor of Physiology at the University of Tennessee in Memphis, to make a local case study of the AAA's effects upon the sharecroppers. Amberson, who did some of the basic work that made blood plasma possible, organized this study, with the help of students and sharecroppers. The largest "farmer" in the area was the Chapman and Dewey Lumber Company, which ran a plantation of 17,000 acres. It was immediately clear that they, and other planters, well subsidized for not planting cotton, reduced the number of sharecroppers and field hands (who were lucky to earn 75 cents a day when they could find work) as they cut down their cotton acreage. The Amberson report revealed that between 15 and 20 per cent of the sharecroppers had lost their employment as a result of the crop reduction program, and noted that the contract prescribed by the government did not protect them from exploitation as day laborers or from dismissal.

Thomas wrote Wallace again. The Secretary of Agriculture reiterated his "serious concern" about the problem, but offered no assurance that the eviction of sharecroppers would be stopped. Wallace did send Mrs. Mary Conner Myers, an AAA attorney, to Arkansas to investigate complaints about sharecropper evictions, but refused to release her report for publication. Dr. Calvin B. Hoover, of Duke University, conducted another investigation for Secretary Wallace, which again confirmed that the sharecropper was getting a bad deal. No action was taken by the Agicrultural Department to protect the interests of sharecroppers.

However, Thomas' visit to Arkansas and his impassioned speech were to have effect. In July, 1934, twenty-seven white and black men, clad in overalls, gathered in a rickety old schoolhouse in Poinsett County, just south of the little town of Tyronza. Most of the men had never been in a union but they knew that they could get nowhere trying to negotiate individually with the landlord. Soon the inevitable question arose. "Are we going to have two unions, one for the whites and one for the colored?" One man said that since the churches divided the races, maybe the union should do likewise. Another man observed that the planters would be angered if whites and blacks mixed in one union. An old Negro rose to his feet, maintaining: "It won't do no good for us to divide because there's where the trouble has been all the time." The men decided he was right. The union would welcome Negro and white sharecroppers, tenant farmers and day laborers alike into its fold. Then they went to H. L. Mitchell and Clay East for help in building the union, which was incorporated as the Southern Tenant Farmers' Union.

Despite intimidation of sharecroppers and threats of eviction, the Southern Tenant Farmers Union kept on organizing. Word came through the grapevine that the planters were buying machine guns, so union members took down their old shotguns, oiled and cleaned them. It was not unusual to see sharecroppers and their families walking to a union meeting with shotguns slung in a businesslike fashion under their arms. But Mitchell, East and the other union leaders disapproved of gun-carrying, realizing that the planters were itching for an excuse to wipe out the union in blood as they had done in earlier years. In order to remove every provocation, the union officials asked the men to leave their guns at home and to hold meetings in the open fields under the bright southern sky. Even so, as such meetings were held, planters and their riding bosses would gather on the fringe of the meeting and amuse themselves by shooting over the heads of the crowd to intimidate the speaker and frighten his listeners. In using this technique of non-violent resistance, the union served as a forerunner of Martin Luther King and the Negro students in the South.

Outside the town of Marked Tree, Ark., was an abandoned warehouse which the union used as its headquarters. An old colored preacher, the union chaplain, A. B. Brookins, would lead the assembled unionists in union songs adapted from hymns. Naomi Mitchison, a British historian who accompanied Jennie Lee, a Labor Member of Parliament in February, 1935, on a trip to Arkansas, wrote Thomas that the sharecroppers sang:

> "I'm on my way to New York and I shall not be moved,
>   I'm on my way to New York and I shall not be moved,
> Just like a tree that's planted by the water,
>   I shall not be moved.

> "Just to see Norman Thomas, and I shall not be moved.
> Just to see Norman Thomas, and I shall not be moved.
> Just like a tree that's planted by the water,
>   I shall not be moved."

"You see," wrote Miss Mitchison, "they sang your name with a religious simplicity and intenseness which I have never heard before. You *are* someone divine for them—you can't help being. Those verses were written by a man who had been badly beaten up—his face showed it—and in prison for forty days. And again, in one Negro home of Union members, they told me how they'd heard you on the radio: 'To think he could be thinking of us! Ain't it wonderful!' I think all the radios in Arkansas must have been crowded round that afternoon you spoke."

Thomas decided to make another tour of the area in March, 1935, to focus national attention on the shame of Arkansas. After a long and fruitless interview with Governor J. Marion Futrell, Thomas spoke to thousands of sharecroppers, some of whom walked seventy miles to hear him. While driving over the plantation roads he witnessed one of the many evictions. A white sharecropper's family, household goods and all, were dumped by the roadside. The man and his wife had tried to arrest a plantation rider who had kidnapped and raped their 14-year-old daughter. Instead of arresting the rapist, officials had arrested the father on a trumped-up charge of "stealing two eggs." After he was released from jail, the father, a staunch union member, had been brutally beaten and his family evicted while the riding boss, a relative of the plantation owner, still kept his job.

Not all of Thomas' experiences were that grim. One night he paid the hotel bill for McAlister Coleman and himself with the small change collected at a meeting. Coleman noted how the hotel keeper kept looking at the nickels and dimes and quarters, and then made a phone call to the Police Department. Eavesdropping unashamedly, Coleman heard: "That you, Chief? Listen. Watch out for a travelling dice game operated by a tall feller going by the name of Norman Thomas."

On the last day of the tour, Thomas came to the little town of Birdsong, where he had been invited to speak by the officials of the colored church. When Thomas commented on the town's poetic name, a native soberly replied, "Stranger, they had orter call it Hog Waller." As some five hundred sharecroppers, mostly colored, began to assemble, thirty to forty armed and drunken planters forced their way to the front of the church. Howard

Kester, a Southern clergyman (and a pacifist Socialist who had brought the concept of non-violent resistance to the share-croppers) opened with, "Ladies and Gentlemen, we are met here at the invitation of this church—" A raucous voice broke out from the white mob: "There ain't no ladies in the audience and no gentlemen on the platform." The gunmen surrounded the speakers and denied that the speakers had any invitation. Thomas, holding a copy of the church's letter of invitation in his hands, insisted that this was a legal meeting. The planters' mob, cursing monotonously, admitted that the meeting was "legal all right" but warned that as citizens of the county they were going to run it to suit themselves. "We don't need no Gawd-damn Yankee bastard to tell us what to do with our niggers and we want you to know that this is the best Gawd-damn county on earth. There ain't going to be no speakin' here." Thomas went on talking, until one man stepped out from the mob, identified himself as a deputy sheriff and ordered Thomas to close the meeting since, as he said, "I cannot protect these innocent women and children." As the mob carelessly brandished guns, one of them hit Jack Herling, secretary of the Strikers Emergency Relief Committee, on the head. The Committee members were pushed into their waiting car. Several carloads of planters' thugs followed the car to the county line. Thomas said he would have enjoyed the ride more if there had been shatterproof glass in the rear window.

The Rev. Abner Sage, pastor of the Marked Tree Methodist Church and secretary of the planters' association, told Raymond Daniel of *The New York Times*, "It would have been better to have a few no-account shiftless people killed at the start than to have all this fuss raised up." Added Mr. Sage, "We have had a pretty serious situation here, what with the mistering of the niggers and stirring them up to think the government was going to give them forty acres."

When the Socialist national executive committee wired Roosevelt in March, 1935, asking for an investigation of the Arkansas "reign of terror" against the Southern Tenant Farmers' Union, Secretary Wallace replied for the President that it would be hard for the Federal government to step into the situation. Thomas scorned this argument. "A government that has interfered as extensively as yours has in the cotton economy of the South," he retorted, "has a moral responsibility to act in view of the wholesale evictions I've seen with my own eyes."

Thomas also appealed to Under Secretary of Agriculture Rex Tugwell and to Chester Davis, AAA administrator, to use their influence for an open investigation. Both passed the buck. He visited various Agriculture Department officials but soon became convinced that fear of powerful Southern Senators paralyzed them from any effective action. In desperation, Thomas wrote Felix Frankfurter, begging his intercession with Roosevelt; but Frankfurter replied that "My relation to the President is not at all what the silly papers make it out to be" and that, since he knew little about agriculture, it would be improper for him to raise the matter with Roosevelt.

Thomas then urged Senator Robert F. Wagner to include protection for sharecroppers and other agricultural workers in his National Labor Relations Bill, and to safeguard their civil liberties. Wagner replied regretfully that he had excluded agricultural workers "only because I thought it would be better to pass the bill for the benefit of industrial workers than not to pass it at all, and that the inclusion of agricultural workers would lessen the likelihood of passage so much as not to be desirable."

With prophetic foresight, Thomas appealed to William Green for help. "As long as there is a reservoir of white and colored workers as badly exploited as these plantation workers," he declared, "the employers always have an advantage in the struggle with organized labor." While the AFL responded by unanimously adopting a resolution deploring "the inhuman levels to which the workers employed in the cotton fields had been reduced" and urged a federal investigation of their conditions, the unions failed to give any substantial aid to the hard-pressed Southern Tenant Farmers Union.

Finally, Thomas wrote directly to Roosevelt about the "veritable reign of terror" in eastern Arkansas. Both Tugwell and Aubrey Williams, Harry Hopkins' deputy in the Federal Emergency Relief Administration, said Thomas, were "frankly in fear of the powers of Southern Senators" and could not act. (Tugwell had once put it to Thomas, "Well, what in the world would you do if you had to deal with committees, the chairmen of which are such people as 'Cotton Ed' Smith and Joe Robinson?") Roosevelt's reply was noncommittal but he finally agreed to see Thomas.

The Socialist leader had met with Roosevelt on many previous occasions and knew the clever way in which the President handled interviews. He would charmingly reminisce and try to keep the conversation in his own hands. After Roosevelt began to tell Thomas of his wrath at the reactionary behavior of some chamber of commerce at a particular meeting, Thomas took a deep breath, plunged in with, "And so are the Southern planters," and reported briefly on the woes of the sharecroppers. When Thomas asked the President if he had read the AAA's Cotton Acreage Reduction Contract clause, which had allegedly been written by the manager of one of the world's largest plantations, Roosevelt said that he had not. "Would you mind reading it?" asked Thomas. "Certainly," replied Roosevelt.

"The producer," read Section 7 of the contract, will *"endeavor* . . . to bring about reduction as to cause the *least possible* amount of labor, economic and social disturbance, and . . . shall *insofar as possible*, maintain . . . the *normal* number of tenants, shall permit all tenants to continue in the occupancy of their houses . . . free . . . (*unless any such tenant shall so conduct himself as to become a nuisance or menace to the welfare of the producer.*)" Roosevelt handed the contract back to Thomas, half laughing, and said, "That can mean everything or nothing, can't it?" Replied Thomas, "In this case, Mr. President, nothing. Over at the Agricultural Department they have just fired Jerome Frank, Gardner Jackson and Lee Pressman, partly because they tried to make this contract mean something."

Roosevelt, a little impatiently, interrupted Thomas and said, "Oh, Norman, I'm a damned sight better politician than you are." Thomas made the obvious retort, "Certainly, Mr. President. You are on that side of the table and I'm on this." Roosevelt ignored this and went on to say, "I know the South and there is arising a new generation of leaders in the South and you've got to be patient."

How did the Administration react to Thomas' charges? Wallace wrote an article in *The New York Times* conceding that displacement of tenants had increased and that the operation of the cotton contracts had probably added to their difficulties, but blamed the bitterness of the sharecroppers on "Communist and Socialist" agitators in the South. President Roosevelt, in an "unscheduled address" to a "spontaneous" demonstration of pro-AAA farmers, held in Washington in May, 1935, excoriated those with "special axes to grind" who were trying to mislead America by "lying" about the farm program.

But the Thomas campaign had acquired too much momentum. As articles about the unhappy predicament of the sharecroppers appeared in national magazines and northern papers, and as their plight was aired over the radio networks, Roosevelt decided that action was needed.

On July 1, 1935, the Resettlement Administration was established to provide emergency relief and a long-range rehabilitation program for a selected group of farmers. Roosevelt also announced support of the Bankhead-Jones bill to provide low-interest loans amounting to $50 million a year to tenants for the purchase of farms. While the AFL's president, William Green, and Catholic, Protestant and Jewish social welfare agencies backed the bill, Thomas criticized it as "simply a gesture" to divert attention from evil results of the AAA and "in particular the enormous hypocrisy of Section 7 of the cotton contracts." He urged that the bill be amended to permit the government to encourage "cotton cooperatives under expert management." Secretary Wallace himself was forced to admit that at an annual outlay of $50,000,000, it would take 230 years to find farms for the existing number of tenants at a cost of $4,000 per farm.

In May and June of 1936, five thousand Arkansas sharecroppers went on strike. Many strikers were assaulted and others were arrested on the usual charge of vagrancy but a new charge was added: "interference with labor." When two Socialists, Miss Willie Sue Blagden and the Rev. Claude Williams were whipped near the town of Earle, Thomas called upon the President to take effective action. Roosevelt asked the governor of Arkansas to appoint a committee of citizens to investigate the matter, which Thomas caustically characterized as like "asking Al Capone in his prime to investigate conditions in the underworld in Chicago."

In the end, all of Thomas' efforts failed to win justice for the sharecroppers, but he had been the first person to awaken America not only to the plight of the sharecroppers, but indeed to the very word. When Thomas spoke throughout the nation, reporters frequently interrupted to ask if he did not mean "crop-sharers" instead. And Thomas spoke so frequently about the sharecroppers, Maynard Krueger relates, that when one Chicago Socialist heard that Thomas was coming to Chicago to speak at a dinner meeting, he groaned, "Oh, Lord, that means we'll have sharecroppers again for dinner."

Years later, reflecting upon his experiences with both Wallace and Roosevelt anent the sharecroppers, Thomas felt that Wallace was the kind of man who was so self-righteous that if you called attention to flaws in his administration about which he could do nothing for political reasons, he was compelled to prove that "it ain't so." Or, as one of Wallace's close associates put it when discussing the very real possibility in 1940 that Wallace might succeed to the presidency, "He has the mind and heart to be one of the country's best Presidents. But he may be one of the worst because of his dangerous habit of rationalizing his yielding to political pressure as 'dictated by the voice of God' made known through one of the mystical channels which he explores assiduously."

Roosevelt was different. He would see Thomas, where Wallace would not, and did not try to deceive Thomas. Instead he would imply, "It's too bad, but what in the world can I do about it? After all, I need Southern support to get anything." And then he would demonstrate his pride in his political skill, a pride that sometimes made him think of politics as a game rather than a problem of principles.

Sharecroppers were not the only victimized Americans whom Thomas tried to help. In July, 1935, AFL unionists had gone on strike at the Columbian Stamping Company in Terre Haute, Indiana. When management recruited a force of strikebreakers from big city underworlds, the AFL had called a two-day protest general strike. Governor McNutt sent in the National Guard and imposed martial law; the general strike had ended but some soldiers remained and the Governor maintained "military law" in the county to help smash the Columbian strike.

In August a quiet, young Socialist organizer, Leo Vernon, decided to hold street corner meetings in Terre Haute, in accord with time-honored Socialist tradition. He was immediately arrested and clamped in jail. No charges were filed against him. The militia's Major Weimar, boasting of his absolute power in the county, ordered the jailer to hold Vernon incommunicado and Sheriff Baker told Vernon, "You can rot in your cell before you'll see an attorney."

As soon as word of the arrest leaked out, Powers Hapgood, a member of the Socialist national executive committee and Socialist candidate for Governor of Indiana in 1932, insisted upon his right to visit Vernon. He promptly joined Vernon in the lockup but was put in solitary.

Meanwhile, local unionists appealed to Thomas to make a test case in Terre Haute. He flew in to speak on August 30th, but was much worried lest an arrest keep him away from his wife on their 25th wedding anniversary on September 1st. When the Major learned that Thomas was coming, he hurriedly released Hapgood and Vernon but warned them to leave town. It was not until Thomas, accompanied by Vernon and Hapgood, climbed the Court House steps to address a crowd of 2,000 people that they were officially informed that McNutt, through his Adjutant General, had revoked his ban on the meeting. The audience was very enthusiastic and a committee of leading Terre Haute and Indiana citizens was set up to carry on the fight against McNutt's abuse of power.

Ordinarily martial law is invoked only when riots, rebellion or civil disaster threaten the operation of civil government. In Vigo County, under McNutt's bastard form of martial law, soldiers did not patrol the streets. A man passing a red light would be dealt with as usual by civil courts. But if he tried to hold a socialist or labor meeting, or support strikers in their legal right of peaceful picketing, he would be arrested by a policeman or deputy sheriff—and then told that he was being held under military law.

"If this sort of thing works in Indiana," said Thomas, "it will work elsewhere . . . Here is something better than an injunction, even more truly in line with the irresponsibility of fascist tyranny." Thomas' protests were successful. The Governor abandoned his unique verson of martial law. Nevertheless, this abuse led Thomas to call Paul McNutt the "Hoosier Hitler," a label which somewhat hampered McNutt when he unsuccessfully sought the Democratic presidential nomination in 1940.

Another civil liberties case soon erupted. On Dec. 1, 1935, Thomas received a melodramatic telegram from a young Florida Socialist, Frank McCallister: "BRUTE POLICE TERROR BROKE OUT TAMPA SATURDAY NIGHT. PEACEFUL MEETING ILLEGALLY RAIDED. SIX HELD FOR INVESTIGATION AS COMMUNISTS, INCLUDING JENSEN, SOCIALIST STATE SECRETARY, ROUSH, MEMBER STATE EXECUTIVE, POULNOT, PARTY MEMBER AND PRESIDENT FLORIDA WORKERS ALLIANCE, ROGERS, PARTY MEMBER, SHOEMAKER, CHAIRMAN MODERN DEMOCRATS. JENSEN ROUSH RELEASED AFTER INVESTIGATION. SHOEMAKER, POULNOT, ROGERS KIDNAPPED BY UNIFORMED COPS, TAKEN RIDE, BEATEN UNCONSCIOUS. SHOEMAKER NOT EXPECTED LIVE. POULNOT ROGERS VERY SERIOUS EFFECTS BEATING TAR FEATHERS. MOBILIZE DEFENSE. ABSOLUTELY NO FUNDS HERE. WISH PROSECUTE KNOWN ASSAILANTS. WIRE PROTESTS MAYOR CHANCEY, CHIEF POLICE TITTSWORTH DEMAND SHERIFF MCLEOD PROSECUTE FULL EXTENT LAW. LETTER FOLLOWING."

Thomas immediately sent such wires but was appalled to find the full story even more bloodcurdling than the telegram. It was known that the Ku Klux Klan, with the help of plantation and factory owners, sought to destroy unions, enforce its own standards of personal morality and protect Tampa's gambling ring, whose take in the early thirties was alleged to be over three million dollars a month. The ring bribed public officials, who were also Klan leaders. The Klan relentlessly persecuted "agitators" who challenged either the exploitation of the workers or the power of the gambling syndicate.

On Saturday evening, November 30, the executive committee of the Modern Democrats, a reform group in Tampa politics consisting of New Dealers, Socialists, unionists and the unemployed, met. This group, under Joseph Shoemaker, had been so successful in the municipal election that, according to Tampa newspapermen who watched the polls on election day, they would have taken office if there had been an honest count.

At the instigation of the Klan, ten uniformed detectives raided the meeting without a warrant, seized all six men present and arrested them for investigation as "communists." At the station, Eugene F. Poulnot was taken into a private room for questioning and then was "released." A policeman led him to an auto, saying: "We've caused you enough trouble, we'll take you back." When Poulnot refused to enter the car, a man in the rear of the car told the officer: "Don't argue with him. Put the —— in here!" Three policemen forced Poulnot into the car, they drove for a few minutes, then stopped. Soon another car arrived and Joseph Shoemaker, who had been hit on the back of his neck with a blunt instrument and who weighed 220 pounds, was pushed on top of Poulnot.

Sam D. Rogers, questioned after Poulnot and Shoemaker, was then forced into a third car, which drove into some woods. Rogers was stripped and held over a log and beaten. Then he was tarred and feathered. Shortly afterward, the car with Shoemaker and Poulnot arrived. The two were stripped and flogged with rubber hoses and iron chains. The torturers held Shoemaker's leg over a fire, rubbed hot tar into the wounds and covered him and Poulnot with feathers. The three kidnapped men were then abandoned in the woods. Half naked and freezing, Poulnot and Rogers made their way back to Tampa, but were forced to leave Shoemaker behind. Poulnot had to enter a hospital at once, but Rogers organized a search party for Shoemaker, whose head was crushed and his throat so badly wounded that he was not able to speak. Nine days later, Shoemaker died.

Thomas quickly spread news of this outrage throughout the country. William Green, AFL president, announced that the AFL would remove its scheduled convention from Tampa unless the guilty persons were vigorously prosecuted. People in Tampa had little confidence that the guilty would be punished. They agreed with the huge billboard at the Southern Lumber and Supply Company, which read:

TAR . . . TODAY
WHITEWASH TOMORROW
TAMPA: THE YEAR ROUND CITY

Thomas agreed to speak at a Tampa mass meeting on Sunday, January 19th, 1936. There were dire warnings that the city auditorium would be bombed to prevent Thomas from speaking, but no one molested Thomas, and Mayor Chancey even called on him at his hotel to protest his innocence. Thomas addressed a wildly cheering throng which packed 2,300 people inside the hall and left 1,000 more listening outside to a loud speaker. In his talk, he named the officials responsible for plotting the crime and emphatically demanded their conviction. When he was finished the audience gave him a standing ovation.

Thomas' speech was editorially commended by the *Tampa Times* as "a verbal flogging (to the floggers) more lacerating than their own lashes, more scorching than their own tar." Added the *Times:* "The visit and the speech of Norman Thomas will have helpful effect in heartening the sentiment of the community and strengthening the arm of officials. We are glad that he came and that he spoke."

While Thomas agreed that the talk was one of the most effective he ever made, he doubted that it was effective enough to justify defense counsel Pat Whitaker in winning a change of venue to Polk County on the grounds that Thomas' speech and other activities had made a fair trial impossible in Tampa.

In selecting the jury, Whitaker questioned the jurors about their attitude toward Norman Thomas, referring to him continually as "the nationally known communist and propagandist." Objections from the prosecution brought a ruling from Judge Robert T. Dewell (specially designated to hear the case by Governor Dave Sholtz) that the characterization was permissible "for purposes of identification." Another interesting ruling in the case was Yale graduate Dewell's decision that evidence concerning pistol whipping around the head could not be introduced because the indictment specified that Shoemaker had been "flailed about the body and limbs" and the judge held that the head was not part of the body. As McCallister put it, "This is certainly an opinion that will go down in legal history."

Despite judge and defense counsel, the jury brought back a verdict of guilty and the murderers were sentenced to four years in jail. Some jurors explained to newsmen that they had been unanimous on the first ballot. "Communism and all that stuff had nothing to do with it," one juror said. "We saw right through that. Those defense lawyers didn't stick to the case."

An appeal was brought by Whitaker to the Florida Supreme Court, which reversed the decision of guilt on the grounds that the indictment was improperly worded. The judges ruled that all evidence of an illegal raid on a private home by the defendants and their detention at the police station for questioning would have to be ruled out. When new trials took place, the defendants won a directed verdict of "innocent" from Judge Robert T. Dewell on the charge of murdering Shoemaker.

The action was no surprise to Thomas, who had been repeatedly told in Florida that the State Supreme Court would "never sustain convictions against members of the Ku Klux Klan and supporters of the dominant political ring in the city of Tampa."

Thomas became involved in another civil liberties problem in 1937 in Anderson, Indiana. General Motors strikers there encountered trouble, despite the fact that the parent GM sitdown strike in Flint, Michigan, had been victoriously settled. Anderson, formerly a hot bed of the Ku Klux Klan, was a haven for vigilantes who assaulted union organizers, broke up picket lines at the GM Guide Lamp plant, and smashed union headquarters. When news came of the strike settlement in Flint, United Auto Workers organizer Victor Reuther, aided by his wife Sophie, called a mass meeting to explain the terms of the settlement. They rented the ramshackle closed Crystal Theater, and more than 1,500 people packed the hall. At 8 p.m. Reuther started to speak, but had said no more than three words when shots rang out. Well-armed and internally lubricated vigilantes surrounded and shot into the hall, yelling for Reuther to come out. The chief of police told Victor Reuther, "If you submit to protective arrest, the mob outside will leave." Reuther refused.

By five in the morning the vigilantes went away and the unionists and their children were able to leave the theater. Reuther spoke to Governor Townsend, who refused to guarantee the right of free assembly for the union, but instead proclaimed martial law. Since the national GM strike was over, the press throughout the nation paid little or no attention to events in Anderson, an isolated section of the GM empire. Victor Reuther got in touch with Norman Thomas, then in Flint. Thomas came to Anderson, talked to unionists and city and state officials, and called a press conference. National publicity resulted and the vigilantes promptly dispersed. Said Victor Reuther to me twenty-five years later, "Norman Thomas literally saved my life. Without his intervention, I am sure those vigilantes would have got me."

During these several crises—the general strike in Terre Haute and the reign of military law that followed; the murder of Joseph Shoemaker in Tampa; and the cotton-choppers' strike in Arkansas in the summer of 1936—ad hoc defense committees were formed. Thomas proposed the formation of a national labor and socialist defense committee to coordinate these broad activities, and with the help of Aron S. Gilmartin (who had served as secretary of several emergency committees initiated by Norman Thomas) and David L. Clendenin, the Workers Defense League was created. It planned not only to give legal aid to workers unjustly accused of law violation, but also to take legal action against employers or public officials who abused their powers.

An early case in which the League was active involved "I Am The Law" Mayor Frank Hague of Jersey City, one of the last of the old-style city machine bosses. When the Congress of Industrial Organizations first got under way, Hague denounced it as communist controlled and refused to permit it to function in Jersey City. Hague was not just a city boss. He was vice-chairman of the Democratic National Committee and Roosevelt invariably appointed as Federal judges or District Attorneys in New Jersey only endorsees of the Hague machine. The CIO, aided by Morris Ernst of the American Civil Liberties Union, brought legal action to establish its right to meet and organize. Hague responded to this threat by saying before the Jersey City Chamber of Commerce, "As long as I am Mayor of this city the great industries of the city are secure. We hear about constitutional rights, free speech and the free press. Every time I hear these words, I say to myself, 'that man is a Red, that man is a Communist.' You never hear a real American talk in that manner."

As May Day, 1938, approached, the Socialist Party, which had demonstrated on May Day for decades in scores of American cities, applied for a permit to hold a meeting with Norman Thomas as the main speaker in Jersey City's Journal Square. Hague's Director of Public Safety, Daniel Casey, refused the permit, in order "to avert trouble threatened by the Catholic War Veterans if Thomas was allowed to speak." Thomas announced that he would speak anyway. More than 2,000 people poured into the Square to hear him. When the Socialist leader arrived in an open car, a spontaneous cheer went up from the crowd. But Thomas was roughly shoved into a police car by Hague's police, forcibly driven to the Jersey Central Railroad Ferry slip where he was deported to New York with several others, and warned not to come back. At the same time, policemen in the Square went immediately into action with nightsticks, fists and feet. Morris Milgram, secretary of the Workers' Defense League of New Jersey, was cracked across the eye with a billy and his glasses were broken. A policeman struck Violet Thomas on the jaw as she tried to reach her husband's side. Her first reaction was wholly feminine. She thought to herself, "Oh, dear, I hope none of my children see me with my hat askew and my hair so untidy." Later her son Evan wrote from school that if she persisted in going to such meetings, he would have to leave school to take care of her.

In a radio speech a few days later, Thomas challenged President Roosevelt to take Hague to task. "You are hero and leader to millions of Americans," said Thomas. "You have repudiated for yourself, your party and your country the degradation of lands where men are slaves of dictators. . . . Is it only foreign dictators whom we are to fear and fight?" Roosevelt took no action.

Roosevelt's Republican opponent in the 1936 election, on the other hand, took a strong position in support of civil liberties. Speaking in Rochester and Watertown, N.Y., Alf Landon lashed out at Hague's dictatorial acts and praised Thomas.

The Socialist Party of Newark, just six miles from Jersey City,

Nine months old. Norman, born November 20, 1884, was the first son of Welling and Emma Thomas.

Seven years old. At this time Norman attended a small school taught by one of his father's parishioners.

Below, new sister in the family. Norman *(left)* and his brothers helped with household chores.

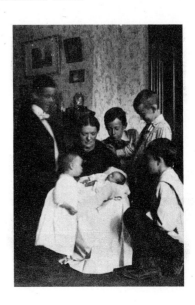

Princeton graduate. Following an interest in public speaking, Thomas was a member of three varsity debating teams.

Emma and Welling Thomas with (*left to right*) daughters Emma and Agnes; sons Arthur, Ralph, Norman, and Evan. "I am so old-fashioned as to be glad that I lived in a home, a time and an environment in which sin and moral vices were realities to be forgiven and cured but not condoned."

Thomas with his first son, Norman, Jr., who died at the age of ten.

On September 1, 1910, Norman Thomas married Frances Violet Stewart. The young couple's first home was on West 42nd Street. Violet (*center*) with Thomas' young sisters.

Norman Thomas in rickshaw on early visit to China.

1924. Thomas poster in first Socialist campaign for office.

FOR GOVERNOR

NORMAN THOMAS

N.Y. JOURNAL-AMERICAN PHOTOS

"This is the first stump speech I ever made from a stump." Norman Thomas testing constitutionality of Bergen County riot law in 1926 Passaic, New Jersey, silk strike. *Below* police interrupt Thomas' speech and arrest him for defying riot law.

Left, first Presidential campaign. Norman Thomas with James H. Maurer, Socialist Vice Presidential candidate in 1928 and 1932. Thomas' campaign tours reawakened Socialist interest and revived the Party. *Right*, last Presidential campaign. Although he urged the Socialist Party to name a new candidate, Thomas reluctantly accepted the Presidential nomination for the sixth—and final—time. Here, Thomas with his running mate, Tucker P. Smith, at the Party's national convention, 1948.

Left, McAlister Coleman interviewing Candidate Thomas during 1929 New York Mayoralty campaign.

Right, U.S. Senatorial nominee Norman Thomas and wife Violet at the polls in 1934.

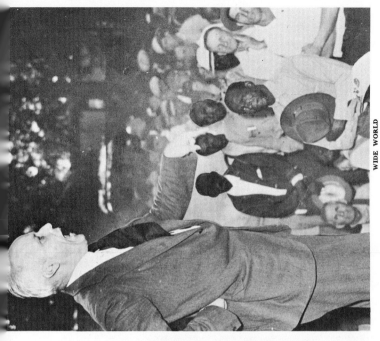

Left, Thomas at campaign stop in West Virginia in 1936. When traveling by train, Thomas often slept in an upper berth to save campaign funds.

Right, Bayridge, Arkansas, 1937. Sharecroppers listen as Norman Thomas tells them, "You are the people who raise the cotton, and have so little to clothe yourselves."

Hostile demonstrators, at instigation of Jersey City's Mayor Frank Hague, hurl rotten eggs and light bulbs to disrupt Thomas rally in Newark, June 4, 1938. The demonstrators, many wearing veterans' caps, marched into Military Park with a band which drowned out Thomas' voice. This photograph won a prize as one of the most important news pictures of 1938.

After being prevented from making a May Day speech in Jersey City, 1938, Norman Thomas is escorted to State line by Jersey police. With Thomas are his brother Evan and wife Violet.

Below, Thomas bareheaded, is guarded by police as he walks to address rally in Newark. Police protection was necessary because of rotten-egg bombardment three weeks earlier. A crowd of 4,000 enthusiastically cheered Thomas' hour-long speech.

Thomas confers in Prague in 1937 with Siegfried Taub, Socialist vice president of the Czechoslovakian Parliament, and with Dr. Paul Hertz, former Social Democratic member of the German Reichstag.

Below, Norman and Violet Thomas are greeted by son William on their return from 1937 European tour. While the Thomases were in Valencia, the city was bombed by Franco planes.

NEW YORK POST

Thomas indulges a secret desire to be an orchestra leader on Cal Tinney's radio show, "If I Had the Chance." Members of the orchestra include: William C. White and Peter Arno (*piano*); Clement Wood (*ukulele*); Cal Tinney; Arthur Garfield Hays (*mandolin*); Rockwell Kent (*flute*); Eugene Howard (*violin*); and Frank Norris (*drums*).

Below, political foes forget their differences at an off-the-record "Political Rally" in which Presidential possibilities were subjected to good-natured ribbing. *Left to right, seated:* Paul V. McNutt; Senator Arthur H. Vandenberg of Michigan; Jesse H. Jones; Thomas E. Dewey. *Standing:* Attorney General Robert H. Jackson; Representative Bruce Barton of New York; Senator Burton K. Wheeler; Norman Thomas; and Senator Bennett Champ Clark of Missouri.

WIDE WORLD

A pencil drawing of Thomas by Miriam Troop which appeared with his article, "Republicans and Democrats are Stealing from My Socialist Platform," *in Look,* August 17, 1948.

Below, Norman Thomas and colleagues gather for weekly radio program, "The Callboard," over Station WFDR. *Left to right:* Rev. Donald M. Harrington; Harry Fleischman, Thomas, and Aaron Levenstein.

Poet Robert Frost and Henry Wallace chat with Thomas at NBC's Tenth Anniversary of "American Forum of the Air."

Union leader A. Philip Randolph and Norman Thomas with a group of trade union leaders in Japan in 1952.

Friends share a joke with Thomas at seventieth birthday party at New York's Town Hall. *Left to right:* Donald M. Harrington, Virgilia Peterson, A. Philip Randolph, and Thomas.

Granddaughters Louise and Wendy Thomas supervise as Norman Thomas cuts the cake. Party to celebrate Thomas' seventy-fifth birthday was held at the Waldorf Astoria.

Above, December 1959. Norman Thomas and Harry Truman meet at Four Freedoms Award dinner of Italian-American Labor Council. Truman had asked to be photographed with Thomas.

Below, United Auto Workers leaders enjoy Thomas' direct approach at luncheon meeting held at Solidarity House in Detroit, in 1960.

Right, Thomas exhibits film clips from "Communism on the Map," a movie produced by the extreme-right-wing National Education Program. He attacked Armed Forces use of film which supported John Birch Society views.

"So long as he is alive . . . those who are alienated and excluded are not entirely mute." Norman Thomas joins sympathy picket line (New York, April, 1963) protesting segregation in Birmingham, Ala. Others in line include: Rev. Donald Harrington; James Farmer, leader of CORE; Cleveland Robinson, vice president of Negro American Labor Council; and David Livingston, president of District 65, Retail, Wholesale and Department Store Union.

decided to hold a meeting at which Norman Thomas would explain the situation in Jersey City. No trouble was expected since many radical meetings had taken place in Newark without incident. The meeting was held on June 4th in Military Park, and as Thomas rose to speak a brass band advanced down the street, blaring loudly to drown out Thomas' booming voice. Following the band was a mob of hoodlums, armed with vegetables, eggs and light bulbs, with which they pelted Thomas while the band played on. Thomas insisted on continuing the meeting and called on the police to provide protection. They pleaded inability to do so and adjourned the meeting.

Waving proudly throughout the crowd were dozens of little American flags, which the garbage throwers carried in one hand while pitching refuse with the other. The same placards which had appeared four weeks earlier in Jersey City loomed over the crowd: "Norman Thomas, Roger Baldwin and Stalin—One for all and all for one. KEEP OUT," and "The working people of our city are contented— REDS KEEP OUT."

At the next regular meeting of the Newark City Commission, Thomas appeared and demanded an investigation into the riot. He was not alone. Fifteen hundred citizens packed the City Hall chamber while more swarmed in the corridors and nearby streets. Local 144 of the International Ladies Garment Workers Union called a brief stoppage so that its members could parade to City Hall in support of Thomas. Before the hearing, Thomas had learned that a number of the thugs recruited by Hague's henchmen to break up the Thomas meeting had criminal records. Among them was a Democratic ward leader who had been arrested for breaking into a butcher shop, fornication and white slavery. Another was a teamster union business agent who had 16 arrests since 1923, on charges including seduction, bastardy, grand larceny, assault and battery and carrying concealed weapons.

The Commission granted Thomas' request for an official investigation of the police and protection for another meeting in a Newark park. The meeting was held June 25th, and 4,000 people cheered Thomas' call for a finish fight against Hagueism. President Roosevelt, responding to the widespread protests against his party's vice-chairman, had denounced Hague in a radio fireside chat the night before (but without mentioning his name). "The American people will not be deceived by anyone who attempts to suppress individual liberty under the pretense of patriotism."

When Thomas called upon the President to implement his remarks by removing patronage from Hague, Roosevelt withheld his answer. But after the fall elections, when Thomas wrote him again about a Federal appointment in New Jersey, Roosevelt plaintively voiced his dilemma in the following "private and confidential" note:

"Dear Norman:
    I am glad to have your letter about the New Jersey judgship [sic]. Mr. (blank) is apparently an able and fair judge—and on the other hand, the man suggested by Southern New Jersey does not seem to measure up in his qualifications. I am looking around hoping to find someone who will not owe his appointment to anybody but me! But it is a difficult job.
    I hope to see you one of these days soon.
                                          Very sincerely yours,
                                          Franklin D. Roosevelt."

Meanwhile Thomas, aided by expert legal advice from Morris Shapiro of the Workers Defense League and Arthur Vanderbilt of Newark (who later became Chief Justice of the New Jersey Supreme Court), began various proceedings in the state and federal courts. The major accomplishment, despite the opposition of the Federal district attorney, was to pressure a Hague grand jury to ask for an investigation by the F.B.I. During this period, Frank Murphy replaced Homer Cummings as Attorney General and promised Thomas a fearless "hewing to the line" by the F.B.I. Thomas later learned that the F.B.I. report, never officially released, was very damaging to the Hague machine. But by this time, the original CIO case against Hague had reached the U.S. Supreme Court and resulted in a great victory for civil liberties. Hague was instructed by the Court not to interfere with meetings of any kind.

TWELVE

Socialist Factionalism and the New Deal

≈§ IN THE SPRING OF 1933, Socialists had been hopeful that the New Continental Congress as proposed by Clarence Senior would resuscitate the La Follette coalition of 1924 and lead this time to a new Farmer-Labor Party. But the groups which gathered in Washington—organized labor, the unemployed, hard-hit farmers —soon began to look to Roosevelt for succor. Nor was it only Socialist sympathizers who moved toward the Roosevelt camp. Many Socialist Party members, from both left and right wings of the Party, found in the Roosevelt camp an irresistible lure. In the fall of 1933, Upton Sinclair had announced his EPIC plan (End Poverty in California) through which he would seek the Democratic nomination for Governor. Thomas attacked Sinclair on the grounds that he was "once again trying the discredited way of making one of the old capitalist parties something else than it is instead of trying to build a party of workers with hand and brain who know their own interests and definitely seek their own emancipation." Meanwhile, Sinclair won the Democratic nomination, but was defeated by Governor Merriam, the GOP nominee, after a vicious and dirty campaign.

Thomas was particularly saddened when Paul Blanshard, one of his closest associates first at the LID and then at the City Affairs Committee, resigned from the Socialist Party to back Fiorello La Guardia for Mayor of New York. Others followed similar paths out of the Party because of discouragement over Socialist lack of electoral success rather than disagreement with Socialist principles.

While La Guardia and Roosevelt were attracting many Socialists and sympathizers, the Party became more and more involved in deep factional warfare that was to wind up in a split. Among the issues which exercised Thomas greatly were what he considered anti-Socialist and undemocratic actions by right-wing Socialists in trade unions. For instance, when the right-wing Furriers' Union got an injunction against the communist-controlled union, Thomas insisted that "I cannot possibly be expected to go all over the United States arguing for socialism with such a weight around my neck without dissociating myself from any such position as this." Socialists, he said, should aid the right-wing union only if it became "democratic in organization and principle" and abstained from "anti-Socialist methods with regard to injunctions." Stressing his dislike of communist unions, and his knowledge that both right and left wing unions had resorted to tie-ups with gangsters and corrupt police, Thomas nevertheless averred that "the Socialist Party is coming close to suicide when it is so much quicker to see the sins of communism than the sins of capitalism or the embryonic fascism in America."

The Old Guard, which had tried unsuccessfully to have Clarence Senior fired as national secretary, suffered a crucial blow when its outstanding leader, Morris Hillquit, died in October, 1933. As a matter of fact, it was a blow to the whole party, because, if Hillquit had lived, he might have been able to work out compromises that would have prevented a party split.

As the 1934 party convention in Detroit approached, all factions geared for battle. Thomas worked with both the Militants and Centrists in lining up support, hoping to insure that the new national executive committee would be more in tune with his thinking, and more willing to push effective Socialist activity. When some left-wingers wrote an "Appeal to the Socialist Party from 47 Members," he severely criticized its drafts as "infantile leftism" and warned of the immense harm "the manner and phraseology of these extraordinary resolutions" could do to the Socialist Party as "the acknowledged leader of a mass movement."

At the convention, Thomas lined up with the Militants and

Centrists behind what came to be known as the Detroit Declaration of Principles. He was not enamored of the statement written by Devere Allen, who shared Thomas' general point of view, but felt that it was the best that could be done under pressure of time and the convention's pulling and hauling. In later years, he regretted not having taken a more vigorous part in its shaping prior to the convention. The Old Guard, led by Algernon Lee, Louis Waldman, and ailing James Oneal, savagely attacked two parts of the Declaration. One, dealing with Socialist action in the event of capitalist war, was in many respects similar to the St. Louis Declaration of 1917, which most of the Old Guard had supported.

Socialists, it declared, "will meet war and the detailed plans for war . . . by massed war resistance, organized so far as practicable in a general strike of labor unions and professional groups in a united effort to make the waging of war a practical impossibility and to convert the capitalist war crisis into a victory for socialism."

Even more controversial was a section which said: "If the capitalist system should collapse in a general chaos and confusion, which cannot permit of orderly procedure, the Socialist Party, whether or not in such a case it is a majority, will not shrink from the responsibility of organizing and maintaining a government under the workers' rule."

Waldman stigmatized the Declaration as "anarchistic, illegal and communist," but the delegates voted 99 to 47 to adopt it. The Party's ultra-left wing, the Revolutionary Policy Committee, (a happy hunting ground for stooges of the Communist Party and Trotskyist and Lovestonite communist factions) attacked the declaration as not radical enough. A later Party referendum endorsed the Declaration by a vote of 5,993 to 4,872. In view of Socialist strength at the time, the Declaration can only be viewed as a pious, if quixotic, hope, but it stirred passions within the party very deeply.

After the *New Leader* became the virtual house organ of the Old Guard, the national executive committee withdrew official party endorsement and the Militants and Centrists started a new paper, the *Socialist Call*, with Thomas transferring his weekly column to that paper. Louis Waldman persisted in saying publicly that Thomas was "the conscious or unconscious tool of the Communist Party" while the communists continued to maintain that Thomas had sold out to American reactionary and imperialist interests.

In spite of all the factional fighting at the Detroit convention, the party in New York waged a vigorous campaign in 1934. Charles Solomon, an Old Guard lawyer, was picked to run for Governor and Thomas for U.S. Senator.

Thomas, for the first and only time in his Party life, faced strong opposition to nomination as the senatorial nominee. Louis Waldman nominated James Oneal, editor of the *New Leader,* and since the vote on Governor had been 79 for Solomon against 33 for Coleman Cheney, it looked as though Thomas would be defeated. However, many Old Guardists, including Usher Solomon and Julius Gerber, called upon Oneal to decline in the interests of Party harmony. Even when he did so, the vote for Thomas was 58 to 38 against, with 16 abstentions.

Thomas deliberately concentrated on upstate New York and Long Island, speaking in more than seventy cities and towns, while Solomon campaigned mostly in New York City. Violet joined Norman and traveled thousands of miles with him in their Chevrolet. In small towns, Violet would hang signs on the car, Norman would stand up on the rumble seat and start speaking. The townspeople displayed the expected rural suspicion of outsiders; they would listen—but from a safe distance. Often, Thomas exhorted them to come in closer, saying that he didn't have smallpox and the worst thing they could catch was socialism. Meetings in schools, at factory gates, at Rotary clubs and farm cooperatives, plus many local radio interviews and talks helped organize a number of new Socialist locals and helped boost the Socialist vote. Solomon polled 126,580 votes for Governor while Thomas rolled up 194,952 as the senatorial nominee as compared to 176,-045 votes when he ran for president in 1932. More than 64,000 of those votes were polled upstate, the highest upstate vote ever recorded for a Socialist candidate. Even though he failed of election, the campaign results tended to buttress Thomas' theory that the Party could afford to have very considerable differences in theory about long-range ideological problems if its members could unite on a program of immediate action.

After the election, Thomas urged the appointment by the national executive committee of a representative committee to work out a statement, following the lines of the Declaration of Principles, which could win wider party support and prevent or mitigate unwholesome controversy during the 1936 presidential campaign. Thomas rejected the possibility of organic unity with the Communist Party but called for an inclusive Socialist Party, saying he wanted men in the Party both to the right and left of his own position. He stressed that "We don't have to agree on everything in order to work together for the cooperative commonwealth." In late 1935, the Party executive committee had voted to make the Party an "all-inclusive" Party. It invited into its ranks all independent, unaffiliated and other homeless radicals. Followers of Ben Gitlow, Herbert Zam, Jay Lovestone and a few Trotskyites all marched into the Party and worked to make over the Party in their own image.

As a rank and file young Socialist, I cheered Thomas' brilliant speeches at scores of meetings, but I was by no means enamored of his political views. I thought them too conservative, deeming myself a left-winger. In 1935, fourteen young Socialists, myself among them, signed a "manifesto" which could be charitably characterized only as half-baked Leninism. Thomas called us together and gave us a tongue-lashing. He said it was bad enough having to combat right-wing Party factionalists without having well-meaning but politically irresponsible youngsters giving them precious ammunition. Sober reflection made many of us concede that Thomas was right.

To Old Guard complaints that adoption of the Detroit Declaration of Principles in 1934 had broken the connection between Socialists and the labor movement, Thomas could report the following activities with unions: at the request of the national leaders of the Textile Workers, he spoke at general strike meetings in New York, New Jersey and North Carolina. He talked for the National Biscuit Company strikers in New York and Philadelphia; for white and colored laundry strikers in Birming-

167

ham, Alabama; for onion strikers in Ohio; for lead and zinc miners in Picher, Oklahoma; for shipyard strikers in Camden, N.J., and striking seamen in New York; for auto workers' organizing meetings or strikes in St. Louis, Toledo and Detroit; and he was arrested while picketing with May Department Store strikers in New York.

Yet all this activity also had its negative side for the Party. Ex-Communist Benjamin Gitlow exaggerated when he said later that "Norman Thomas, who was opposed to a split, was so engrossed in his own activities, which kept him moving all over the country and busily speaking day and night, that he had no time to watch his own house." But still there was a germ of truth in Gitlow's statement. Moreover, so bitter had factionalism within the Socialist Party become that the split was inevitable.

Taking advantage of this situation, the Communist Party approached the Socialist Party in late 1935 with an attractive proposition. Earl Browder offered to debate Norman Thomas in Madison Square Garden, with all proceeds going to the national office of the Socialist Party and the *Socialist Call*. The national office and the *Call* accepted the offer, but the Old-Guard-controlled New York City executive committee ordered Thomas to withdraw from the debate, which they called a "united front." The national executive committee countered with a ruling that the Thomas-Browder debate did not violate party discipline and censured the *New Leader* for its articles on the Party situation in New York. The Old Guard leaders thereupon labelled the *Socialist Call* a dual organization and ordered expulsion of all members supporting it. The next move in the chess game was for the Militants to set up a new New York central committee of the Party and arrange for an emergency state convention. The national executive committee then voted eight to two for Darlington Hoopes' motion to suspend the charter of the New York state organization and set up a temporary state committee of fifteen to reorganize the Party. This the Old Guard refused to recognize, thus making it necessary for both sides to appeal to the forthcoming 1936 national convention.

Legally, the national convention represented not only dues-paying members but voters enrolled as Socialists under primary election laws. Thus, for the first and only time in Socialist Party history, the fight for delegates was taken into the spring primaries in New York state. The majority of the left-wing slate was elected, which pleased Thomas, but he commented sadly on primary night that his only electoral victory was over Party comrades.

Although Thomas had emphasized, in accepting Browder's offer to debate, that it would be no "love feast," Browder was not greatly exercised about who would "win" the debate. His objectives of further intensifying the division between the Old Guard and the Militants had been accomplished. In the debate itself, which drew a capacity crowd of over 20,000, the communist rank and filers had not yet learned their new "Popular Front" line. When Thomas excoriated the Soviet Union for aiding Mussolini's conquest of Ethiopia by saying, "Those who died on the battlefield do not understand international diplomacy; they only know that they were killed by Mussolini's tanks driven with Soviet oil," communists in the audience booed and hissed. Browder ignored Thomas' strictures and appealed again and again for a "people's front" with Catholics, Republicans and Democrats.

Early in 1936, the communists approached Thomas and his associates first to urge the formation of a Farmer-Labor Party and then to press a joint Socialist-Communist presidential ticket that year with Thomas for President and Browder as his running mate. In February Thomas told Browder that he would not consider such a joint ticket. When the Socialist Party national convention met in Cleveland in May, Browder volunteered to reporters that he would still welcome a joint ticket with Thomas as the presidential nominee—an offer Thomas forcefully repudiated. This maneuver only served to strengthen the suspicions of the Old Guard against Thomas and the Militants.

On the opening day of the 1936 convention, both left and right wing delegations from New York appeared and demanded to be seated. The convention voted immediately to seat the Militants. When the Old Guard leaders realized that they would be outvoted in the convention, they stalked out and announced the formation of a new party to be known as the Social Democratic

Federation. Ironically, at the 1936 Socialist convention, the Party voted for a resolution to put an end to any further united front negotiations with the communists and also modified the 1934 Declaration of Principles. Had this policy been adopted several years earlier, it is possible that the split might have been averted.

In 1936, after the national convention, the official Trotskyites asked to be admitted into the party as individuals, promising that they would have no caucus. Thomas, who had been nominated again as the Socialist candidate for President, was busy with the campaign, but willingly countenanced the admission of the Trotskyites into the party—a mistake that he was soon to rue.

As the 1936 campaign went on, a strange development occurred. The Communist Party, which had denounced Norman Thomas in 1934 for trying "to hide from the masses in this country . . . that it is the White House that is the central headquarters of the advance of fascism," suddenly blossomed forth as an ardent supporter of Roosevelt's campaign for re-election. The communists had nominated Browder for President, but carried on a campaign in which they repeated the thesis of Georgi Dimitrov at the Seventh World Congress of the Communist International, that the real threat of fascism in America came from Big Business critics of Roosevelt. Accordingly, the communists dubbed the Republican candidate, Alf Landon, the "front man" for American fascism.

Young Socialists made the most of the quick switch in the communist line. Number One on their "hit parade" was a parody, "Our Line's Been Changed Again," sung to the tune of the old Negro spiritual, "Dem Bones Shall Rise Again." Verses of the song, written by Alton Levy, included the following:

United Fronts are what we love, our line's been changed again,
From below and from above—our line's been changed again.

CHORUS: I knows it, Browder; I knows it, Browder;
I knows it, Browder; Our line's been changed again.

The plenum says the time has come, our line's been changed again.
Don't call a Socialist a bum, our line's been changed again.

Imperialist war we once attacked, etc.
But since the Franco-Soviet pact, etc.

We're now a party with finesse, etc.
With bourgeois groups we'll coalesce, etc.

A Labor Party's too left by far, etc.
We Communists choose FDR, etc.

Ironically, those right-wing Socialists who had been very suspicious that Norman Thomas wanted to support Roosevelt, or at least not nominate a candidate against Roosevelt, found themselves in the American Labor Party campaigning for Roosevelt. And, at the same time, these Old Guard leaders, who had bolted the Socialist Party on the grounds that Thomas wanted united fronts with communists, found that within a few weeks after the split, the communists had moved into bed with them in the American Labor Party and in support of Roosevelt.

Thomas actually did not want to run for President in 1936, knowing that the result would be anti-climactic. He did not think that the Socialist vote would be lessened by the defection of the right wing but felt that the loss would come from other sources. "Our great loss," he wrote, "will come anyway on account of the Roosevelt sentiment, and many of the votes that our right-wing friends think they can control would have gone to Roosevelt anyway." Yet, while Thomas was of the opinion that Roosevelt's achievements had been tremendous, he did not feel that the New Deal was enough of an answer to America's problems as to make a Socialist campaign unnecessary. He was irritated by the suggestion, popularized by James P. Warburg and Al Smith, that Roosevelt had carried out the Socialist platform of 1932. "Roosevelt did not carry out the Socialist platform," said Thomas sarcastically, "unless he carried it out on a stretcher." At the same time, Thomas refused to call Landon a fascist, as the communists insisted, and found himself attacked by William Z. Foster, who asserted that Thomas aided "Fascist demagogues" by failing to make a distinction between Landon and Roosevelt. Thomas knew that Landon was a decent liberal, somewhat to the left of most of his Republican colleagues.

During the campaign Thomas had a unique experience, a

running debate with an immense Townsend Plan convention in the huge Cleveland municipal auditorium. In the hot summer weather of mid-July, Dr. Townsend had gathered together nine thousand of his followers from all parts of the country. Among the rabble rousers who addressed his convention was Father Charles Coughlin of the National Union for Social Justice. Father Coughlin aroused the Townsend audience to heights of enthusiasm by a kind of clerical strip tease in which, under the influence of the heat and the wild response to his own eloquence, he discarded various articles of his clerical garb, including the clerical collar itself.

Dr. Townsend had formally invited all presidential candidates to appear and express their views at his convention but only Norman Thomas was brave enough (or foolhardy enough) to accept the invitation. Thomas felt strong compassion for the thousands of elderly men and women in the audience, who sat about the auditorium in the heat, worn and tired, eating the remains of lunches they had brought from home. When Thomas began his speech by expressing sympathy for these whose old age had come with so little security, he was greeted with considerable applause. But then Thomas told the Townsendites why their plan could not work. He said that no economic or political system would be willing to pay more to people for not working after they had retired, than it was paying on the average to workers currently employed.

As boos began to fill the air, Dr. Townsend, who was presiding, made an unsuccessful effort to quiet the audience. After all, he reminded his followers, Norman Thomas was the only presidential candidate who had accepted their invitation to address the convention. Thomas suggested, as a kind of compromise, that the Townsendites allow him to finish a sentence or a paragraph and then they could boo. And this was what happened. When Thomas condemned Father Coughlin and likened the Townsend Plan to "treating tuberculosis with cough drops," the protest sounded like a Greek chorus—with Thomas giving the solo and the audience responding antiphonally with boos.

The election returns were what Thomas had expected: Roosevelt won in a landslide, creating the new political slogan, "As goes

Maine, so goes Vermont." Thomas and his running mate, George Nelson of the Wisconsin Farmers' Union, polled only 187,342 votes —a far cry from the 903,286 in 1932. The Socialist vote in New York dropped from 177,397 to 86,897, with large numbers of former Socialist voters swinging to Roosevelt on the American Labor Party line, where the latter received 274,924 votes.

Thomas accepted these results philosophically. Replying to a questionnaire from *The United States News*, he stressed that great masses of the people backed Roosevelt because of their "exaggerated belief that a Landon victory would mean the end of relief, a virtual outlawry of labor unions, and perhaps an erection of concentration camps." The outstanding fact of the campaign was "popular support for Roosevelt" which had "elements of conscious working class solidarity in it." This, Thomas said, "almost wiped out numerically minor parties for the time being" because to hundreds of thousands of minor party voters "the defeat of Landon seemed to be the outstanding necessity."

During this period, Thomas was disturbed that Americans evidently did not realize the evils of fascism as they applied to the United States itself. Kent School in Connecticut, attended by his youngest son, Evan, followed the practice of flying the flags of the homelands of its foreign students. When a German student enrolled, a swastika flag was hoisted over the school. Thomas wrote headmaster Father F. H. Sill, "This is the flag of a party which has forced its rule upon Germany by great cruelty . . . Surely I need not remind you of what the Church, both Catholic and Protestant, have suffered by the effort to make the flag supreme over the cross."

Evan, then in the sixth form, was captain of the crew and was enjoying himself thoroughly. He did not want to leave Kent, but was convinced that his father was right. On one occasion, Evan heard his father and Headmaster Sill quoting Bible verses to each other, and it was apparent that Sill had more than met his match. He also heard a couple of boys of German national background, who roomed across the hall, say, "Let the bloody Socialist go." The final upshot was that the swastika flag was taken down, and Evan stayed at Kent.

Another example of moral myopia about fascism occurred at the time that Mussolini invaded Ethiopia. Mayor La Guardia, always anxious to keep the Italian vote, was careful not to denounce Italian fascism and would inveigh magnificently against Nazism instead. Generoso Pope, then a strong supporter of Mussolini, was promoting a Madison Square Garden rally for Italian War Relief. When Italian anti-fascists tried to see La Guardia, he stalled them off. When Thomas intervened, he finally agreed to see him —on the very day of the meeting. La Guardia, a superb actor, played the role of the overburdened executive, harassed not only by a multitude of affairs but by those who ought to be his friends.

"Oh, Norman, you mean I can't even go to see *Aida?*" he asked. Thomas replied that the plot of *Aida* was very different from this other plot. When Thomas showed him that it was the pro-fascists in the Italian community who were supporting the rally, La Guardia still refused to promise not to attend. In the end he compromised by going but not sitting on the platform. Instead he sat in a box, and was called upon to stand up. Thomas felt this wasn't one of La Guardia's most heroic efforts.

These incidents in America were only minor symptoms of a major threat to democracy rapidly growing in Europe. The danger became acute in July 1936 when the Spanish Civil War broke out with a rebellion by Spanish fascists, under the leadership of Francisco Franco. The rebellion, Thomas insisted in a letter to President Roosevelt, was not "an uprising of the exploited masses against autocracy. It is a singularly cruel and dangerous military revolt engineered by the economic royalists of Spain."

President Roosevelt, appealing to American sentiment for neutrality, soon upheld the State Department's "moral embargo," which hindered the sale of arms to the legitimate Spanish Government. When American companies applied in December 1936 for licenses to export arms and planes to the Spanish Loyalists, Roosevelt acted with unaccustomed speed. On January 6, 1937, he called for an arms embargo law which Congress passed the same day. In a Baltimore speech, Thomas called Roosevelt's action hypocritical:

"The danger that the United States would be involved in war by permitting a friendly Spanish Government to buy military supplies, which we have freely permitted the conservative governments of China, Japan, and other countries to buy for use against insurrection, was very slight. . . . To the degree that it [the sudden refusal] strengthens the fascist cause, it is far more dangerous to peace than it would be to permit to Spain the rights that heretofore have always been acknowledged."

A month earlier, Thomas had met with Spanish Ambassador Fernando de los Rios, who stressed the Loyalists' need for arms but added that well-trained American technicians could also be helpful. In the middle of December, New York Socialist secretary Jack Altman had proposed that the Party recruit a Eugene Victor Debs Column of 500 volunteers to fight with the Loyalist army in Spain, and that $50,000 be raised to transport them. Local New York voted overwhelmingly for the proposal, which was announced in the press the next day. Upon Thomas' initiative, the national executive committee arranged for the creation of a new group, Friends of the Debs Column, to raise funds and assist volunteers to get to Spain, and, more than incidentally, to insure that the Party would not be involved in any legal problems. Among its sponsors were Roger Baldwin, V. F. Calverton, John Chamberlain, Clifton Fadiman, Charles Yale Harrison, Sidney Hook, Ludwig Lore, A. Philip Randolph, Upton Sinclair and Carlo Tresca. Poet Carl Sandburg declared, "Were I younger, I should be fighting shoulder to shoulder with the workers against Franco."

But many pacifists, Socialists or sympathizers reacted with dismay and anger at the spectacle of the anti-militarist Socialist Party recruiting men for armed warfare. John Haynes Holmes, one of Thomas' closest friends and collaborators, wrote sadly that "Times have changed apparently since you and I were young, and in 1917 saw the Socialist Party refuse to support a war in which not a foreign but our own country was involved!" Bitterly Holmes added: "By which right does any Socialist today profane the sacred name of Debs by using it to designate a regiment of soldiers enlisted for the work of human slaughter? . . . You and I, Norman, have been through this business before. We stood fast when Belgians lifted cries as pitiful as those lifted by Spaniards today, and when Paris was beset no less terribly than Madrid . . . Are we to stand by idly now when a new generation, tempted as we were tempted, yields to the appeal for another fight to save democracy, and one more war to establish peace?" Concluded Holmes: "Let us send food, clothing, medical supplies in abundance, but not a gun, not a bomb, not an airplane to prolong the war, and extend the area of devastation and death."

Heartsick, Thomas replied to Holmes that "in many ways I would be a much happier man if I could agree with you." But in a memo to his pacifist friends, Thomas added that "victory by the Spanish fascists" would "menace the peace of the world by the encouragement it would give to fascist aggression." . . . Sadly, Thomas noted: "I myself have not for many years found it possible to accept the type of religious pacifism which I accepted during the World War. Life has forced me to change in many respects my philosophy of those years . . . I know the heaviness of heart which many of you feel when the Socialist Party is obliged, as in the case of Spain, to use military violence against Fascist Rebels. . . . This situation, however, differs greatly from the support of international war between capitalist nations."

As to the use of Debs' name for the Column, Thomas recalled that "in spite of some extremely pacifist utterances, at many times in his life Debs said and did things which argued that he would have supported this Column."

A few days later, Morris Ernst came to Thomas' home and told his wife (Thomas was not at home) that word had come that the Department of Justice planned to indict all those acting to aid the Loyalists, using as basis the old neutrality laws dating back to the 18th Century and the French Revolution. Thomas decided that the time had come for him to try to speak personally about the situation to Cordell Hull, and an appointment was arranged. Hull was friendly, spent most of the time questioning Thomas about the differences between Trotsky and Stalin, said that he had no plans to press for any action against supporters of the Loyalists but then suggested that Thomas should see some people at the Department of Justice. Gratified, Thomas ventured to say:

"Mr. Secretary, thank you so much but do you mind if I ask you a question? Why does our Government follow a policy which so clearly helps the fascists?"

Replied Hull: "Well, Mr. Thomas, you see the French and the British do it that way and they are much nearer than we are." Then apparently noting the look on Thomas' face, Hull quickly added, "Not, of course, that our Spanish policy is a mere copy of theirs."

Thomas then went to the Department of Justice where he saw many officials. When the Justice Department lawyers said, "Now, Mr. Thomas, this is a government of laws and this is what we have to do," Thomas countered with, "I'm too old to tell that to. The government never used the old laws against American volunteers in the Allied armies before U.S. entry in the World War; against Irish-Americans who aided the struggle against British rule; or even against Italian-Americans who fought for Mussolini in the war against Ethiopia."

Within the week Thomas was invited to meet with the New York District Attorney and an F.B.I. man, where a similar discussion ensued. By this time, Frank P. Walsh, a labor lawyer, Catholic and an old friend of Thomas from the days when Norman was one of the few Protestants to speak for the cause of Irish freedom, offered to defend Thomas. Moreover, Walsh added, "I'll bring the court evidence of the way they didn't enforce the law against the Irish Republic and its American friends." The Justice Department quickly dropped all talk of prosecution.

Yet, while Thomas effectively inhibited government action against American volunteer aid to the Loyalists, the Debs Column itself was a weak and ineffective form of such aid. The communists, with their International Brigade, raised far more money and sent many more recruits to the Loyalist armies.

On March 31, 1937, Norman and Violet Thomas sailed on the *SS Aquitania* for Europe, planning to visit Spain, England, France, Austria, Czechoslovakia, Poland, Russia, Finland, Sweden, Denmark, and Belgium.

In England, Thomas visited Ernest Bevin, then head of Britain's largest union, the Transport and General Workers Union, and later Foreign Minister of the Government. Bevin, who in many ways resembled John L. Lewis, began a tirade in which, for nearly ten minutes, he denounced Thomas for daring to criticize the

British Labor Party's support of Prime Minister Chamberlain's non-intervention policy in Spain. Bevin told Thomas, "We are good Socialists and when our French comrades ask us to do something, we do it." Thomas finally managed to get in a word, and said, "I don't believe Leon Blum asked you to do it. What's more, I'm going to Paris and I'm going to ask him." Bevin's temper cooled and then, with a twinkle in his eye, he said, "Remember, I have a lot of Irish Catholics in my union."

Later, when Thomas saw Blum, Socialist Premier of France's Popular Front Government, he inquired whether or not Blum had ever asked the British to adopt non-intervention as a policy. Blum replied that, on the contrary, he had expected to carry out the treaty provisions of the French Government and provide aid to the Spanish Loyalist Government, but that the British had insisted on non-intervention and that his Radical Socialist (roughly similar to our Democrats) colleagues in the cabinet backed the British policy. Added Blum optimistically: "I suppose you've noticed how loose were the interstices of the net across the Pyrenees and the French border."

Thomas, no military expert, failed to realize until much later that the openings in Monsieur Blum's net never let through tanks or planes for the Loyalists and that what decided the war was the comparatively small number of tanks and planes that Germany sent the rebels to carry on small-scale blitz tactics. It was indeed a rehearsal for World War II.

In May, 1937, Thomas visited the battle fronts in Spain. It seemed to him that the war was being conducted in a completely amateurish manner. He observed the great price the Loyalists were paying Stalin in gold for small help against the fascists, and also that the communists had secured a very high degree of control over all foreign volunteers. Thomas decided then that the Socialist Party should no longer take any actual or moral responsibility for volunteers, even though he still supported the Loyalist government under Negrin. While heavily infiltrated, he felt that the legal government was not completely controlled by the communists.

Upon his return to the United States, Thomas took to President Roosevelt, at the request of Negrin, a copy of the Loyalist White

178

Book which gave documentary evidence that Mussolini had plotted with Franco even before the revolt started. He urged Roosevelt to enforce the Neutrality Law against the Germans and Italians who were waging an undeclared war against the legal Spanish Government. Roosevelt replied that he thought we were sending very little arms to Germany and Italy and added that "when it was clear to the world, as he knew it was clear in fact, that Germany and Italy were really attacking Spain," the U.S. would have to act. "The trouble," Roosevelt went on to say, "was that England and France hadn't recognized breaches of neutrality." Then Roosevelt adroitly switched the subject and told Thomas how liberal in economic matters certain Catholics, particularly Cardinal Mundelein, were. Thomas took this to mean that Roosevelt would be unwilling to do anything against Hitler's and Mussolini's intervention in Spain unless the Cardinal approved of such a policy. In fact, Roosevelt personally blocked any modification of the Neutrality Law even when isolationist Senators Nye and Wheeler were ready for it.

Interior Secretary Harold L. Ickes talked privately with the President about the desirability of lifting the embargo on the Loyalists, and Roosevelt silenced him by claiming that "to raise the embargo would mean the loss of every Catholic vote next fall and that the Democratic members of Congress were jittery about it and didn't want it done." This, confided the disgusted Ickes to his diary (*The Secret Diary of Harold Ickes*, Simon and Schuster, Inc.), "was the cat that was actually in the bag, and it is the mangiest, scabbiest cat ever."

In a letter to Thomas in October, 1938, Ambassador Claude Bowers had expressed disappointment that Roosevelt had failed to heed warnings that the Spanish Civil War was likely to be the curtain-raiser for World War II. "It is easy to keep peace," wrote Bowers. "All that is required is to truckle to the dictators, betray liberty and democracy and receive ovations. Maybe there is no other Democracy in the world outside that of Spain that has the guts to fight." Finally, in March, 1939, Roosevelt summoned Bowers to return for consultations. At that time, the President conceded, as the Spanish Republic lay on its death-bed, "We have made a mistake."

179

Before Thomas embarked on his trip to Europe, he had felt hopeful that the Socialist Party was making progress in building an inclusive Party, a vanguard organization which would not be isolated from the masses. But when he returned, he discovered that the watchword in the party had become fission, not fusion. With the Old Guard contentedly herded into the greener pastures of the New Deal's American Labor Party, the Militants had split into two wings: the Altmanites, led by Jack Altman, secretary of Local New York; and the Clarityites, led by Herbert Zam, a former Lovestone Communist, and Gus Tyler, then editor of the *Socialist Call*. The Trotskyites, who had (with fingers crossed) promised the Socialist leaders that they would dissolve their organization and maintain no factional caucus, made the third group.

The Altman group, including such active Socialists as Aaron Levenstein, Murray and Sam Baron, Hal Siegel and Murray Gross, was allied with the trade union activists of the Wisconsin party of Dan Hoan and Paul Porter, itself a part of the Farmer-Labor Progressive Federation in that state. They were anxious to work closely with the labor movement to build a mass base.

The Clarityites had strength in many weaker locals of the Party. Among its leaders were Maynard Krueger of Chicago, David Felix of Philadelphia, national labor secretary Frank Trager and Bob Delson. They backed Zam and Tyler in the effort to make the Socialist Party "more revolutionary." When Altman proposed that the Party run no slate of candidates in New York against the American Labor Party's councilman choices but instead cooperate with the ALP, the Clarityites insisted that the party should refuse to cooperate with any party that was not completely independent of old-party politics.

After his return from Russia and Spain, Thomas constantly warned against the danger of Trotskyism as well as Stalinism. "I have stood up for Trotsky's right of asylum and for a fair inquiry into the charges against him . . . At the same time I am sure that if Trotsky had won we should have had similar denials of civil liberty, a similar refusal to build a political structure permitting legal opposition, and a similar Jesuitism; that is to say, a great emphasis that the end justifies the means . . . No American party can safely be guided by observations taken always from the latitude and longitude of Moscow, Madrid or Mexico City, or whatever might be the temporary home of the exiled Trotsky."

Thomas did not know that, with the Trotsky Investigation Committee ready to publish its report exonerating the latter from Stalin's plot charges, the Old Man, as his adoring followers called him, had given orders to split the Socialist Party. In a "confidential" letter to James Cannon and James Burnham (later to become one of the leading "philosophers" of the right wing in America), Trotsky gave marching orders to meet what he described as a new "turning point" in history.

The Trotskyists enthusiastically mobilized to carry out Trotsky's orders, and were so vicious in their attacks against the Socialist Party, its policies and its discipline that Trotsky's timetable was exceeded. By September, 1937, they had been expelled from the Party, taking with them about three hundred converts.

What hurt the Socialist Party was not so much the loss of a few hundred members, but the debilitating effects of the many wasted months of internal party struggle when the Party might have been active as an organized force in aiding the drive for industrial unionism sparked by John L. Lewis, the Congress of Industrial Organizations and the militant sit-down strikers. Faced with the choice between endless and often fruitless wrangling within the Party and inspiring and rewarding activity within the burgeoning labor movement, many of the Party's most able, courageous and vigorous members assumed active roles in the unions and drifted away from Party meetings.

THIRTEEN

Communism Reappraised

৶৳ WHEN NORMAN THOMAS and his wife visited Russia in the spring of 1937, he had still hoped that what he saw would allay his fears and doubts concerning the development of totalitarian tyranny. Alas, his major fears were confirmed. Not that Thomas made a thorough study of Russia on this tour. He visited the usual tourist sights, Moscow, Leningrad, Kiev. He was taken to some of the collective farms and to Bolshevo, which appeared to him to be a model prisoners' community. But he was deeply depressed when he saw forced laborers "under armed guard finishing the aqueduct which is part of the Moscow Volga Canal project." Thomas realized that these people were members of that "large group of Russians who suddenly disappear from their homes and accustomed places, usually without any trial worthy of the name."

Thomas was also shown through the publishing plant of *Pravda*, and noticed that the new and pretentious buildings were already beginning to crack. In pointing out various features of the plant the guide, properly propagandized, would maintain, "*The New York Times* hasn't anything like that." Thomas refrained from saying that in *The New York Times* building an officially guided party would not have had to show a pass five times to fully armed soldiers as was done at the *Pravda* plant.

The Soviet regime showed little official interest in the Thomas visit, except that the Intourist guide tried to be with Norman and Violet all the time. She appeared deeply grieved when she learned that Thomas had evaded her and gone with an American resident in Moscow to the railroad station late at night, where he saw many people sleeping on the floor. Thomas was anxious to see and hear for himself all that he could, and was later told that in his few days in Moscow he had made more use of the American Embassy's fact-collecting office than had Joe Davies, then familiarly known in Moscow as the "absentee ambassador."

The Thomases saw and heard Stalin at the May Day parade and then, on their last night in Moscow, saw him at the Ballet. He sat in the back of the old imperial box, entering as the curtain rose and leaving as it fell. Before Stalin arrived, an officer in the box directly over his stood up and inspected the audience. Maj. Faimonville, the American military attaché, whispered to Thomas: "That's my old friend, General Feldman, very high up and very close to Stalin. I think Uncle Joe must be coming and has him looking over the house." Thomas forgot the incident until, less than a month later, he read in a newspaper the list of generals executed in the great army purge. General Feldman's name was on the list. Whatever the General's alleged offense, Thomas later wrote, it was "obvious that he was no vulgar assassin for I had seen him pass up a chance such as John Wilkes Booth never had."

When Thomas returned to the States he began to write his impressions of the trip. In an article in the June 5th *Socialist Call*, it is obvious he was still eager to find signs of progress. "After the horrible nightmare of anti-Semitism in central and southeastern Europe," he wrote, "it is a great thing to come to a country without a Jewish problem within its borders." (Not until a number of years later did Thomas learn about Soviet anti-Semitism.) Even the severe shortage of housing, food and other consumers' goods he excused as perhaps necessary because of arms expenditures required by the Nazi threat.

What bothered Thomas, however, was his "strong feeling . . . that Russia was not moving toward a classless society, but on the contrary, perpetuating and even strengthening new class divisions." Noting that Stakhanovites were paid as much as 2,000 rubles a month while unskilled workers in the same factory made only 100 rubles, Thomas said: "Don't let anyone tell you that there is no feeling of class distinction between the poorer paid workers and the high officials or even the Stakhanovites! . . . The speed-up system as practiced in Russia seems to me to contain many perils not only to individual well-being, but to Socialist ideals."

Torn between his hopes and his fears, Thomas concluded that: "Many things in Russia exceeded my expectations. The masses impressed me as generally happy, but there is an incalculable and poisonous weight of fear which if continued will destroy our dreams of socialism."

The continuing purges forced Thomas to exclaim: "More and more the news that comes out from Russia parallels news that we would expect from fascist countries where dictatorship is absolute." And, at this point, almost two years before the Nazi-Soviet Pact, Thomas forecast that: "The methods of Stalin in certain important respects so closely parallel the methods of Hitler that one is obliged to give more credence to the belief . . . that an understanding between Stalin and Hitler is not an impossible development in international affairs."

When the Stalin-Hitler Pact actually occurred in August, 1939, the *Socialist Call* printed a cartoon showing a Nazi soldier with a banner beside him—"Friends of the Soviet Union." Thomas denounced Stalin's agreement with Hitler as "a piece of infamy beside which Munich was an adventure in ethics, and the hypocritical nonintervention agreement in Spain a model of international good faith . . . Stalin's infamous pact with his fellow dictator has at last made the issue plain: His communism is the ally, not the foe of fascism; the enemy, not the friend of democracy and the worker's cause." Said Thomas: "Stalin has not yet vied with Hitler in anti-Semitism or tribal nationalism. But he has shut out Jewish refugees from a country which has room for, and need of, hundreds of thousands of well trained artisans and professional men. Perhaps, like Mussolini, he may yet follow Hitler into the depths of racial intolerance." The one ray of hope to Thomas was that: "The world isn't big enough for three gods. Mussolini, Hitler and Stalin have every reason to distrust each other. The very intensity of their nationalism will divide them . . . The religion of totalitarianism will provoke such conflict."

The young Socialists were singing Al Levy's new "Song of the Nazi-Soviet Pact," to the tune of "Three Little Fishes."

> Down in the Kremlin where Trotsky's attacked,
> Sat three little fascists who were after a pact.

Sign, said the Fuehrer Fascist, sign or you'll burn—
So they signed on the line with the Comintern.

What a disgrace and what a sight,
GPU and Gestapo unite!

We're off, cried Stalin, to a very good start,
For we are no longer Poles apart.
Hitler said, Comrade, now that we've signed,
You'll find that we have no more axis to grind.

It sounds peculiar but this is the tune,
Foster's uniting with Fritzie Kuhn.

Down in the Kremlin sits the King of knaves
While all the old Bolsheviks turn in their graves,
Laughing up his sleeve at his latest stunt—
Russia's in the anti-Comintern front!

Believe it or not, me-oh-my,
And they killed Bukharin as a Hitlerite spy!

As if to prove the point, after the Russians had occupied their
section of Poland, Stalin telegraphed von Ribbentrop, in reply
to birthday greetings: "The friendship of the peoples of Germany
and the Soviet Union, cemented by blood, will long remain firm."

In the United States, the communist policy immediately underwent a drastic change. Instead of loudly proclaiming that "The
people demand a halt to Hitler," communists carried placards
saying "The Yanks Are Not Coming." Their erstwhile hero, President Roosevelt, suddenly became a warmonger and the communist
hit parade included these lines:

Oh, Franklin Roosevelt told the people how he felt;
We damned near believed what he said.
He said, I hate war, and so does Eleanor,
But we won't be safe 'til everybody's dead.

Even before the Nazi-Soviet Pact, Thomas became involved in
a considerable controversy with communists within the American
Civil Liberties Union. Dr. Harry F. Ward, a long-time fellow-
traveller, was chairman both of the ACLU and the Communist-
controlled American League for Peace and Democracy. Thomas,
supported by other members of the ACLU board, argued that
"Communists belong on the Board of the Civil Liberties Union as

much or as little as fascists who also want the protection of the Bill of Rights—until they seize power."

With incredibly poor timing, three days after the Nazi-Soviet Pact was signed, Ward was part of a "Committee of 400" which issued a statement claiming that "Soviet and fascist policies are diametrically opposed . . . The Soviet Union continues as always to be a bulwark against war and aggression, and works unceasingly for a peaceful international order . . . Its epoch-making new constitution guarantees Soviet citizens . . . civil liberties, the right to employment, to leisure." Among those joining Ward in that bit of Stalinist apologetics were Mary Van Kleeck, Corliss Lamont, Robert W. Dunn and Elizabeth Gurley Flynn.

Thomas and his colleagues on the ACLU board were successful in securing the resignation of Dr. Ward and the expulsion of Elizabeth Gurley Flynn. At the annual meeting of the Union in February, 1940, a resolution was adopted declaring it inappropriate for any person to serve on the governing committees or the staff of the ACLU who was a member of any political organization which supported totalitarian dictatorship in any country, or who by his public declaration and connections indicated his support of such a principle. The banned groups included not only Communist, Nazi and Fascist parties, but native anti-democratic groups like the Ku Klux Klan, the Silver Shirts and the Christian Front.

While successfully urging the ouster of communists and fellow travellers from the ACLU, Thomas continued to plead for civil liberties for communists. For instance, when Princeton University refused to permit its students to invite Earl Browder to speak, on the grounds that he had admitted under oath that he had violated a federal statute by travelling on a passport obtained by fraud, Thomas urged Dean Christian Gauss to permit the Browder talk. In reply, Dean Gauss asked, "Does Browder deserve a reinvitation because he has been backed into a position where he must admit having secretly violated federal statutes for the purpose of evading a law against which he has never protested?" Said Thomas: "I do not think that free speech is something we owe to Browder as Browder, but something we owe to ourselves as the best method in a democracy. The case for letting Browder speak, as was done in Yale (is that) 1. His type of communism thrives more on martyrdom than it does on self-exposure to speak. 2. It is exceedingly dangerous to set justice on a principle of refusing an opportunity to speak to a man who has been indicted."

What concerned Thomas even more was his fear that laws "passed to reach Nazis or communists" would hit instead "some innocent bystander." Thomas declared: "A New Jersey law ostensibly directed against the Nazis has been used, as you probably know, against the children of those Witnesses of Jehovah who don't like to salute the flag because to do so is a form of idolatry. . . . It is this sort of thing which makes me lean over backwards in this field of legislation."

Yet, while urging the right of students to invite communists to speak, Thomas questioned the wisdom of such practices. "I do, however, think the students in these various colleges made a serious mistake in rushing to invite Browder just because he was indicted. He had no contribution, whatever, to make on the subject of civil liberty or indeed on any other subject unless it is in the arts of Machiavellianism."

It may be well to review here some of the myths which have persisted since the thirties regarding communism in the United States. On the one hand we have the myth of an America, as Norman Thomas and Maurice Goldbloom put it in 1955, "whose vitals were gnawed away by communist termites who had succeeded in penetrating it root and branch; of a period in which communists not only pulled the strings of political life, but completely dominated schools and colleges, the arts and the means of mass communication." This, we are told, led to all the world's evils today and we are still suffering from the many "years of treason." And, on the other hand, the legend persists of a period in which "all right-minded people were thrown into the arms of the communists, because only they kept aloft the banner of uncompromising opposition to the fascist threat, only they fought with courage and determination to remedy the injustices which our country had inherited from the Hoover era."

Norman Thomas and anti-communist liberals, then as now, were smeared by Martin Dies and ex-communist-fronter J. B. Matthews as "communists or communist agents." And the communists and their fellow-travellers, like wolves in sheep's clothing, paraded ostentatiously in the robes of "twentieth-century Americanism," insisting that any opponents were agents of Hitler, Mussolini, Franco and the economic royalists.

What was the truth? In actual fact, nowhere did the communists play a major role in planning, instituting or carrying out the great changes which affected American political life during the thirties. These changes reflected efforts to find piecemeal solutions for urgent problems that could not be solved within the traditional framework. There was no sharp line of cleavage between Mr. Hoover's Farm Board and Mr. Roosevelt's AAA, and the Reconstruction Finance Corporation's loans under Hoover to former Vice-President Dawes' Continental Trust Company of Chicago put the government into a wide variety of businesses—including the publication of daily newspapers. Even the Wagner Act, labor's Magna Carta, was less revolutionary than the Norris–La Guardia Act, signed by President Hoover in 1932. Moreover, the first Federal program for direct relief to the unemployed was initiated under Hoover.

But while the communists were not responsible for these changes, they were able to turn many of these changes to their own advantage. For a time, they were able to wield an influence far beyond their membership, to produce impressive-sounding manifestos signed by a host of "innocents," to win control of many strategically located unions, and to place supporters in many key positions in government.

However, except for espionage in some government posts, the communists do not appear to have determined major policy decisions. They were able to make hay with their Popular Front Line, because they and the liberals were going in the same direction. When they sought to change the line of march, the army of fellow travellers almost melted away. In the strategic unions which the communists controlled, where, according to communist theory, they should have been able to influence American foreign policy by paralyzing the economy and the nation's military potential, their main effect was to pass resolutions. After the Nazi-Soviet Pact, when they pulled crippling strikes in the Allis-Chalmers plant, which produced tanks, and in the North American Aviation factory in Inglewood, Calif., they were careful to refrain from even suggesting strikes for overtly political ends. And, while the communists bitterly attacked Britain as an aggressor against the peace-loving Nazis, a large part of the flow of aid to Britain was manufactured in plants whose workers were members of one communist-dominated union and transported through submarine-infested waters in ships manned by seamen who belonged to another. This was a measure of the real weakness which underlay communist strength, even where it seemed greatest.

Many people in the thirties accepted the communist claim that the only way in which it was possible to fight reaction and fascism was to cooperate with or join the communists. The facts, of course, are that the vote for Norman Thomas in the 1932 presidential campaign far exceeded the highest figure the communists ever polled. What is more, it represented a larger percentage of the vote than Wallace secured in 1948. And Socialist influence on American thinking and policy was far greater than communist influence, then and later.

What the communists brought to America was a concept of radicalism destructive of the old ethics that had hitherto prevailed. Among earlier radicals, the idea of hiding one's beliefs in order to undermine and take over other organizations was inconceivable. Not only socialists, but anarchists and syndicalists, including the Industrial Workers of the World (I.W.W.), were proud of their views. No Fifth Amendment stand for any of these old-timers. Instead they insisted upon declaiming their views at every opportunity.

The communists brought into radical circles the policy of lying, cheating, disruption, treachery—even murder. They would enter organizations claiming to be simple liberals, deny without compunction membership in the Communist Party, and bore from within to subvert the groups to communist ends. In unions communists would filibuster at meetings until most normal members became disgusted and went home. Then the persevering communists, now a majority of the bleary-eyed remnant of the meeting, would pass pro-communist resolutions and bleed the treasury

189

for communist causes. The communists were aided by the fuzzy-mindedness of many "innocents" who accepted the communist claim that since there was agreement on specific issues of fighting fascism, one should not examine or question the totalitarian nature of world communism. These views helped bring under communist control the Workers Alliance, the largest organization of unemployed workers in the country, which had been started by Socialists. Until the siren song of "unity" led to a merger, which Thomas opposed, of the socialist-led Student League for Industrial Democracy and the Communists' National Student League to form the American Student Union, the communists had been relatively weak in the student field except for a few large cities in which communist membership was concentrated. Again the communists were able to maneuver themselves into control of the merged movement.

Especially in the situations where new and dangerous ground was broken, communists were conspicuously absent. Among the Southern sharecroppers and tenant farmers, it was Norman Thomas and the Socialists who took the lead; the communists arrived like jackals later, trying to disrupt what others had built. In the coal mines of West Virginia and Harlan County, Ky., the fight against terrorism by company and public officials was carried out by members of the I.W.W., Socialists and United Mine Workers. The communists were satisfied with exploiting the situation for publicity and to raise funds, ostensibly for the miners, but actually for party purposes. This pattern was repeated in case after case, although the communists had no objection to claiming the credit for the work of others, and were frequently helped by the insistence of reactionaries to smear liberals and Socialists with the epithet "communist."

FOURTEEN

The War Clouds Gather

~§ ALTHOUGH THOMAS was no longer a religious pacifist and had even supported efforts to send American volunteers to fight in Spain in 1936, he was still strongly opposed to war as a means of settling differences. He saw clearly the magnitude of the Nazi menace but was more than ever determined to keep America out of the world conflagration which seemed to be brewing. He had never forgotten the day when one of his sons came home from school and asked him, "Daddy, will there be another war and must I fight in it? Can't you stop it?"

In 1938 Thomas took the initiative in creating the Keep America Out of War Congress, which met in Washington, D.C., over the Memorial Day weekend. More than 1,100 delegates from unions, fraternal, political, religious, farm and youth groups attended.

Then came the shameful Munich Pact, which Thomas viewed as a "logical kind of deal for capitalist powers." Roosevelt first issued a statement on October 25, 1938, commending the "cool heads" who in the European crisis had "pleaded for continuance of negotiation." This he contradicted a couple of days later by denouncing "peace by fear"—an obvious allusion to Munich.

Meanwhile Roosevelt scrapped his earlier pledge "to make certain that the small decisions of each day do not lead toward war." Although he had invoked the Neutrality Act against Loyalist Spain, now Roosevelt secured the repeal of the Neutrality Law, gave destroyers to Britain, repaired her warships in our ports, extended the enormous aid provided under the Lend-Lease Law, jointly occupied Iceland with the British, hunted German U-boats in the North Atlantic, and even convoyed British troops to Africa in American ships.

The American public was tense and uneasy during this period. Isolationist America First businessmen and liberal trade union leaders were equally anxious to keep America out of war. Working with Thomas was Senator Burton K. Wheeler, the liberal Montana Democrat who had been La Follette's running mate in the 1924 Progressive presidential race. Labor was particularly fearful of the government's Industrial Mobilization Plan. "Under this plan," wrote Rose Stein in *M-Day*, "labor will have to either work or fight. The individual will have no choice in the matter." On Labor Day, 1939, CIO head John L. Lewis said: "Labor wants the right to work and live—not the privilege of dying by gunshot or poison gas to sustain the mental errors of current statesmen . . . Let those who will seek the votes of the workers of America be prepared to guarantee jobs for all workers and freedom from foreign wars." And William Green of the AFL, at odds with Lewis on most issues, chimed in with: "Labor throughout the length and breadth of the United States is opposed to sending another generation into the trenches of war . . . There must be no European entanglement and no involvement in European wars." Union after union adopted resolutions calling for a war referendum amendment to the Constitution. On the other hand, until the Nazi-Soviet Pact, those unions under communist control whooped it up for collective security.

When the Socialist convention opened in Washington, D.C., on April 6, 1940 (the 23rd anniversary of the U.S. entrance into World War I), it was a foregone conclusion that Norman Thomas would be nominated for President. The key issue at the convention was the problem of war, peace and fascism. While strongly anti-fascist, the party was so vigorously anti-war that it never resolved the dilemma of how to destroy fascism without resort to war. Thomas argued that steps "short of war" to aid the allies would soon involve us in war itself. A small but highly articulate minority, led by Jack Altman of New York; Paul Porter, editor of *Kenosha Labor* and Alfred Baker Lewis of Massachusetts, a millionaire Socialist and one of the Party's top contributors, urged aid to the allies.

The convention, held in the National Press Club auditorium, in the world's news center, had excellent press coverage. Reporters for the four Washington papers, the wire services, and the Washington bureaus of more than a dozen major out-of-town papers, all jockeyed for the insufficient press seats in the front of the auditorium. As Les Finnegan, *Washington Daily News* correspondent, put it, "For nearly all the reporters, covering a Socialist convention was a new experience, unique and more than a little baffling. Those who had covered Capitol Hill for years were on a first-name, back-slapping basis with the top GOP and Democratic politicos. But only three or four of the reporters knew the Socialist leaders by first name; obviously there weren't going to be many behind-the-scene dope stories."

Party officials had persuaded the three major networks to carry Norman Thomas' speech accepting the presidential nomination late Sunday afternoon, which would enable millions to hear him. But as the afternoon wore on, debate over the Party's plank on war continued. It was an absorbing and exciting discussion but apparently it was going to continue into the precious network time. As the radio deadline approached, several Party officials and delegates proposed that the remainder of the debate be deferred until after Thomas' nomination and acceptance speech.

This, however, Thomas would not accept. Bluntly but affably he told the convention he would not consider acceptance of the presidential nomination before the platform was adopted. For other parties, he reminded the delegates, the platform might be unimportant, but for a Socialist it was a matter of over-riding principle. There was muted consternation in the hall among the socialist leaders who had sweated blood to get the network radio time. At the press tables, the reporter for the *Washington Herald* turned to Les Finnegan and exclaimed, "My God! Can you imagine anything like this happening at the Democratic or Republican conventions! Why they'd browbeat their candidate into making his speech in two minutes or they'd threaten to find another candidate!"

A girl reporter from Chicago said, "That settles it. Any man with that kind of integrity gets my support; I'm voting for Norman Thomas." As she and others commented on Thomas' stand, the attitude along the press tables quickly changed from astonishment to outright admiration. "That was politics with a difference," said a woman Sunday feature writer for the *Washington Star*. "By comparison the other conventions look phoney."

By a vote of 159 to 28, the convention adopted the platform plank favored by Thomas and he was nominated with Professor Maynard C. Krueger of the University of Chicago, a brilliant economics teacher, as his running mate. A chant went up throughout the hall. "The workers are eager for Thomas and Krueger." (After Election Day Daniel Bell was to add the rueful refrain, "But when the votes were counted, the results were meager.")

The convention demanded absolute neutrality, a constitutional amendment granting all the voters a chance to vote on entering a war, and opposition to increased military expenditures. Socialists insisted: "We will, to the best of our ability, aid the victims of war and oppression. We will seek with all neutrals at the first appropriate occasion to mediate in behalf of negotiated peace. And to make that peace effective, we will cooperate in disarmament and in all economic arrangements which will lessen the strain of insecurity and exploitation upon the peoples of the world." To defeat the fascists, the party suggested only "The continuance of independent working class action through the medium of workers' boycott of German and Japanese goods."

The day after the convention ended, Hitler invaded Denmark and Norway. The Socialist national executive committee immediately promised "all practicable support in their struggle, now and in the coming years, for the preservation or restoration of their freedom," denounced "Hitler's crime," but wound up with a plea for America to stay out of the war. Thomas was later to write that not even Pearl Harbor "brought more anguish of mind than the relentless push of the Nazi forces to Paris and the Channel . . . whatever might be my opinions of the British Empire, England, Scotland and Wales were in my blood. No choices that I could make seemed wholly right. But . . . the certain evils of American involvement in war seemed greater than the uncertain good we might accomplish in a war which was still without other positive aim than to stop Hitler."

Before the fall of France, Thomas proposed that America should assume the responsibility, with such help as she could get from other nations, for care of the growing number of refugees. He outlined a plan and showed how comparatively modest would be its costs. Roosevelt replied that the plea touched "a most responsive chord in me" and pledged that the government would both study and give immediate attention to the whole problem. But little happened. Others were less kind. For the most part, Thomas' proposals were either ignored or abused, leading him to say bitterly, "I learned first hand how many Americans preferred to fight or have their countrymen fight for the rights of Jews in Europe than to give them asylum in America."

As the Battle of Britain continued, Socialist campaigning became increasingly difficult. Election laws in state after state had been made more difficult, and people were so frightened by the war issue that they were afraid to sign nominating petitions. Thomas wrote Attorney General Robert H. Jackson about the problem and on July 12, 1940 received the following prompt reply:

> "I have your letter of July 9, relating that many people believe that nominating petitions for the Socialist Party will be automatically turned over to the Federal Bureau of Investigation and each signer investigated as a Fifth Columnist.
>
> "It is regrettable that such a story should gain the slightest credence in this country. The Socialist Party under your leadership has not been regarded as representing or as being under the influence of foreign governments. It is a lawful political party and an American citizen is not subject to harassment because he exercises his right as a citizen in signing your nominating petitions."

During the conventions, both the Democrats and Republicans had failed to support conscription. Once the conventions were out of the way, Roosevelt backed conscription strongly and Willkie, as Thomas put it in a letter to Roosevelt, "has shown a surprising capacity to resist all inquiries concerning his stand." When Thomas accused the President of wanting conscription and "the executive power which it gives you," Roosevelt protested "the grossly unfair suggestion . . . that I am in favor of some form of conscription because of the executive power which it gives to me personally. That is unworthy of you." Added Roosevelt: "You and I may disagree as to the danger to the United States—but we can at least give each other credit for the honesty that lies behind our opinions . . . Incidentally, though you are a student and thinker, I cannot help feeling that my sources of information are just as good and probably better, for the reason that they come from so many places, than yours are."

Thomas hastened to reply that "neither in public nor in private do I mean to imply that you want power for power's sake . . . While you might want that power (for conscription) only to use it for your conception of defense, there is no telling what another executive might desire."

While opposing conscription, Thomas did not oppose all national defense measures, holding that "the old socialist absolutism concerning the similarity of all wars and all armaments needs modification. There are differences. Unless one is an absolute pacifist one can oppose *all* military defense only if one believes all nations are about equally good or bad, or if one believes that war will result in a general revolution against it on both sides." At the same time, Thomas and Krueger feared the development of a garrison state, and the conscious or unconscious attempts of American capitalists to escape from depression and unemployment by expensive and provocative "boondoggling of militarism." (Millions of workers were still unemployed until the defense boom got under way.)

In a nationwide broadcast from Los Angeles on September 21, Thomas warned that "Both the President and Mr. Willkie are so far committed to a program of all steps short of war in aid not only of England but her empire, that they may easily find themselves over the step of war before which they intended to stop short . . . War may easily arise out of our defense of Shanghai against the Japanese whom this Administration has both insulted and aided with extraordinary impartiality—so that in any war with the Japanese militarists, our boys will be drilled by weapons bought with the profits of the sale of Japanese gold to our

Treasury Department."

Incensed by this speech, the *Army and Navy Register*, a magazine of national circulation in military circles, called for Thomas to be jailed. Thomas and others who wanted to repeal the conscription law, the magazine insisted, were a "menace" to the future defense of the nation and should be treated as were Alexander Berkman and Emma Goldman, "who got their just desert during the last war." (Berkman and Goldman were arrested and imprisoned in 1917 and then deported to Russia in 1919.)

The American Legion in Carbondale, Ill., quickly attempted to follow through on the *Army and Navy Register's* advice. Mayor Johnson, after Legion protests, banned a Thomas talk in this city and forced the owners of the Rogers Theater to cancel a projected Thomas meeting, even though the hall had been rented and paid for by William Cox, a leading Carbondale Socialist. As Illinois state secretary of the Socialist Party, I was with Thomas in Springfield, Ill., when Cox phoned to tell of the mayor's action. Thomas told Cox to announce that the meeting would be held even if it had to be on a street corner in the rain.

Then news came that Ruth Adams, a young Socialist who was driving to Springfield to take us to the Carbondale meeting, had been killed in an auto accident. Another Socialist, Nate Egnor, insisted on driving us. The rain was coming down in sheets when we arrived in Carbondale. We went to the railroad station and saw a large crowd there. Fearing that these people might be Legion vigilantes, I left the car to reconnoiter and found that others had had the same idea. The throng was composed of fraternity boys from Southern Illinois Normal University there to protect Thomas should Legionnaires start some rough stuff. Dr. Roscoe Pulliam, president of the University, offered the use of the University auditorium, with a seating capacity double that of the Rogers Theater. The time had come, he said, to cease appeasing dictators —even local, home-grown ones. University students painted a sign, "Jersey City," and hung it over the Carbondale signpost at the entrance to town.

A capacity audience of more than 1,400 students and townspeople jammed the auditorium and cheered Thomas' defiance of the "little Hitlers" who had tried to prevent his speaking.

As the Thomas campaign centered more and more on keeping America out of war, some Socialist Party members veered strongly in the opposite direction. Jack Altman and a group of his supporters joined William Allen White's Committee to Defend America by Aiding the Allies. Responding to Thomas' plea to avoid creating a new factional struggle, these men left the Party more or less quietly.

Meanwhile Roosevelt and Willkie kept reassuring the people about peace. "The American people," declared Wendell Willkie, "do not want war . . . They are determined to keep America at peace. In that determination I stand with them. I am for keeping out of war." Speaking on October 30, after France had fallen, President Roosevelt gave this solemn pledge to the country: "And while I am talking to you mothers and fathers, I give you one more assurance. I have said this before, but I shall say it again and again and again. Your boys are not going to be sent into any foreign wars. They are going into training to form a force so strong that, by its very existence, it will keep the threat of war away from our shores. The purpose of our own defense is defense."

During the campaign, Thomas thought and said there was a case for going into the war with our eyes open, although he believed the case for staying out was stronger. But what angered him and made him fearful for the whole democratic process was what he considered "the business of fooling or lying the people into war." Certainly, the promises of Roosevelt and Willkie to keep the country out of war were effective among the electorate. Roosevelt swept in to an unprecedented third term, with 27 million votes against Willkie's 22 million. The Thomas vote dropped from 187,342 in 1936 to 116,796 in 1940, with almost all the loss accounted for by the drop in interventionist New York state from 86,879 to 20,500.

Thomas sent a note of congratulation to Roosevelt on his election victory, and Roosevelt answered graciously:

"Dear Norman:
That is a mighty nice note of yours and I appreciate it. Do run down here some day soon. I want to have a good talk with you. I am really a bit worried about the trend of undemocratic forces in this country."

When Thomas testified for the Party against a bill for lend-lease aid to Britain, a number of former Socialist Party leaders issued a statement opposing him. A couple of months later, they, and others who had resigned in protest against the Party's anti-war stand, formed the Union for Democratic Action, which later was transformed into Americans for Democratic Action.

Meanwhile, the America First Committee had been organized and Thomas was asked to speak at its meetings. This isolationist group had General Robert E. Wood as its chairman, and its leadership included such diverse elements as General Hugh S. Johnson, Kathryn Lewis (sitting in for her father, John L.), Edward Rickenbacker, William Benton and Chester Bowles. Thomas spoke at several mass meetings, stressing his Socialist position. He felt that the America First program was inadequate but that it was not pro-Nazi or fascist, and that its leaders took vigorous and effective measures to prevent fascist or communist interpenetration. When Thomas spoke at Madison Square Garden with Colonel Charles Lindbergh, liberal interventionists were outraged. To their protests, Thomas replied that Lindbergh had made "a good speech" at the Garden rally and that "I had a chance before a vast audience to speak for a unity of brotherhood, against anti-Semitism, etc. and these sentiments were applauded. Where could I get a better chance to do the same sort of work?"

Lindbergh, Thomas was convinced, was a patriotic American who was the victim of an unscrupulous smear campaign. He had made reports on German military aviation to the British and American governments but both governments ignored them. He was a political conservative but, Thomas insisted, was neither anti-Semitic nor pro-Nazi. His anti-war sentiments were inherited from his father, a progressive and anti-war Congressman from Minnesota during the first World War. As a youngster, Thomas noted, Lindy had helped to distribute from the air his father's anti-war speeches. Thomas added that Lindbergh's repudiation of the pro-fascist Verne Marshall and his "No More Foreign War Committee," plus Lindy's statement that the defeat of Great Britain would be a tragedy, revealed his true attitudes.

Then Lindbergh blundered into his ill-fated Des Moines speech, widely regarded as anti-Semitic. That speech exaggerated the role of American Jews in pushing the nation toward war. Thomas immediately issued a statement hitting sharply at Lindbergh's speech. "Many groups and elements in this country," he said, "are attempting to drive us into war. This issue cuts across all racial lines. No one race is responsible. The Socialist Party has many Jews in its ranks and these take their stand with the Party against American involvement. . . . We are glad that Lindbergh puts himself on record against the Nazis as he did when he said that 'no person with a sense of dignity of mankind can condone the persecution of the Jewish race in Germany.' . . . But when Lindbergh singles out the Jews as a race for major responsibility and speaks of their power and influence as apart from others in American life, he helps to create the conditions which give rise to the very wave of persecution he warns against." Nevertheless, Thomas remained convinced that Colonel Lindbergh was not guilty of intentional anti-Semitism and resented the "character assassination" in which many "liberals" indulged.

Because of his anti-interventionism and his cooperation with America First, Thomas himself was smeared on a number of occasions as "anti-Semitic." He was heartened when James G. McDonald, then president of the Brooklyn Institute of Arts and Sciences and later to become America's first ambassador to Israel, expressed shock that anyone could be so "absurd" as to charge Thomas with "intolerance and anti-Semitism. . . . The current practices in some quarters of answering arguments by hurling abuse at individuals is a depressing manifestation of lack of self-control . . . Though you and I are far from agreement today, I have written this note to tell you I am confident that no one whose good opinion is worth having could, except in complete ignorance, think of your public activities as other than those of a devoted and public-spirited citizen."

As America edged closer to entrance into World War II, Hitler attacked his erstwhile partner, Stalin. On June 22, 1941, the Nazi-Soviet Pact which, as Stalin put it, "cemented in blood" the friendship of Germany and the U.S.S.R., came unglued. The invasion of Russia switched the locomotive of history to another track and communists in America changed their line from "The Yanks Are Not Coming" to "The Yanks Are Not Coming—Too Late!"

Writing to philosopher Morris Raphael Cohen, who had asked Thomas for his views on isolationism and the war situation, Thomas conceded that the "complete victory that Churchill, Roosevelt and Stalin desire" might be won, but "at a frightful cost . . . (which) could mean the perpetuation and intensification of conditions that once produced Hitlerism." Prophetically Thomas added: "Unless Russia should remain actively in the picture, I do not think there could be, under any circumstances, complete victory, and if Russia does remain in the picture, it will be Stalin rather than either Roosevelt or Churchill who in five years will dominate most of Europe and a large part of Asia. Alas, with sorrow I have been driven to the conclusion that there is not enough difference between Stalin's and Hitler's totalitarianism to warrant the cost of war."

About a month before Pearl Harbor, Norman's son Evan, who was in his senior year at Princeton, and thus far strongly opposed to American participation in war, decided that he wanted to help personally in defeating the Nazis. Yet he was reluctant to take up arms. A friend who had served with the British Ambulance Corps announced his intention of sailing for Egypt with the American Field Service, and Evan chose to go too. The news was a shock to Norman and Violet, but they respected Evan's reasons and gave their blessing and such financial help as was needed. At this time, Thomas also wrote the following letter to Evan:

"My very dear son:
"You know how hard it is for our family to say what's most on our hearts. But on this day of parting, and all the days that come, I want you to know how we love you, how much we've hoped for and from you, and how proud of you we are. In a cruel and ugly world you never made you've chosen what is for you, I'm sure, the best possible course. I'm glad that we can help you in it. In the months that lie ahead you'll find opportunities of great service to others and real education for yourself. I am very confident of the spirit and the intelligence with which you'll meet what life and fate will bring.

"Of course I dread the dangers that await you and also the long days of boredom that will bring their own temptations. It isn't, I think, Puritanic in any barren, life-denying sense to tell you that all your life—and, after all, the chances are that your

days may be long in a world you'll help to make a better place—
if you'll steer clear of the temporary consolations and forgetful-
ness of too much liquor and the far more powerful urges to sex
satisfactions of a sort always easily obtainable, you will rejoice.
This sort of continence will deepen the priceless joys of marriage
with the girl of your choice.

"I suspect that you will find much that makes for cynicism
about us men and our ways, but I've found it a help to consider
that if God must be disappointed in us so must be the devil in
the presence of such courage and loyalty and comradeship as
plain people show.

"More than I can tell, we shall be missing you and loving you
and wishing for you the external good fortune and, still more,
the inner courage and hope which may sustain you. Despite our
follies and madness men are made for better things than constant
exploitation and ever recurring wars—it will be a great happiness
always to carry your watch till you return to claim it. Love,

Dad"

On December 7, 1941, Norman and Violet drove to Princeton
to pick up some of Evan's belongings and paid a visit to one of
Evan's professors. The professor's young son, who had been lis-.
tening to the radio, rushed in with the news about Pearl Harbor.
For Thomas it was the "irreparable defeat" of his dearest hope:
that the generation of his children should not know World War.
What tortured him most was the conviction that he had to accept
war, "the monster he had so utterly loathed," because there was
no "conceivable political alternative." Thomas chose critical but
active support of the war, describing his own position as accepting "a circle of hell below which yawned even more horrible
depths."

FIFTEEN

World War II

✍§ AT THE 1942 MILWAUKEE CONVENTION of the Socialist Party, almost half the delegates favored Thomas' call for "critical support" of the war, while about the same number backed Travers Clement's line of "political non-support." I was among a handful of delegates who abstained, arguing that there was no meaningful difference between the two positions, since both Thomas and Clement backed the same program of *action* in regard to the war. A compromise resolution was adopted which tacitly permitted both positions. (Following the convention, the national executive committee elected me national secretary, a post I held for eight years. Ever since that election, I have worked closely with Norman Thomas.)

On a hundred or more platforms, Thomas had said that in the event of war, he would do whatever he could to frustrate his own dark prophecies of a war-induced drift to domestic totalitarianism. The nature of the Japanese attack on Pearl Harbor helped in that endeavor. While it was a military disaster, it was a political godsend to Roosevelt, because it virtually united the entire American people. If the attack had not occurred, and an attempt to declare war had necessitated a vote by Congress, the country would have remained bitterly split. Entrance into war under such conditions might well have required totalitarian efforts and widespread repression of civil liberties by the government—even more than in World War I—to silence the opposition.

As it was, a skirmish in defense of civil liberties occurred the very week after Pearl Harbor. Prior to American entrance into the war, a CALL Radio Bureau had organized a Norman Thomas

203

radio series which received considerable support from pacifists and others anxious to keep America out of the war. On the basis of a Thomas talk on "The War and Democracy," half of the most important radio stations carrying the Thomas radio series cancelled the address. The Don Lee network on the West Coast knocked out the broadcast because of the sentence: "Conceivably American arms may ultimately win the war and American democracy lose the peace." Stations WOL in Washington, D.C., and WISN in Milwaukee also cancelled the contracts. Ironically, the cancellations occurred on Sunday, December 14, the day that radio programs were stressing the Bill of Rights in anticipation of the 150th anniversary of its ratification and only a few hours before President Roosevelt declared that "we will not, under any threat, or in the face of any danger, surrender the guarantees of liberty our forefathers framed for us." Few groups joined with the Socialists in protesting the censorship of the address.

A new Thomas radio series was started by transcription in March of 1942 and was broadcast over more than 30 stations, including several in Alaska and Puerto Rico. The recordings of the first two talks were impounded for a long time in the New York Customs House, and then the chief clerk in charge of "restricted merchandise" banned their transmission to Alaska and Puerto Rico. Reasons given were references made by Norman Thomas to the anti-Negro race riots around Detroit's Sojourner Truth housing project and to the treatment of Japanese aliens and American Japanese on the West Coast. When Thomas protested to Treasury Secretary Morgenthau, Assistant Secretary Herbert E. Gaston promptly cleared the recordings. Gaston, it will be recalled, was city editor of the *New York Leader* during Thomas' editorship of that brief venture.

Democracy was even more severely wounded in the house of its friends when President Roosevelt signed an order giving generals the power to evacuate wholesale from the West Coast not only Japanese aliens but American citizens of Japanese origin, to remove 110,000 of them from their homes and jobs and, without trial or hearing, to put them into concentration camps, euphemistically called "relocation centers." Thomas bitterly attacked this act, which, while far more humane than the decrees which led to Hitler's concentration camps and gas chambers in Europe, was based on the same racist and totalitarian concepts of the rights of the state versus the individual. Because these people were evacuated almost overnight, many lost their homes, farms and businesses. The racist basis of this action was clear. The United States was also at war with Nazi Germany and Fascist Italy, but no one seriously suggested that German or Italian aliens, let alone Americans of German or Italian ancestry, be placed in detention camps—even though it would have been harder to detect them, if they chose to serve as spies or saboteurs, than the Nisei.

When Thomas first spoke out on this issue, only a few groups like the Post War World Council (which replaced the Keep America Out of War Congress after Pearl Harbor), the Socialist Party, the American Friends Service Committee and the Workers Defense League, opposed the relocation program. Thomas considered resigning from the American Civil Liberties Union because of its timidity, but was dissuaded by John Haynes Holmes. The ACLU soon reversed itself and backed full equality for the Japanese and Japanese Americans. The communists, who were now 200 per cent behind the war and pressing for a "second front" to aid Russia, wanted no agitation on this subject. On at least one occasion they tried to break up a meeting on the Japanese Americans, chaired by Norman Thomas, because it "hampered the war effort."

Another area in which Thomas contended that liberty took a beating was the handling of conscientious objectors. The alternative service law was more liberal than in World War I, but it was carried out in a way which reduced the CO's to a kind of forced labor in civilian public service camps, where the men received no pay and had to provide their own maintenance. At the end of World War II, there were almost seven times as many prisoners of conscience in jail as at the end of World War I. Thomas then noted the curious paradox that Allied courts were "punishing Germans for not being conscientious objectors to military orders to kill; in the United States, after peace had come, we were punishing Americans for being conscientious objectors to participation in the wholesale killing of war."

As a commuter, Thomas daily traveled the road from the station past the upper end of Cold Spring Harbor to his home. Rarely did he pass it without seeing in his mind's eye Evan and his companions when they were about eleven or twelve years old and sailed little dinghies on the long summer days. "One could see and hear the boys as a group afar off but scarcely distinguish them in their boats, so alike were they, their crew haircuts, and browned bodies. So vivid was memory that for an instant I would look for them again. And then would come the realization in what dangerous places all over the earth I should have to seek them." More than ever, he determined to do all in his power so that they might return to a world free from war and injustice.

After Pearl Harbor, the other Thomas son, Bill, went to Egypt with the American Field Service. A slight injury he suffered in the desert became seriously infected and he was invalided home. Upon recovery he went into the Red Cross, with which he is still associated. Meanwhile, Evan drove the last ambulance out of Tobruk in the British retreat before Rommel's attack. As soon as he could return to the United States he joined the Navy.

During the long summers of World War II, the Thomases stayed in Cold Spring Harbor on Long Island and gathered in the household as many children and grandchildren as they could. Both children and grandchildren affectionately called Norman "Big Daddy."

Hitler's attack on Russia, followed by the Soviet alliance with America and Britain, led to a love affair between the American people and an idealized image of Russia. Not only did the American Communist Party and its front organizations flourish, but pro-Soviet sentiment received encouragement from many conservative quarters, as Paul Willen later documented in an *Antioch Review* article, "Who 'Collaborated' with Russia?" (Volume XIV, Number 3). Bishop Manning thundered on August 24, 1942: "Anything in the nature of anti-British or anti-Russian propaganda . . . is a dangerous and particularly despicable form of sabotage." In December, 1943, *Collier's* magazine editorialized that Russia was "evolving from a sort of Fascism . . . toward something resembling our own and Great Britain's democracy." Walter Winchell told millions that "the fear of Russia" is a "bogey."

Life magazine devoted its entire March 29, 1943, issue to "Soviet-American cooperation" in which it described the NKVD, Russia's secret police, as "a national police similar to the F.B.I." whose job was to track down traitors. Joseph Davies, former American envoy to the Soviet Union, answered for *Life* the question, "Can we assume that the rulers of Russia are men of goodwill toward other nations and that they desire a peaceful, stable world?" "Yes," Davies replied, "the Soviet Union is not a predatory power like Germany and Japan." He added, with no dissent from *Life*, that he expected complete Soviet cooperation in building a strong postwar China under Chiang Kai-shek's leadership.

Airline executive Eddie Rickenbacker, upon his return from a trip to the USSR, was "particularly impressed" with the "iron discipline in [Soviet] industrial plants, the severe punishment for chronic absenteeism, incentive pay, compulsory overtime work and 'no labor difficulties.'" He was delighted to find that, contrary to his fears, workers were not in control in the Soviet Union. Rickenbacker also welcomed Stalin's dissolution of the Comintern in 1943 as "sincere and permanent."

Even Winston Churchill, after the Yalta Conference early in 1945, told the House of Commons:

"The impression I brought from Crimea . . . is that Marshal Stalin and the other Soviet leaders wish to live in honorable friendship and democracy with the Western democracies. I also feel that no government stands more on its obligations than the Russian Soviet Government."

The lonely and often frustrated democratic left shared none of these illusions. When Henryk Ehrlich and Victor Alter, two leaders of the Polish Jewish Socialist Bund, were executed by Stalin, thousands jammed Mecca Temple and spilled over into the streets to hear David Dubinsky, president of the ILGWU; AFL president William Green; and CIO secretary-treasurer James B. Carey denounce Stalin for this "political murder." Norman Thomas, the *New Leader* and the *Call* played up the protests, the daily press played them down.

Again, when the Katyn Forest massacre by the Russians of thousands of Polish prisoners of war was publicized by the Germans, the mass media treated this as Nazi propaganda. Thomas, *The Call, New Leader* and *Commonweal* were among the few who took the massacre seriously and tried to warn of its meaning for America.

Meanwhile the advocates of "unconditional surrender" spread hate throughout the land. Major George Fielding Eliot demanded that all the Japanese be reduced to the abject poverty of primitive agriculture, without modern laboratories or tools, or "so much as a book which tells how these things are made." George Weller, author of the widely-selling book *Singapore Is Silent* insisted that we fight Japan "until the land . . . is plowed with salt, its men dead, and its women and children divided and lost among other people." Another lurid book, *Germany Must Perish*, demanded that all Germans be sterilized so that no more German children could be born to curse an innocent earth. Writers Clifton Fadiman and Rex Stout were high on the list of those singing hyms of hate. Thomas was fond of quoting philosopher Irwin Edman's lines, copyrighted 1943, *The New Yorker* Magazine:

TO SOME BLOODTHIRSTY WRITERS

At the Stork Club very late,
Let us drink and drum up hate.
Another round, and while we swill,
Arrange to kill, kill, kill, kill, kill!
Let's make sure when Victory's won
We'll be more savage than the Hun.
What does Freedom triumph for
Except for men to kill some more?
Why else are other people slain
But that we bluster might and main?
Let others do the dying, drilling,
It's we who'll plan the post-war killing;
Soldiers have little time for loathing,
That's for us chaps in tailored clothing.
Waiter, some caviar, some wine,
We're planning blood baths on the Rhine.
And we'll be here to toast in gin
Nice peacetime slaughters in Berlin.
It's up to us, far from the front,
To bay like wolf packs on a hunt,

It's up to us who think and write
To fume and writhe and rage and bite.
All Germans must die! But us no buts,
The dirty job's for guys with guts.
Do we mean us? Oh, clearly not!
We'll keep our brave typewriters hot.

"Suppose we white Americans," suggested Thomas, "were to be judged by the standards applied to our enemies? Imagine the indictment an American Indian could frame against our capacity for honor and peace on the basis of our unbroken record of broken treaties through three long centuries! Or suppose our accuser was an American Negro who remembered that the first slaver brought his people to our shores a year before the landing of the Pilgrim Fathers. . . ." Moreover, it was "illogical to believe that the United States can settle the tangled racial problems of the world although it cannot or will not prevent discrimination against Negro soldiers in a war for freedom. There are restaurants in America which will feed German prisoners of war but not Negro troops."

"We are willing to fight Hitler," said Thomas, "partly because of his anti-Semitic cruelty, but we have not been willing to take any bold and aggressive action to rescue Jewish refugees or even temporarily to modify our immigration laws in this historic land of asylum. Anti-Semitism is a barometer which measures pretty accurately the climate of democracy and peace."

When Hitler announced that he planned to exterminate all the Jews, men, women and children, Thomas pleaded with Roosevelt to open America's doors. However, at the Anglo-American Bermuda Refugee conference in 1943, the United States refused to relax its immigration laws and Britain refused to permit Jewish children to enter Palestine. No action was taken at the conference except for the issuance of a generalized statement concerning the fate of the refugees of war and Nazism. The one result, as British historian Malcolm Hay stresses in his book, *Europe and the Jews*, "was to strengthen Hitler's conviction that the world did not really care very much what happened to the Jews, and to fortify his resolution to exterminate them." Both the British Foreign Office and the American State Department "knew that the Germans could be bribed, that they were willing to sell Jewish lives for

Allied money." But, reveals Hay, the Allies would not pay the comparatively trifling sum the Germans were ready to accept —two to ten dollars for a life. Hundreds of thousands of Jewish children could have been saved at the cost of a few million dollars.

"Where should we be," Mr. Randall of the British Foreign Office asked Moshe Shertok of the Jewish Agency, "if the Germans should offer to dump a million Jews on us?" Nor was the American reaction any more compassionate. For a year and a half after August 1942, when the Nazi extermination plan was issued to the world, "the American State Department did practically nothing." As Henry Morgenthau later pointed out, "Officials dodged their grim responsibility, procrastinated when concrete rescue schemes were placed before them, and even suppressed information about atrocities in order to prevent an outraged public opinion from forcing their hands."

Norman Thomas had hoped not to have to run in the 1944 campaign. His choice for the presidential nomination was Maynard Krueger, his 1940 running mate and an eloquent educator. But Krueger refused and Thomas felt that no one else was in a position to secure the kind of publicity needed for a hard-fighting campaign. With Thomas running for the fifth time, the Socialist convention in Reading, Pa., chose as his vice-presidential partner Darlington Hoopes, who had served three terms in the Pennsylvania legislature.

The platform, with Thomas as its main author, opposed both appeasement of Nazism and unconditional surrender. New war would not be averted by a "triple alliance of the major powers . . . even though such an alliance with its already obvious rivalries may be masked behind a plan for a vague association of nations. Yet this is the pattern for the future which most Republican as well as Democratic leaders accept." Similarly, the platform opposed an "America First or isolationist imperialism" as equally "dangerous to democracy and peace."

The platform called instead for a political peace offensive pledging equal rights for all peoples and self-determination plus organized political and economic cooperation to remove the causes of war, settle disputes, conquer poverty and guarantee security.

It urged the united nations to free the European nations overrun by Germany and guarantee speedy self-government to colonial territories overrun by Japan or under white rule. It proposed a United States of Europe or strong regional federations to supplement a world federation. And, three years before the Marshall Plan, Thomas urged the Allies "to extend material aid for immediate relief and reconstruction of devastated countries without using such aid as a weapon for political domination." The platform also pressed the united nations, after the establishment of peace, "to follow the disarmament of the enemy countries by ending their own competitive armaments and military conscription and working out international guarantees of mutual security."

Domestically, the platform stressed the traditional Socialist proposals for socialization of the commanding heights of the economy plus a variety of civil rights and civil liberties planks.

Despite Thomas' consistent record in demanding asylum for Jewish (and other) refugees, a number of Jewish papers attacked him strongly during the campaign. The *Jewish Morning Journal*, for instance, printed a cartoon headed "Messenger of Peace as a Hitch Hiker." It depicted Thomas flying as a Socialist candidate for president with the devil, as appeaser Quisling, on his back. And the *Jewish Daily Forward* claimed that the Socialist platform proposed that "the Allies should offer peace to Hitler and his satellites."

An even dirtier smear came from the Teamsters, leading to a $500,000 libel suit by Thomas against Daniel Tobin, president of the International Brotherhood of Teamsters and chairman of the Democratic Party's national labor committee. Also named in the suit was Lester M. Hunt, editor of the *International Teamster*, for an article he wrote in that magazine entitled "Conscription is Essential to Peace." Among the objectionable passages were the following:

"Norman Thomas has a postwar plan. It is the kind of a plan you would expect from a man who has spent so much of his time fawning on the Germans and Japs while they were killing Thomas' fellow countrymen.

"His 'plan' fits in perfectly with Hitler's plan for future conquest, which is not surprising when you remember that Thomas

211

is the head of the Socialist Party in the United States while Hitler is the leader of the Socialist Party in Germany.

"Just a couple of socialist boys looking at the world through blood-smeared glasses."

It took a couple of years for the case, handled for Thomas by Socialist lawyer Joseph G. Glass, to wend its way through the courts. Before it finally came to trial, but after pretrial court actions upheld Thomas, the case was settled. The Teamsters paid all court costs and printed a retraction by editor Lester M. Hunt in the December, 1946, issue of their magazine, which said in part:

"We acknowledge that the fact that Mr. Thomas is opposed to peace-time military conscription is not a reflection upon his patriotism or loyalty as a citizen of the United States. In the course of the discussion of the subject, various persons and organizations, including labor organizations, have divided; some, as does the International Brotherhood of Teamsters, favor peacetime conscription, and others oppose it.

"We have learned that Mr. Thomas was one of the earliest critics of Fascism and Nazism and at no time in any way condoned any of Hitler's crimes . . . While we have not agreed with Mr. Thomas in his stand before Pearl Harbor, we acknowledge that his conduct in no way amounted to sabotage of the war, but was within his rights as an American citizen."

Hunt was eventually fired by Tobin. A final footnote. When a testimonial luncheon to Thomas took place in 1950, following his 65th birthday, Dan Tobin served as one of the vice-chairmen.

Prior to the 1944 campaign, Congress had passed a Soldier Vote Law which provided that equal radio time, for broadcast to the armed forces overseas, must be provided to each political party having a presidential candidate in at least six states. When I wrote to Major General F. H. Osborn asking for time for Thomas to speak, he replied that, while the law provided for equal time for all candidates, no time had yet been granted to any candidate and he was uncertain as to whether or not any would be given. Then, more or less as an afterthought, he asked whether I considered the speech that President Roosevelt had made at Bremerton, Washington, on August 12 to be "political."

I answered in the affirmative, because of Roosevelt's reference to the war guilt of the Japanese people, and Major General Osborn wrote back August 25th offering us equal time. A few hours later, Acting Secretary of War John J. McCloy reversed the decision on the ground that the President had made a "report" and not a "political" presentation. At a press conference, President Roosevelt, in a characteristically whimsical manner, suggested to reporters that his Bremerton speech was on a par with a report he was planning on the care and treatment of his Christmas tree.

I was not amused. In the President's Bremerton talk, I pointed out, "Roosevelt stated that the common people of Japan are equally guilty with their warlords of imperialist grabbing and promoting warlike policies, and that the people, as well as their rulers, cannot be trusted. We Socialists emphatically disagree with this political position. We urge a political peace offensive [which] would shorten the war by inviting revolt in Germany and Japan, would save American lives and would lead to a lasting peace. But whether or not the War Department prefers Roosevelt's policies to those of the Socialist Party, certainly the soldiers should have a chance to hear both sides of this political discussion."

To the accompaniment of front page headlines, editorial comment and cartoons, the War Department reversed itself and issued a ruling for a series of weekly talks to soldiers by representatives of five recognized political parties—Socialists, Democrats, Republicans, Socialist Laborites and Prohibitionists. Thomas made the broadcasts but they had no effect on the election returns.

Thomas received 80,518 votes, his worst showing in any presidential race. Despite this, he is proudest of the 1944 campaign, feeling that history has vindicated the policies and principles he advanced, albeit to a then apathetic public. The approach to a settlement through regional and worldwide federation, he felt, might have delivered us from the cold war, or at least greatly lessened Russian and communist capacity for aggressive expansion.

On Lincoln's Birthday, 1945, the Big Three released their statement on the Yalta Conference, which prompted Thomas to note that: "A war began ostensibly to guarantee the integrity of Poland and entered presumably by the United States on the basis of the principles of the Atlantic Charter (which condemns 'terri-

213

torial changes that do not accord with the freely-expressed wishes of the peoples concerned') ends with Stalin in possession of the territory that he took forcibly from Poland in alliance with the Nazi aggressor and with a government in charge which is his creation."

When President Roosevelt died in April, Thomas paid tribute to Roosevelt's early New Deal days but remained strongly critical of his foreign policy. Said Thomas:

"There would have been an element of shock and even tragedy about the sudden death of any man who with the support of millions of people enjoyed such power over the world as President Roosevelt possessed. In his case, the public's sense of loss was more personal because of certain outstanding qualities: his charm, his great courage—witness his gallant struggle against his paralysis —and his sympathy for the underdog.

"It is hard to appraise his significance in history in the passions of this hour, but I do not think there will be much dispute that in the crisis of 1933 he magnificently restored confidence, that in his first term he caught America up in the field of social legislation, and that he appreciably revived faith in the ballot among the masses . . .

"He was, I think, genuinely interested in establishing the kind of world order that would make for peace, but again he went far to frustrate his own purpose by his costly slogan 'unconditional surrender' and his failure to lead his people in working out in time an honest program of inclusive world cooperation instead of a disguised and uneasy triple alliance imperialism."

On V-E Day, Thomas was puzzled by his own emotions and the public reaction. There was far less elation than might have been expected. Perhaps, he thought, "Our minds have been numbed by the tragedy of the years . . . But I suspect there was an even deeper difference of feeling between Armistice Day in 1918 and May 7th and 8th, 1945. The former day brought with it an exaltation of thanksgiving and hope which no words can describe. It marked, I was sure, the end of war, on a world-wide scale, at least for my own and my children's generation. What happened to deny that faith is history . . . Disillusionment has not brought understanding but has tended instead to produce a fatalistic acceptance of the passions and prejudices, the thirst for power and profit, which breed war . . . Already it is evident that the only victor in this war of annihilation against Japan—besides chaos and dark night—will be Stalin."

Nor did the ending of the Japanese war bring any lift to his spirits. He was thankful that "the cruelest war in human history" had ended and that he could "look at my son, home on leave, without being tortured by the thought that it is but a respite from hell. . . . Yet as an American, I cannot rejoice over the ending of a victorious war without a sense of shame for the horror which the atomic bomb released upon the earth. I shall be told that it was the bomb which ended the war. As things were, that is probably true, but I shall always believe that the war might have been ended before the first atomic bomb was dropped on Hiroshima, bringing death to at least a hundred thousand men, women and children . . ." In connection with this belief Thomas quoted a Chinese report to the effect that "Japan had been ready to offer up her war leaders as hara-kiri victims and retreat to her 1931 boundaries as conditions of peace even before the first atomic bomb fell and the Soviet Union entered the war."

"Certainly the bomb should not have been dropped on a crowded city without warning . . . it would have been within our power to direct the world's attention to the destructive capacity of an atomic bomb at some designated point, not crowded with human beings. It was wholly inexcusable to drop the second bomb on Nagasaki . . . We shall pay for all this in a horrified hatred of millions of people which goes deeper and farther than we think."

Thomas felt sure that the masses of the world, two-thirds of them colored, would insist that we used the atomic bomb on Japan rather than on Germany because the Japanese were "not only devils; they were *yellow* devils."

At first, not many Americans agreed with Thomas concerning the use of the atomic bomb, but as the years went by his position gained more and more favor. Writing in 1947, Thomas soberly noted that:

"It is the absolute certainty that at this moment the United States of America could impose its will on the world were it prepared to use its present temporary monopoly of a stock pile of atomic bombs to that end. It is the conscience of America in which lies today the world's safety. . . .

"As nations now are going, we shall not long have either a monopoly of atomic bombs or possess so little inclination to war . . . It becomes of the first importance to get it into the heads of peoples and rulers that so universal will be the devastation of the next war that there can be no victor but death. The method of war which has long tended to the destruction of the noble ends for which occasionally it has been involved, is now only the road to suicide, if not for all mankind, then for human civilization."

Since the end of World War II, this has been the passionate theme which Thomas has stressed over and over again. In it lies his one hope for a future for mankind.

SIXTEEN

Violet and Norman

❧ The pessimism thomas felt about the future of the world was mitigated by the radiant happiness of his family life. The love between Norman and Violet was so great that it spilled over to the rest of mankind. Yet it never grew mawkish or openly demonstrative. Violet had great tenderness of heart and toughness of mind which impressed all who knew her.

Despite the long sieges of illness which plagued her for almost thirty years, Violet was an exceedingly happy woman who told friends that she had had the most interesting life in the world. Any Thomas home, Violet insisted, also had to be headquarters for her husband. She wanted to share his life fully. Once when she was being interviewed by reporter Inez Robb before a crackling fire in the huge combined living room and library of the Thomas brownstone, Violet bobbed up a dozen times to answer the telephone.

"I hope you don't mind," she said to Inez Robb, "but I try to take care of all the phone calls so that Mr. Thomas' secretary can get a little work done."

"I've done dictaphone work for him, too," Violet added, "especially when he was working on books. After the children were in bed, I'd get at the dictaphone, and if I was never an expert, at least I could cope with it."

Violet, diminutive and mild in appearance, enjoyed having a heretic and a fighter as her husband. She never made a political speech in her life, but her aristocratic background did not deter her from distributing leaflets among audiences gathered to hear Norman. She served as his secretary on many campaign trips, and, on those occasions when he campaigned alone, would be in constant touch with the Socialist Party's national office to check on latest reports—how large were his meetings, were the audiences enthusiastic, what was Norman's reaction to the meetings?

Thomas' failure to be elected she attributed to a regrettable lack of intelligence among the general citizenry, but she was proud that he had contributed to the education of thousands of persons and to the acceptance of many social reforms. She was reconciled to the fact that he would never retire until the world became "peaceful or perfect."

In 1943, Violet and Norman moved to an apartment at 20 Gramercy Park. The rooms were big but the ceilings fairly low. It was a curious sight to see Norman and his brother, Evan, both over six feet, pacing the living room like caged lions as they discussed foreign or domestic affairs. The two men towered over Violet as she looked up at them and listened.

The telephone in the living room had an extra-long cord so that Norman could walk up and down while carrying on a conversation. In that room, as in all her living rooms, Violet grew African violets—her favorite plant. A big French poodle generally added another note of warmth and domesticity to the scene.

Christmas eve of 1943 Norman and Violet spent alone and Norman wrote this note to express feelings he found hard to say aloud.

"My best Beloved:

"This, as we've been saying, is the first Christmas since Tommy was born that we've been without chick or child. And it won't matter much to me because I still have you. And that's a blessing so great I should like to thank some personal God very personally for a boon that makes a dark world bright. For, you see, it's you, but it's you and the children and the grandchildren for whom you seem to me to be so much responsible, not just biologically, but as the nicest kind of matriarch!

"So together we'll face life tomorrow and I hope for many many more tomorrows and that will be life's richest Christmas gift to me."

An incident which further reveals how close was the relationship between Norman and Violet occurred when Friedrich Adler, at one time secretary of the Socialist International, visited the Thomases. He told of his experiences in World War I, when much to his dismay the Austrian Socialists had supported their government in the war. As the war continued, the government had ruthlessly suppressed socialist papers and refused to convene Parliament. When the Premier, Count Stuergkh, refused to restore constitutional government, young Adler had shot and killed the Premier. He had been sentenced to death, but the penalty was commuted and he was released in the fall of 1918.

Describing the assassination of Count Stuergkh, Adler related that when he was hungry his hand would often shake, so just before the shooting he rushed into a restaurant to get a full meal. He added that he had shot the Count as a purely individual act, telling no one about it in advance.

Asked Violet Thomas, "Didn't you tell your father about it?"

"Oh, no. He was pro-war and the leader of the Austrian Socialist Party. I couldn't tell him."

That seemed reasonable enough to Violet, who then asked, "Well, did you tell your wife?"

"No. It was an individual act. I told nobody."

Whereupon Violet incredulously asked, "Do you mean to say that you assassinated the prime minister without even talking to your wife about it beforehand?"

Violet let Norman take care of world affairs, but she took care of people. On many occasions, when illness or trouble befell one of the Party's workers, she would visit and help that person. She was kind and generous. Her ready wit combined with a deep sympathy for suffering showed itself in countless quiet services to obscure and oppressed people who came for sanctuary to the Thomas home, and never went away empty-handed.

These were qualities which Thomas later felt he himself lacked to some degree. While he had fought all his life for the cause of justice and brotherhood, he criticized himself as being often impatient, gruff, overbearing and sometimes rude in the small personal encounters of day to day—with colleagues, neighbors and tradesmen. Noting the paradox between fighting for justice and love in the abstract, while denying it in the immediate and individual particular case, Thomas determined to try for a better balance between social and individual ethics.

When World War II ended, the Thomases moved to 71 Irving Place. With the organization of the United Nations and its location in New York, their home became a center for international hospitality. Receptions were held for the many Socialists in the delegations of European, Asian and Latin American countries. Ordinarily, Violet never served alcoholic beverages, but for the sake of international amity she offered sherry as well as coffee and tea at the receptions.

At one reception, Victor Kravchenko, a Russian engineer who broke with communism and defected to the West, spoke at the Thomas home to a gathering of experts on communism. Many of the latter, themselves ex-communists, castigated Kravchenko for not having broken earlier with communism. This bothered Mrs. Thomas, who whispered to me that apparently these ex-communists could only believe that supporting communism was understandable until the date they rejected it, but impossible for any sane person to support thereafter.

Violet loved to have young people around, and though she knew that they sometimes talked sheer nonsense, she knew too that in their idealism and courage rested a real hope for a better tomorrow. McAlister Coleman told of seeing her at a Socialist meeting at her home where the argument was hot and the tensions high. Violet was knitting in a corner, following every turn of the argument, smiling a little to herself at the repetition of phrases which the young speakers evidently thought were startlingly novel, but which Mac and Violet had early learned by heart.

"Well, Violet," Mac whispered after they had heard an emotional left-wing outburst, "it sounds familiar, doesn't it?"

"Yes, but it sounds good too," she replied. "I like the spirit of these youngsters."

During 1947, Violet had several recurrences of her heart ailment and Norman was reluctant to travel away from New York, but she insisted that he carry on as usual. He made a lecture tour of the South and West, but his phone calls and letters were preoccupied with the state of her health and he rushed home as quickly as possible. In August, when he was at a meeting of the socialist national executive committee in Reading, Pa., word came to Norman that his beloved Violet had died.

The funeral was private with Norman's old friend, Sidney Lovett, officiating as Norman had done many years earlier at the funeral of Sidney's first wife. Both Norman and Violet shared a strong dislike of public funerals, desiring instead a place in the memory of friends as "living beings sharing in the wonder and tragedy of life, in its comradeship of success and failure."

Even to his children, Thomas found it hard to express fully his feelings about their mother. In a letter a few weeks after her death he wrote:

"My very dear Children:

"I'd like to try to tell you in writing what I've said inadequately in speech. That is how much your love, loyalty, consideration for me and bravery in your own grief have meant to me. How proud and grateful Mom would have been! My thanks are to all of you! Anne—so fine in meeting the first shock, Mary, Herb, Jack and John. It's grand to have such a family and such in-laws.

"Now I want to try to explain to myself and you why I am peculiarly lost without Mom. Parting is the common lot of men and I've had 37 wonderful years. I'm not fool or ingrate enough to say 'no sorrow is like unto my sorrow.' But circumstances as well as her own character made me unusually dependent on Mom —or should I say made us mutually dependent?—for strength and joy. Her love and loyalty, her interests in life, her resourcefulness made for me a peculiar haven of happiness and security in a storm tossed world. Just living with her and doing things together was fun . . .

"I never thought of Socialism as either an equivalent (for me) to religion or compensation for it, but belief in it and work for it brought its own satisfactions and hopes. I believe as much as ever that democratic socialism is the world's best hope. But I have learned in the bitter and tragic years how empty is any hope of sure progress through mere acceptance of any social creed . . .

"In all these experiences I have kept love of life and much faith in human fellowship. And that's largely due to Mom. Her wisdom, conscious or instinctive, and her comradeship in the routine of living kept me aware of the fun of life and the variety of its interests. She'd let me talk about problems and worries and often helped me by her shrewd common sense; she was loyal to the same ends but she never, thank God! turned home into another church meeting or socialist debating society . . .

"I am rich in memories and your constant affection. I have friends and causes and some strength still to serve them. But if I seem to live as in a dream it will be no lack of affection or interest

221

in the strange and wonderful stream of life in which we are caught but because something rare and for me entirely irreplaceable is gone.

"And yet I would rather have it so than that she should have known a kind of lingering invalidism that she often feared. To be spared that, to meet death in the midst of life's happiness with your main job well done, is a thing greatly to be desired. And that she had."

SEVENTEEN

The Last Campaign

◆§ DESPITE THE disastrously low socialist vote in 1944, when 1946 rolled around Thomas was hopeful that a change was in the wind, and that prospects of a new political alignment were improved. The defeat of Winston Churchill by the British Labor Party and the rapid growth of the socialistic Cooperative Commonwealth Federation across our northern border in Canada seemed optimistic portents not only to Thomas but also to a number of union and liberal leaders.

A Chicago conference was called, attended by 125 delegates, and a National Educational Committee for a New Party was set up with A. Philip Randolph as temporary chairman. The committee carried on educational activities for a time, hoping to build a new party when "the time was ripe." But the time never became ripe, because the "new party" slogan was stolen by the communists.

The communists had been wooing Secretary of Commerce Henry Wallace, who was becoming more and more critical of President Truman's foreign policy. In September, 1946, Wallace, in a speech before a communist-packed audience at Madison Square Garden and in a letter to President Truman, broke wide open many of the simmering differences within the Democratic Party. Wallace rightly criticized talk of preventive war and reactionary features of American policy such as the Bikini atom bomb tests and continued production of atom bombs, plus efforts to secure air bases over half the world. But instead of the "get-tough" policy which Secretary of State Byrnes proposed, Wallace offered only a theory of isolationist imperialism which Thomas described as "peace by division of the world into an American and Russian sphere of influence."

Wallace, Thomas pointed out, hit at British "imperialism" while ignoring the fact that the Labor government was giving independence to India and Egypt. At the same time, Wallace evidenced tender concern for Russian "security," and neglected to comment on Russia's aggressively imperialist grab of hundreds of thousands of square miles of territory. These views made the communists hope that Wallace would be the standard bearer of a new party which they could bring into existence.

The 1946 elections abetted the communist scheme; the Democratic Party suffered a real shellacking. Partly, this was due to a swing to the right, but it was also due to anger on the part of many liberals and unionists against Truman's proposals for a labor draft and peacetime military conscription; plus his failure to enact fair employment practices and anti-lynching legislation; and the ending of price controls. Instead of voting Republican by way of protest, this group stayed away from the voting booths entirely. Socialists had a low vote in state elections but, perennially hopeful, gazed optimistically at a *Fortune* magazine poll which reported that 23 per cent of American unionists favored formation of a new party, a longtime Socialist hope.

However, the same figures and the same disenchantment were used by the communists to build up steam for a Wallace presidential try. The Progressive Citizens of America, under communist influence, announced on December 17, 1947, that it had decided to back Wallace even though he supported a so-called "dynamic, democratic capitalism," and urged immediate formation of third-party machinery to put him on the ballot. And although the Amalgamated Clothing Workers, still in the Democratic Party camp nationally, threatened to withdraw from the New York American Labor Party if it backed Wallace, the latter was sufficiently under the communist thumb to openly declare his candidacy on December 29.

Most of the groups that had supported Wallace in 1944 for the Democratic vice-presidential nomination—old line New Dealers, the CIO Political Action Committee and Negro leaders—shied away from him. They remained committed to the Democrats and the two-party system. Only the communists and a handful of old New Dealers firmly embraced him. The National Educational Committee for a New Party called Wallace's decision to run "a distinct disservice to the cause of a peaceful world and a democratic America" because it would have "a deterrent effect on the formation of a genuinely democratic farmer-labor-progressive party which the N.E.C.N.P. is anxious to see emerge on the American scene after the next presidential election."

Thomas attacked the Wallace move because his support of "dynamic, democratic capitalism" was inadequate to America's domestic needs and because his policies might help promote war with Russia. Wallace, said Thomas, backed all the errors of Yalta and Potsdam, peace by the appeasement of Stalin, and indiscriminate vengeance against all Germans. As a *Call* editorial put it:

"The communists support Wallace, not because they want peace, but because they want the war, which they consider inevitable, to come on the best possible terms for Russia. Political chaos in America, like economic chaos in France, is grist to the communist mill. We are not Russia-Firsters. We are not America-Firsters. We are Humanity-Firsters. We want a peace that can last."

At the New York state convention of Americans for Democratic Action, Benjamin McLaurin, international representative of the Brotherhood of Sleeping Car Porters and an ADA vice-chairman, urged ADA to call upon Thomas to run for president. Instead, ADA, anxious to have a "winner" in the presidential sweepstakes, organized a "spontaneous grass-roots" drive to draft Eisenhower. Henry Epstein, former Solicitor General, questioned Truman's leadership and was followed by A. A. Berle, Liberal Party leader, who urged an Eisenhower draft. The convention delegates overwhelmingly adopted a resolution, stating: "The present head of the Democratic Party can no longer lay claim to the support of the voters of this state. He has forfeited this claim by his failure to supplement liberal messages with liberal action."

These Eisenhower fans admitted that while ADA was on record against universal military training and the draft, Ike had just testified in favor of both. Although ADA opposed Jim Crow in the armed services, Eisenhower had recently told a Senate Armed Services Committee, "When you put [black and white] men in the same barracks and make them live together in intimate conditions, we have trouble." He said "complete amalgamation" would work against the best interests of Negroes. Nevertheless, said these ADAers, Eisenhower could win and one had to be practical.

As the presidential campaign approached, Thomas felt that the Socialist Party should have a new candidate. He urged the nomination of A. Philip Randolph, the outstanding Negro union leader, in an effort to speed the drive for a fair employment practices law. Thomas and I met with Randolph, who seriously considered the offer. However, after discussing the matter with fellow unionists and Negro leaders, Randolph came to the reluctant conclusion that he could be more effective in the drive for an FEPC law if he were not himself a political candidate.

Thomas then asked his 1940 running mate, Maynard Krueger, to run, but the latter preferred to try an independent race in Chicago for a congressional seat. By the time the Socialist Party convention opened in Reading, Pa., on May 7, Thomas was reconciled to running once again—for the sixth and final time—as the Socialist presidential nominee. He feared that otherwise pro-Socialist and pro-peace votes might go by default to Wallace and his appeasement party. Thomas' running mate was Tucker P. Smith, head of the economics department at Olivet College, Olivet, Mich., a former organizer for the United Auto Workers, and a former regional director of the United Retail, Wholesale and Department Store Employees, CIO.

Editorials on Thomas' unexpected decision to join the race were profuse and for the most part friendly in tone. "It is easy," said *The New York Times*, "to agree with Mr. Thomas on quite a number of points . . . His socialism is of the democratic variety . . . It is good to have Mr. Thomas in the field."

The *Washington Post* chimed in with: "Mr. Thomas is a radical in a sense of the term not quite understood by the House Committee on Un-American Activities. He would go to the root of what he deems wrong with the American society. . . [His] impact is thoroughly healthy, prodding complacency and fostering progress."

"We suspect he's really more interested in issues than in office," said the *Baltimore Evening Sun*. "Campaign years just give him an opportunity to make sense as he sees it. More often than not, the sense is pretty good."

Even the *Jewish Daily Forward*, which had been highly critical of Thomas in every campaign since 1932, said: "All genuine liberals and radicals, outside of New York, who will want to express their protest against both old parties, will have an opportunity to do this by voting for Norman Thomas, rather than for the confused 'totalitarian liberal' Henry Wallace."

There was a dissenting voice to the chorus of praise. "It cannot be doubted," said the *Daily Worker*, "that Wall Street's build-up of its 'Socialist' Party is related to the perspective to form a spurious, pro-imperialist third party as a counter-movement to the Wallace-led forces, as a 'Third Force' against the people's coalition."

Despite the favorable editorials when Thomas was nominated, and the *Daily Worker* charge that Wall Street was trying to build up Thomas, it was difficult to place stories in the daily press and socialist campaign finances were almost non-existent. Then Thomas recalled that in one campaign, just before William Jennings Bryan was selected as the Democratic nominee, he served as a journalist covering the Republican convention. Thomas decided to go Bryan one better. I phoned Palmer Hoyt, publisher of the *Denver Post*, who had recently invited Thomas to write a guest editorial, and asked, "How would you like to have Norman Thomas write daily columns from the Republican, Democratic and Progressive Party conventions?" Hoyt replied, "It sounds interesting, but give me a couple of days to think it over." Two hours later, he called back. "It's a deal."

Hoyt put together a patchwork syndicate of 14 papers, mostly Midwestern and Western, to carry the columns and paid something like $3,000 (which went, via the *Call*, into our campaign kitty) plus expenses. Among the papers, with a total circulation of 3,000,000, were the *Los Angeles Times*, the *Portland Oregonian*, the *San Francisco Chronicle*, the *St. Louis Post Dispatch*, the

227

Seattle Times, the *Milwaukee Sentinel,* the *Indianapolis Star,* the *Trenton Times* and the *Phoenix Gazette.* Thomas joined the American Newspaper Guild and I went to the conventions with him, serving as his legman.

At the Republican convention Thomas reported that he found outside the convention hotel a rubber elephant which seemed highly symbolic. This elephant, evidently defective, had to be inflated every hour or so with hot air. He also reported that a real baby elephant, leaving Taft headquarters, started to walk backward with a determination that seemed to Thomas "prophetic."

When Herbert Hoover stood on the platform, again denouncing "collectivism" as the enemy of liberty, Thomas wondered in his column if Mr. Hoover's mind, like his, went back to 1928. In that year "rugged individualism" meant that "every man a capitalist" had conquered poverty. It was the government's business to interfere as little as possible with private enterprise. But by 1948, noted Thomas, the Republican convention which cheered Hoover to the rafters unanimously and without discussion adopted a platform calling for government action to end inflation; expand the merchant marine and air transportation; aid small business; control collective bargaining; enforce soil conservation and support farm prices; develop water resources for navigation, flood control and power; and carry out an extensive program of social security. A far cry, noted Thomas, from Hoover's "free enterprise."

The chairman of the Alabama Republican delegation gave Thomas an interesting insight into the democratic workings of the convention. When the vice-presidential nominations were to be made, his delegation waited anxiously for instructions. As the first state in the roll call, Alabama could make the first nomination or yield to another state to make the nomination. Said the Alabama chairman to Thomas: "Boy, was I getting worried this morning! Here it was time for the convention session to begin and nobody told us what to do. But just in the nick of time, Sprague (a Dewey lieutenant) told us to yield to Oregon which would nominate Warren."

Thomas was appalled at the insipid platitudes that poured from speaker after speaker at the convention. When Dewey was renominated despite the least spontaneous demonstration, Thomas quipped that this only proved that you don't have to win friends to influence people.

The presence of the Socialist candidate was sufficiently noteworthy to elicit comment from other columnists. Inez Robb, representing International News Service, wrote about Thomas' meeting with Senator Taft:

"What happened Monday to the Union League Club, sacred headquarters of Philadelphia's most rich and conservative pillars, shouldn't happen to a dog. A reception for Republicans at the Union League Club is just another reception on the society page. But a reception at the Union League Club featuring a Socialist candidate for President is 24-carat-man-bites-dog news . . .

"As Taft and Thomas chatted animatedly and photographers and radio interviewers swarmed about them, the scene was too much for a few old-time Republicans. There was muttering and dignified frowns . . .

"In brief, Thomas stole the spotlight from the Messrs. Taft, Dewey, Stassen, Saltonstall, Joe Martin and Warren." To which Joseph Driscoll of the *St. Louis Post-Dispatch* added: "Norman Thomas was the most photographed reporter at the convention and got more publicity than many of the fat-cats on the platform."

It was immediately clear that the Democrats would put on a far more interesting show than the Republicans. The air was thick with gloom since the delegates appeared convinced that their party had no chance in November. "This convention," Thomas reported, "is like a carnival at a morgue, lined with unburied hopes." Washington columnist Elise Morrows wrote, when the convention opened: "The only spirit the Democrats have exhibited so far has been for Dwight D. Eisenhower and William O. Douglas, both of whom are not candidates. Conventions are traditionally mad, but not this mad. It has all the air of preposterous fantasy in which no one would be surprised if the party suddenly decided to run Norman Thomas for President and Frank Hague for Vice-President."

Americans for Democratic Action first plumped for Eisenhower, then Douglas, then anybody and finally went for Truman. For vice-president, their chairman Leon Henderson came out for

Leon Henderson, William Douglas, and then Helen Gahagan Douglas ("any Douglas in a storm"). Then their former national chairman, Wilson Wyatt, made the nominating speech for Alben Barkley.

At the "Draft Douglas" headquarters, a group of Douglas supporters rushed over to assure Thomas that, if Douglas were not nominated, they would vote for him. Said a *New York Post* reporter: "The only one who's gaining votes at this convention is Norman Thomas."

Meanwhile, outside the convention, Thomas relinquished his "objective reporter" role long enough to join A. Philip Randolph on the picket line to protest the bi-partisan failure to end segregation and discrimination in the armed forces. Inside the convention hall, a strong fight was going on between the Southern bourbons and the ADA liberals on the issue of the civil rights platform plank. Truman had first advocated a vague civil rights plank as a means of placating everyone, but the Southern rebels remained adamant.

Just before Congressman Andy Biemiller of Wisconsin presented the liberal report to the convention, I asked him why only three members of the 103-man platform committee had signed it. Andy replied: "If we tried, we would have gotten a majority of the committee to sign it and then it wouldn't be a minority report." I asked: "How come it wasn't a majority report then?" to which Biemiller replied: "Oh, the bosses were against it yesterday, but they're for it today." Apparently the big-city machines had given up hope of winning the national election, but wanted to lure Negro voters back into the fold and thus sweep in their local candidates. So the civil rights victory was won by ADA, and as a result some Southerners stalked out to raise the "third party" Dixiecrat banner.

Then a strange thing happened. As Thomas reported in his column, after a victory for morality had been won, the convention took on new spirit. And when Truman arrived after his nomination, he made a fighting speech which brought the delegates roaring to their feet and injected life into the erstwhile corpse. Thomas was impressed, but still felt that Truman was bound to lose.

Continuing the pattern established at the Republican convention, Norman Thomas appeared on at least a dozen radio and television programs and was interviewed by innumerable reporters. Newsmen, reputedly blasé, crowded around asking him to autograph their press cards.

The 1948 conventions were the first to be covered on a large scale by television. Since the oratory on the convention floor was usually deadly dull, the networks were eager for "personalities" to be interviewed, and I was kept busy arranging for Thomas to be on one program after another. On one occasion, Thomas was being interviewed over WPIX-TV by Jimmy Jemail of the *New York Daily News*. In the wings was Jim Farley, waiting to be called next. As he watched Thomas, Farley whispered to a friend, "If I hear that man once more, I'm afraid I'll end up voting for him." A member of the WPIX staff tried to persuade Farley to repeat this on the air, but Farley, of course, refused. He did appear on another TV program with Thomas, praised Thomas as "one of our greatest Americans," but said he would still vote for Truman.

The communist-infiltrated Progressive Party convention, like the others, was held in Philadelphia's Convention Hall. But Thomas noted with amusement certain aspects which made it quite unlike the other conventions. For one thing, the delegates were abnormally sensitive to the color red. The Pennsylvania Railroad ordinarily designated its special trains by color. Taking no chances on having their delegates ride a "Red Special," the Wallaceites gave the trains which brought the faithful from New York such names as "Common Man Special" and "World Peace Special." Delegate badges were blue, green and white. Only the press had red badges. Further, when Vito Marcantonio found that his Rules Committee was scheduled to meet in the Pink Room of the Bellevue-Stratford, he hastily had the meeting transferred to the Green Room.

Perhaps the most peculiar episode at the convention was the Henry Wallace press conference which took place on the opening day. Wallace talked for a half hour before allowing questions. He said he would not answer questions about his relations with communists, that he had already explained them. Actually, all he had said was that he was not a communist and that this was not a communist convention. Nevertheless the communists were obviously at the convention in force and in leading spots.

A reporter asked Wallace if he wanted to debate Truman and Dewey. "YES!" Would he also be willing to debate Norman Thomas? "NO!" Why? "Well, because I believe in conserving my strength."

"He shows a certain prudence," Thomas remarked to Elmer Davis, who was sitting next to him.

A few minutes later Wallace was asked, "In view of your refusal to debate Thomas to conserve your energy, would you consider Truman and Dewey justified in refusing to debate you in order to conserve their energies?"

Wallace hesitated and then said, "Uh, yes, from their viewpoint, they would be justified."

Then arose the question of the notorious Guru letters. When Wallace was Secretary of Agriculture, a nationwide concern was the severe drought in the dust bowl. Wallace heard that a former Russian, Nicholas Roerich, a mystic and an artist, had found in central Asia a wheat that would grow with a minimum of water. Wallace persuaded Congress to provide an appropriation to locate that wheat. Meanwhile, Wallace, somewhat of a mystic himself, had been corresponding with Roerich, in letters calling the latter "Dear Guru" or "Master." The existence of these letters had been known for a long time, reportedly as long before as 1940, when Wallace was nominated for Vice-President, but were not used by the Republicans in that campaign. Westbrook Pegler had been particularly excited about the Guru letters and had written many columns about them.

When Doris Fleeson, a liberal columnist, rose at the 1948 convention to ask Wallace about the Guru letters, he said, "I will not answer questions from any stooge of Westbrook Pegler." Then that roaring lion, Pegler himself, nervously got to his feet and repeated the question. Wallace again refused to answer. Finally, H. L. Mencken said, "Now, Mr. Wallace, you know me. Am I a stooge of Westbrook Pegler?" "Oh, no, Mr. Mencken," said Wallace. "Nobody could say anything like that about you."

"Good," continued Mencken. "Now I really don't give a damn about those Guru letters, but since the matter has been brought up, what about them?" Wallace turned red and repeated that he would say nothing about the letters at that point.

Incidentally, every time a reporter asked Wallace a question which he refused to answer or muffed, one of the communist coterie masquerading as the press would get Wallace off the hook by asking, "What about lynching in the United States?" or some such question.

Thomas' reception at this convention was far different from what he had encountered at the Republican and Democratic conclaves. There, both party leaders and rank and file delegates had been extremely cordial. At the Wallace meet, Thomas soon felt like a geiger counter. Hostile stares and rude remarks were fairly obvious signs that he was in the presence of communists and their fellow travellers.

The highlight of the convention was an open-air rally at Shibe Park, where Henry Wallace and Senator Glen Taylor formally accepted the presidential and vice-presidential nominations. The rally, professionally staged, exhibited many dramatic and hypnotic effects. First came speeches by Vito Marcantonio and Paul Robeson, who sang "Los Cuatros Generales" (popularized by communist singers during the Spanish Civil War) and "Old Man River." Then, after an expert collection pitch by William Gailmor, Senator Taylor promised to fight against the "forces that would bankrupt America by spending billions in a futile effort to bribe whole nations into becoming our mercenaries in a senseless struggle for world domination." Following this, Taylor's wife and sons joined him in a rendition of "When You Were Sweet Sixteen."

Then the lights dimmed. Spotlights followed Henry Wallace as his car circled the ball park to the rostrum. His speech, coming almost at midnight, was an anticlimax, as he called again for making deals with the Soviet Union and for making capitalism "progressive." Many in the audience walked out before the speech ended.

As the campaign continued, the Wallace camp became smaller and smaller, while Thomas saw Truman gaining strength. By accident, Thomas crossed Truman's trail a couple of times—once in Texas and the other in Madison, Wis.—and was able to hear at least part of each meeting. The new Truman, who dropped his old hesitations and any effort to speak formally, was surely gaining support with his "give 'em hell" theme. Thomas, having campaigned so often against Roosevelt, noticed an important difference in the crowds. The feeling about Roosevelt among the masses who supported him had been something approaching hero worship. Truman was more one of their own, a spunky fellow who was in there fighting. As a taxi driver put it to Thomas, "I think I'll vote for little Harry. I'm kind of sorry for the guy and he's fighting hard."

Dewey, on the other hand, apparently sure that he had the election in the bag, spoke only in generalities. He was reluctant to discuss anything that might exacerbate any faction within his party. Dewey, Thomas said frequently, probably woke up each morning and asked himself, "What pair of platitudes shall I put on today?"

Nevertheless, Thomas thought Dewey would win the election. At the very end of the campaign, he imagined that Truman might get a bigger popular vote than Dewey, but still felt that Dewey would win because important electoral votes would be drawn off from the Democrats by the Dixiecrats and Wallace. And this, Thomas hoped once more, would lead union and farm leaders and liberals to join Socialists in the creation of a new mass party similar to Britain's Labor Party.

In spite of the traditional lack of funds, the Socialist campaign got more publicity, and a friendlier reception than in many years past. Cynical H. L. Mencken, for instance, deploring the failure of more Baltimoreans to hear Thomas, hastened to add that they would still have gone away, as they came, "with more or less disabled minds, kidneys and morals." But, insisted Mencken, "while they were giving him ear they would have at least enjoyed a rare and exhilarating pleasure, to wit, that of listening to a political speech by a really intelligent and civilized man . . . It is not often in this great Republic that one hears a political hullabaloo that is also a work of art."

The *Progressive* magazine, founded by Robert M. La Follette, Sr., who in 1924 refused communist support when he ran as Progressive candidate for President, denounced the "perversion of progressivism" by Henry Wallace and his communist-influenced "Progressive" Party. The magazine called on real American progressives to back Thomas. "It doesn't make sense," said editor Morris H. Rubin, "for a political party which sincerely believes in freedom to accept as collaborators those who are committed to the destruction of freedom." Rubin added that "a vote for Norman Thomas will speed the development of that long overdue political realignment."

One of the interesting features of the campaign was the last-minute support of Thomas by many interventionist intellectuals and writers who had been bitterly opposed to Thomas in the period before and during World War II. Max Lerner, for instance, who had voted four times for FDR, wrote, "Harry Truman is putting up a spunky fight against odds, and I should like to vote for him if only out of pathos, but I compare what he is saying with what he has done, and I conclude that either he is a cynical demagogic knave now or else he was a poor gullible fool before . . . A vote for Norman Thomas is a vote immediately to make American socialist energies democratic, and in the long pull to make American democracy socialist."

"By the processes of sheer logical reason and on the basis of your record on foreign policy," wired columnist Dorothy Thompson, "I am compelled to vote for you and am saying so in my column." In the column, Miss Thompson pointed out that "we are in the gravest crisis in our history, which has its center in the German capital. This crisis is the result of a chain of actions whose results could be, and were, foreseen by some but not by President Truman, Governor Dewey or Henry Wallace. The only candidate for President who can stand on a record of foresight and principle is Norman Thomas. He, alone, saw how false policies logically must turn out."

Miss Thompson insisted that "all the Republican leaders and Henry Wallace" had supported Truman, not only at Potsdam, but also when the atom bomb was dropped on Hiroshima and Nagasaki, an act which, according to Miss Thompson, damaged "our moral position" and instilled "world-wide fears by demonstrating that the United States regarded the atom bomb as a legitimate instrument of warfare."

Conceding that "because I am not a Socialist" it was "hard" to "vote for Thomas who foresaw the result of all these policies," Miss Thompson concluded that "the issue in the world is not between socialism and capitalism, but between civilization and barbarism" and that "now, if ever, a yes must be a yes, and a no a no."

While Thomas' main theme during the campaign was "winning the peace," domestic problems occupied much of his attention. Housing expert Charles Abrams, in an open letter to candidates, stressed that the Taft Housing Bill, drawn up by the man Thomas called "the most intelligent of the conservative Republicans" and endorsed by Democratic President Truman, was socialistic. Thomas agreed warmly, saying, "It is socialistic simply because free enterprise cannot provide housing, and it is one of the many evidences of the humbug of the conventional American dogma."

In a major speech before the 200-man national administrative council of the Mechanics Educational Society of America, an independent union of 75,000 members, Thomas gave credit to Truman for "showing an admirable political courage" in backing his "Civil Rights Commission" report. But, Thomas reminded the unionists, the majority of the Democrats in Congress voted for the anti-union Taft-Hartley Act and for tax reduction in behalf of the rich. And, even though Truman finally vetoed the Taft-Hartley Act, said Thomas, he had previously "almost jammed through Congress a worse law to draft labor in time of strike." Against that "brain-child of the President," noted Thomas, "there were only thirteen negative votes in the House of Representatives in which Sidney Hillman boasted that labor, through PAC (Political Action Committee) had elected 85 Democratic Congressmen."

During the campaign Thomas again displayed his keen sense of humor, and especially on the occasion when he was chosen to be the 100th "fall guy" of the Circus Saints and Sinners at the tent-top decorated Waldorf-Astoria. As *The New York Times* reported, "He gave as much as he received in making 'fall guys' of his fellow presidential candidates and his non-Socialist audience."

Initiated before 1,200 persons at the luncheon, Thomas laughed heartily at skits lampooning his many "un-elected" election campaigns. When Harold Hoffman, former New Jersey Governor and president of the club, presented Thomas with a "diamond-studded" soap box with a microphone of Station "WIND" attached, Thomas quipped, "I think I know why you gave me this. I'm the only man in America who can stand on a platform. In fact, I'm the only one with a platform to stand on."

Following humorous gibes at both Truman and Dewey, Thomas said he would "settle for more votes and less applause." He won frequent applause during his remarks, particularly when he said: "While I'd rather be right than President, at any time I'm ready to be both."

"That was the curtain line," remarked the Circus Saints and Sinners bulletin, for "one of our greatest luncheons. We left the Waldorf completely convinced of the superior intellect and principles of Norman Thomas. Why, we'd do anything for that guy! Anything, that is, except give him our votes."

And, alas, that was how the electorate reacted. The well-attended meetings, plus radio, TV and press coverage, had encouraged Thomas to hope for a vote approaching half a million. Instead the vote was 140,260. While that exceeded the 1944 vote of 80,518 by almost 60,000, it was still disappointing. Wallace polled 1,156,-103; a much lower percentage than Thomas' vote in 1932.

On election night, I accompanied Thomas to the studios of the TV networks, where we watched the returns come in. As it became obvious that Truman, despite all expectations, was winning, we realized that the Socialist Party's last hope of creating a new political alignment through a new mass party had gone down the drain. Of far greater importance than the meager Socialist vote was the fact that all the labor and liberal forces which had expressed interest during the campaign in a possible new party immediately jumped back on the Truman bandwagon.

EIGHTEEN

The Electoral Fizzle

⚏§ THE DECISION was emotionally painful, but Thomas felt that it had to be made. In a pamphlet for circulation only to party members, he called upon the party to stop spending its "energy on political campaigns which give us only a handful of votes." He urged instead that Socialists work with liberals and unionists in old-party primaries and elections, while consciously stressing socialist education. "We shall lose the great satisfaction for us Socialists that we have a socialist ticket on the ballot for which we can vote with approval . . . but political parties do not exist to save our Socialist souls . . . We do not advance the cause of socialism when, by default or sheer lack of resources, we become less and less able to put Socialist tickets in the field. In 1948 . . . faced with the tangle of state election laws increasingly intended to monopolize the ballot for the two Old Parties, we succeeded by Herculean efforts in putting our national ticket on the ballot in only 30 states, which did not include California and Ohio.

"That isn't all the story. Almost without exception, the more dynamic younger people who at heart are Socialists are refusing to join or, with important exceptions, to stay in the Socialist Party. They want to be free to act in the political field with the great mass of liberals and of labor."

Concluded the veteran Socialist standard-bearer:

"A party which can't or won't live except on the basis of action as we now carry it out is as good as dead. A party which does not see the magnificent job that can and must be done in constructive thinking and action for Socialism outside the nomination of candidates has lost what it takes to make Socialism victorious. If we cannot convince the kind of folks who are in farm organizations, labor unions, cooperatives, and the Americans for Democratic Action, of the necessity of democratic socialism, we shall never convince the American community as a whole.

"I speak from the heart when I say that it is never easy for a man to decide that the way which he has chosen to advance his cause—and the way that ideally he still would strongly prefer —is closed to him and that the march toward a goal must, at least for the present, be taken along another road. Of course, this conclusion involves some sense of frustration or failure. But he is a sorry general who, rather than modify his plan of battle, would abandon the fight or stubbornly await avoidable defeat."

A majority of the Socialist national executive committee, including Tucker Smith and Maynard Krueger, Thomas' vice-presidential running mates in 1940 and 1948; labor secretary Bill Becker; economist Aaron Levenstein; Martin Diamond of Chicago and myself, backed Thomas. But when the issue came before the party's national convention in Detroit in June, 1950, it was obvious that—come hell or high water—the party membership disagreed with us. The convention voted 64 to 42 for a resolution favoring continuation of straight Socialist electoral action on as broad a scale as possible. I resigned as national secretary.

Thomas predicted that "even if we should make an heroic effort and place a national ticket in the field in 1952, without a near miracle the campaign would go almost unnoticed." No miracle occurred. Darlington Hoopes and Samuel H. Friedman ran and polled 20,203 votes. In 1956 they ran again and the disaster became a rout. Only 2,044 votes were counted for them. In 1957, when the Party indicated that it would abandon the electoral field, the Social Democratic Federation merged with it and, soon after, the Independent Socialist League, a group of ex-Trotskyists led by Max Schactman, dissolved and its members joined the Party. As this is written, in 1963, the Fabian role of educational rather than electoral work adopted by the Party, plus its increased activity in the fight for civil rights and world disarmament under effective international controls, has led to a slightly larger membership. But the Socialist Party remains a very small group.

Why did the Socialist Party never become a decisive electoral force in America. What role did Thomas play in this failure? Let us examine some of the factors, and the reasons as explained by the social scientists.

Early in this century, Werner Sombart, a German economist and social historian, pointed to the open frontiers of America, the rising standard of living and the many opportunities whereby the individual could rise in the social scale. In a book entitled *Why Is There No Socialism in the United States?* Sombart wrote that as a result Americans felt little need to band together to overthrow the system. Awed by the fact that the Yankee worker ate almost three times as much bread and meat, and four times as much sugar, as his German counterpart, Sombart exclaimed: "On the reefs of roast beef and apple pie, socialistic Utopias of every sort are sent to their doom."

In his *Theory of the Labor Movement* (Macmillan, 1928), economist Selig Perlman attributed the lack of class consciousness in the United States to the absence of a "settled" wage-earner class; the "free gift" of the ballot (in contrast to Europe where workers had to struggle for such rights); and the impact of successive waves of immigration. This latter, he suggested, gave rise to the ethnic, religious and cultural heterogeneity of American labor and strengthened the ambitions of the sons of immigrants to escape from the working class.

Later, historian David A. Shannon, in *The Socialist Party of America* (Macmillan, 1955), argued that the Party "never fully decided whether it was a political party, a political pressure group, a revolutionary sect, or a political forum" and that it was disinterested in local issues, the bread and butter feature of American politics. But the primary reason, Shannon insisted, was that American workers failed to realize their class status.

Late in the great depression, when millions were still unemployed, Elmo Roper made a study of public opinion about social class which fortified Shannon's view. Of those whose incomes were so small that Roper considered them "poor," 70.3 per cent thought they were middle class. Less than 8 per cent of the total considered themselves of the "lower" class. Of the factory workers polled, only about one-third thought their interests and those of their employers essentially opposed.

Sociologist Daniel Bell, whose monograph on "The Background and Development of Marxian Socialism in the United States" is an important essay in *Socialism and American Life* (Princeton University Press, 1952), has insisted that the major cause of the failure of the socialist movement in the United States was its inability to resolve a basic dilemma of ethics and politics. It could only straddle the basic issues of "either accepting capitalist society and seeking to transform it from within, as the labor movement did, or of becoming the sworn enemy of that society, like the communists . . . It was trapped by the unhappy problem of living *in* but not *of* the world; it could only act, and then inadequately, as the moral, but not political, man in immoral society."

As a party leader, claimed Bell, Thomas had two serious flaws: he distrusted his own generation and surrounded himself with considerably younger men who "stood in an admiring and uncritical relation to him." The other was that, unlike Debs, Thomas was "intent on being party leader" and had a "profound fear of being manipulated." Often a situation would develop, Bell added, when, "if party policy tended in a direction other than his, Thomas would threaten to resign (otherwise how could he speak on an issue with pure conscience?)."

To a certain extent, Bell's charge that Thomas preferred the company of younger men in the Party is correct. But he fails to explain why. In the thirties, most of the older men in the Party were Old Guardists, who elevated inactivity to the dignity of a theory. There were some Old Guard leaders, however, whom Thomas not only respected but warmly liked, such as B. Charney Vladeck and Abraham Shiplacoff. As for the young men, far from being "admiring and uncritical" of Thomas, they were hyper-critical—and usually on flimsy grounds. They considered themselves "more revolutionary" than Thomas and better theoreticians. But Thomas sympathized with their zeal, and felt that time and experience would tone down their left-wing dogmatism. (As one of those youngsters, I can testify that Thomas was right about our development. Most of us agree that he was far more correct then than we were.)

When Bell notes that, unlike Debs, Thomas was "intent on be-

241

ing party leader" and had a "profound fear of being manipulated,"
he fails to realize that it was the example of Debs which caused
that fear. Thomas was often embarrassed by old-timers who
clucked disapprovingly at his activities, reminding him that Debs
never tried to shape policies or platforms at party conventions.
Thomas felt that Debs, especially in his later years, was used and
manipulated by the party. Such a role, Thomas believed, was an
abdication of leadership, not an assertion of it.

As to threats not to run for office unless he could approve of
the platform that was adopted, Thomas argued that he had to insist upon the right to tell the truth as he saw it. Contrary to Bell's
assertion, Thomas did not threaten to resign from the party if
policies of which he disapproved were adopted.

As a man whose instincts are primarily ethical, Bell noted,
"Thomas has been the genuine moral man in the immoral society.
But as a political man he has been caught inextricably in the dilemmas of expediency, the relevant alternatives, and the lesser
evil." Illustrating these dilemmas, Bell in 1947 wrote Thomas as
follows: "You reject capitalism as a social system," said Bell, "but
are called upon constantly to take stands on particular issues which
arise out of it and thus get enmeshed within its web although
formally rejecting its premises. It seems to lead, for example, to
the situation where, as on Spain, the SP supports the Loyalist
government, but fearing capitalist action creates the ambiguous
formula of 'workers' aid' but not capitalist aid. Yet in politics
one must think in terms of the viable and if the Victory of the
Loyalist government is the prime objective then one must not
blanch from the real alternatives at hand. Actually, what I am trying to do is to concretize Reinhold Niebuhr's strictures against
Utopianism and his conception of politics as the issue of the relevant alternatives."

"I never was very well satisfied," replied Thomas, "with some
of our Socialist verbal efforts to talk about an ideal 'workers' aid'
somehow divorced from the realities. I was willing to swallow
much to support a Loyalist victory fully recognizing the defects
of the Loyalist government from several rather contradictory
angles, communist and capitalist. I was not willing to swallow, or
have the party swallow, personal responsibility for individuals by

sending them into a particular situation which we clearly could not control from this distance. If they went on their own account, that was another matter. In no case would we have been able to send enough volunteers to affect the final result. Politically I continued after my return from Spain to work actively for a change in the American official policy.

"The dilemma which you state exists, and I have never been able to find a perfect verbal or logical solution of it. Political action always requires compromise and it is difficult to say in advance with dogmatic certainty at just what point compromise becomes betrayal. I have never said 'fiat justitia ruat coelum.' On the contrary, I remember observing publicly that if the heavens fell, there wouldn't be much left of justice . . .

"I have to confess that I doubt if a responsible ruler of a present day government could act by the ethical standards that an individual might be able to follow. If he tried he might be doing more harm than good. I always had a certain sympathy for Rex Tugwell's remark—when he was in a somewhat despondent mood —that no man could be president of the United States who wasn't a crook, but that Roosevelt was at least a smart and successful crook. Apparently crookedness helped the people. In a moral sense, the whole hope of democracy depends upon its ability rapidly to advance the day when ethical conduct is a 'relevant alternative'! It is even now more often a relevant alternative than we think, and situations in which there is no choice except between degrees of evil usually arise from our earlier neglect of a relevant ethical choice or series of choices.

"Thus, if we are to assume that Niebuhr was right in his judgment about the coming of World War II, we are justified in pointing out that we who feared its ethical and social consequences, no matter how high the alleged aim, were also justified. . . . I have always been aware that a critic might list various factors that qualified my usefulness as a political leader, one of them being my dislike of some of the means that a given situation seems to impose upon a political leader. I have always had a lot of sympathy with Steffens' story about the devil's triumph when truth was organized. Nevertheless, I have admitted the necessity of organization, and I have never been much impressed by Reinhold

Niebuhr's solutions of the dilemma you pointed out. They seem to me to give little concrete guidance, and I think Niebuhr has been as unsuccessful as I in influencing socialist action in the direction we both desire."

Bell's thesis was intriguing, but it fell far short of explaining either the Socialist Party's failure or Thomas' part in it. For one thing, Socialist parties in Europe committed equivalent or worse mistakes than the American Socialists, yet built and maintained strong parties. (American Socialists, for instance, never suffered a blow like the defection of a Labor prime minister, Ramsay MacDonald, to the Tories.) For another, those American Socialists who accepted Bell's line, the Social Democratic Federation which supported intervention in World War II, were even less successful organizationally and politically than the Socialist Party. And Niebuhr's Union for Democratic Action had to lose its Socialist soul before it won even a slight amount of political effectiveness. Even in 1934, when the Socialist Party's factional conflict was at its height, the internal trouble had had little effect on the Socialist vote. In fact, Thomas, running for United States Senator in New York State, got the highest vote the Party ever received for that office, 194,952—but still far from enough for election. The swing to Roosevelt had not yet gotten under way.

It was after 1934, when the drift to Roosevelt began to become a landslide, that Thomas discovered that his audiences would be smaller in campaign meetings than at other times. As one friend said to Thomas after the 1936 campaign: "You haven't seen me at any of your meetings or conferences." "No," said Thomas. "Well," continued the friend, "I'd made up my mind how to vote and didn't want to be disturbed by you."

This is not to say that Thomas made no mistakes as a political leader. He made many, and from the vantage point of hindsight, they can easily be pointed out. He was frequently bored by organizational details, and was generally more ready to discuss specific issues and theory. In public speeches, he would stir his audience and then all too often forget to urge them to join the Socialist Party. When I was able to arrange for Thomas to appear on a national radio or television program, I would always keep my fingers crossed as to whether or not he would remember my admonition to give—and repeat—the party's address, so that we would get the names of interested people. But these are minor shortcomings.

More important, Thomas was too impatient with the Old Guard and not tough enough with the Militants. In his zeal for an all-inclusive party, he mistakenly accepted the Trotskyists who helped wreck the party. His willingness to cooperate with America First in the attempt to keep America out of war, strikes me as having pushed away liberal and labor elements which should have been kept close to the party. I have frequently discussed with Thomas his insistence upon a single standard of values, upon being the moral man. He makes no claim to being "holier than thou." Instead, says Thomas, "if I were the leader of a mass party like Britain's Labor Party, I should have had to compromise a great deal, or abandon leadership. But since we have no mass party, I can at least afford the luxury of being as honest as possible."

Thomas believed strongly that no social group, from the family to the state, could be held together on democratic terms save by a process of give and take which involves compromise. The question was not compromise or no compromise, but rather, is this the best agreement which we can reach? Or is this agreement so bad that to do nothing is better? Does this compromise take us in the right rather than the wrong direction toward attainable goals?

This is by no means the whole picture. The truth of the matter is (and here Bell is right) that Norman Thomas has been the prophet of American Socialism, not its priest. As Bryn J. Hovde, former president of the New School for Social Research, put it: "His function in our public life has been that of planting doubt where other leaders thought they had implanted certainty, that of arousing controversy about alleged divine inspiration in economics, that of holding up always with hands of glowing utterance the shape of a better world than that we have. Norman Thomas, in all his strenuous campaigning, never ran for office. There was never any prospect of his election—to office, that is. He was elected to-be-sure, or to use the language of his profession 'elect,' to serve

245

greater purposes than administration. He is 'elect' in the way of Isaiah and Micah, a prophet among us to chide us when we do wrong and to show us the light."

Prophets, however, are not good organization men. They tend to be lone wolves, to concern themselves with issues of right and wrong even if the organization be split. But this aspect of Norman Thomas was not a major factor in the failure of the Socialist Party. Far more important was the nature of America's political system. And while Thomas long viewed this as an obstacle, it was not until after the 1948 campaign that he recognized it as insuperable.

That insurmountable obstacle arises primarily from the fact that we have a presidential rather than a parliamentary system of government. In parliamentary democracies, such as Great Britain, Norway and Sweden, a socialist or labor party only needed to elect a few representatives in local constituencies and make a good record. Their representation could rapidly snowball. But in the United States, every four years, the election of the President overshadows all congressional races.

From time to time, as Thomas himself has pointed out, liberal, progressive and radical blocs have risen in the House of Representatives and the Senate, but have always foundered because every four years they have had to "subordinate their principles and program to the question: which of the two major party contenders for the presidency would they support?" One could argue eloquently, as Thomas did, that there is no worse way to throw away your vote than to vote for what you don't want and get it; that minority parties and protest votes have had an influence on American politics so great that their supporters were, in a sense, far more important figures on the political scene than an equal number of Democratic and Republican voters. Thomas' arguments made little impression. There was tremendous popular interest in the campaigns of Debs in 1920, for Thomas in 1932 and Wallace in 1948, but the votes were only about a million each, because of the obsession with the two-party presidential system.

Complicating the picture is the fact that we Americans cannot vote directly for President. We vote, state by state, for members of the Electoral College, in which each state has as many members as their Senators and Congressmen combined. The winning party in each state takes all the electors, so that a plurality of one vote in New York State could deliver the state's entire forty-seven electoral votes to the victor. Thus Benjamin Harrison won the presidency in 1888 with 5,440,216 votes, although his Democratic rival, Grover Cleveland, polled 5,538,233. The electoral vote was 233 for Harrison and 168 for Cleveland. Furthermore, under the Constitution, if no candidate should get a majority of the Electoral College, the election is thrown into the House of Representatives, where each state would be entitled to one vote, regardless of population. In the campaign of 1924, Thomas reminds us, the cry "a vote for La Follette is a vote to send the election into the House of Representatives," lost that vigorous campaigner hundreds of thousands of votes, thereby greatly discouraging what had looked like a strong movement toward a mass farmer-labor party in America.

Nor is that all. There are more differences within the two major parties than between them. Each is a coalition of fifty state parties with a common interest in winning office—both in Washington and at home—and little more. The laws for getting on the ballot vary from state to state, and the tendency in many states has been to make it increasingly difficult for any minor party to get on the ballot—unless it starts out with tremendous strength or a lot of money with which to carry on the petition work.

Still another factor in making it hard for any third party to have a lasting effect is our system of nomination under varying state laws by popular vote through primaries—a system unknown in other countries. The Anti-Saloon League, using the primary systems expertly, was able to secure enough Congressional support to pass the Prohibition Amendment. The Non-Partisan League in the Midwest was able to capture various state governments. These and similar situations encouraged many radicals to insist that it was easier to capture an old party than to build a new one. Actually, no third party has ever become a major party in America. When the Republican Party first campaigned in 1856, it started out as a second party, the Whigs having collapsed.

Then, of course, there was Franklin D. Roosevelt. Not only Socialist voters, who were primarily concerned with immediate demands, but also Socialist Party members (both right and left wingers) deserted the Party in droves because in Roosevelt they saw a chance to be "practical"—to get "half-a-loaf" now rather than "pie-in-the-sky" at some unpredictable future date. And the immediate reforms were what primarily concerned them. The support which Thomas and the Party had been winning up to 1934 was born of discontent, rather than philosophic Socialist ideas. What cut ground out from under the Party completely, said Thomas, "was Roosevelt in a word. You don't need anything more."

Incidentally, while Thomas has frequently been critical of Roosevelt, particularly in respect to foreign policy, he pays tribute to the President for overcoming a sense of panic in the nation and then rendering three other services of great value. First, said Thomas, Roosevelt brought America in line with a world-wide trend toward social security legislation. Second, he gave status and bargaining rights to unions. (In 1936, when John L. Lewis and the miners contributed heavily in money and activity to Roosevelt's triumphant reelection, Thomas suggested to some miners in the anthracite region, "I suppose Lewis' support means a lot to Roosevelt." To which the answer was, "Hell, no! Roosevelt's support means a lot to John L.") Finally, said Thomas, Roosevelt restored popular faith in the possibilities of effective democratic action through the ballot box. The masses, before FDR's election, took for granted that "the interests" or "big business" owned both old parties but felt that nothing could be done about it. In his considerable experience with audiences and forums, noted Thomas, "nothing was more marked than the difference in popular attitude toward the possibility of effective action through a democratically elected government between the time of Roosevelt's first and second election. To have produced that change was a real service to democracy and this service Franklin Roosevelt rendered."

But this service which Roosevelt rendered to democracy, while advancing the country toward a welfare state, destroyed the possibility of building a strong electoral Socialist Party. Certainly,

Norman Thomas made political mistakes. But it is my sober conviction that after 1934, no course of action he might have taken could have prevented the electoral decline of the Socialist Party. It might have been far more effective (and I confess I would have fought it at the time) if in 1936 Thomas had frankly repudiated Socialist campaigning on the Socialist ticket and called for work with liberals and labor in old party primaries and political organizations. This, coupled with Socialist education of the sort done by the Fabian Society in Great Britain, might have led to much greater Socialist influence within the American body politic. But those who remained in the Socialist Party in the 1930's, 40's and 50's, rejected this approach solidly—and even if Thomas had come out for such a program, I am sure the Party members would have refused to accept it.

NINETEEN

Peace and Communism

৵ৡ LASTING PEACE AND FREEDOM have been the lodestars of Thomas' existence, and the effort to reconcile the two has been his major struggle. Opposing war, he has disagreed sharply with the "Better dead than Red" warmongers, and is dismayed by those Americans who act and talk as if democracy's superiority over communism is so dubious that it can only be proved by superior powers of destruction. At the same time Thomas is fully aware that resort to war has been so much a part of mankind's common heritage that it has easily prevailed over common sense. While war has brought pain, sorrow and woe even to the victors, it has also brought profit, power and glory immortalized by poets and historians. "The ambivalence with which men have looked at an institution which they have at one and the same time hated and cherished," notes Thomas, "persists even now that by their own achievements men have made it only an instrument of utterly indiscriminate destruction."

Although strongly against war, Thomas has by no means joined the "Better Red than dead" peacemongers. He has consistently shunned appeasement, warning that "Peace cannot be won by thinking that the communist wolf is a sheep dog." To this end, he has sought constantly to expose the wide gap between communism's professed goals of equality, freedom and peace and the reality of communist practice.

It is Thomas' belief that the only real solution lies in competitive coexistence between communism and democracy, whereby the two systems would renounce military destruction but maintain intensive ideological and economic competition. "We, com-

250

munists and non-communists, will have to live together or die together." He feels history proves that such coexistence can be successful, citing the Peace of Westphalia, which in 1648 ended the terrible religious warfare between Catholics and Protestants. That peace changed neither the formal creed of either side, nor one's opinion of the other. But Catholics and Protestants agreed to coexist and turned their competitive energies into other channels. Since the end of World War II Thomas has urged the West to press for a universal war against want, in order to help underdeveloped non-communist lands to build up production, advance education and living standards without the coercions of a totalitarian state. An end to the arms race and its replacement by an East-West war against want has seemed to Thomas a sine qua non for survival.

With these objectives in mind, Thomas visited President Truman in August, 1950, to urge him to address the General Assembly of the United Nations with a specific appeal for world disarmament under effective and continuing international inspection. Remembering the "tragic farce" of the toothless Kellogg-Briand Pact outlawing war, Thomas stressed the need for the creation of an international police force under the United Nations to check or punish breaches of agreement and to maintain international security. Thomas urged Truman to pledge the United States to use the billions of dollars that could be saved by a disarmament agreement for a vastly enlarged program under the United Nations to rid the world of hunger and poverty. He suggested that Truman point out dramatically how much more food, shelter and clothing could be available to each worker in Russia, each peasant in Asia, each citizen in Western Europe, if Stalin would join the United States in agreeing to lift the arms burden off the backs of mankind.

In September, the President, impressed by Thomas' words, wrote Thomas that he was giving careful thought to Thomas' suggestion that he address the UN Assembly on disarmament at an appropriate time. He decided that the world body's fifth birthday, October 24, 1950, was such an occasion and there made a vigorous appeal for "foolproof" universal and enforceable disarmament. He linked it up forthrightly to a cooperative war on hunger by planned industrialization of underdeveloped nations in the boldest American approach up to that time.

While Thomas campaigned steadfastly for disarmament, he coupled that drive with attempts to expose Soviet violations of human freedom. He had nothing but contempt for spiritual neutralists who, in their anxiety for peace, would condone communist tyranny. During the late thirties, the warnings Thomas uttered against the communists and their Popular Front wooing had been rejected by most liberals and even many conservatives. When the Nazi-Soviet Pact was replaced by Soviet membership in the Grand Alliance, again Thomas' admonitions against communist duplicity and imperialism fell on barren ground. Because they failed to heed him, Americans were astonished as well as aghast when Soviet wartime cooperation rapidly was replaced by cold war hostility.

Since 1937, when he had seen slave laborers toiling on the Moscow Volga Canal project, Thomas' investigations had convinced him that the Soviet Union operated the largest slave economy of modern times. He spoke out repeatedly against Soviet forced labor, but had few listeners, a condition that persisted throughout World War II, when Russia became our military ally. With the advent of the postwar era, however, Thomas found a more receptive audience when he spoke about forced labor. More and more, the real facts about the "corrective labor camps" came to light as slave laborers who had managed to escape or who had been freed to return to their homelands after the war told their individual stories. Socialists among them naturally turned to Thomas for help in telling the world about their experiences.

Thomas decided that the time had come for a massive effort to spread the truth and gave his backing to the Workers Defense League in setting up a Commission of Inquiry into Forced Labor. The Commission, chaired by Dr. Harry D. Gideonse, president of Brooklyn College, and with Unitarian minister Albert K. Herling as its staff director, heard testimony from many witnesses and viewed countless affidavits indicating that the Soviet regime ran a vast economic empire exploiting the labor of from eight to twelve million slaves.

Spurred on by the widespread publicity given to the findings of this unofficial tribunal, Thomas and the W.D.L. in 1948 asked the United Nations to set up a worldwide investigation into forced labor. Rejecting any double standard of justice, more than 300 liberal leaders joined him in saying to the UN: "We have fought here against lynchings of Negroes, against racial discrimination, against denial of workers' rights, against totalitarian ideology. Precisely because of our struggle to extend and safeguard freedom here, we feel that it is our inescapable duty to raise our voices against the existence of concentration camps and of slavery anywhere in the world . . . Free labor is not secure while slave labor exists."

The UN was reluctant to anger the Soviet bloc by entering into this area of research, but the American Federation of Labor and the International Confederation of Free Trade Unions raised the issue at the Economic and Social Council of the United Nations. That body, meeting in Santiago, Chile, in the spring of 1951, voted to make a worldwide survey of forced labor, and an Ad Hoc Commission on Forced Labor was set up by the United Nations and its International Labor Organization.

The communists were unable to deny the existence of forced labor, for the UN-ILO Commission had access to more than 200 official decrees of the Soviet, Polish, Chinese and other communist governments attesting to the official use of forced labor. The Commission heard testimony of former slave laborers who described how slavery followed the Red Flag, and how the Communists introduced forced labor wherever they seized control of a country. Again, witnesses revealed that the slave labor camps of the USSR, of Eastern Europe and of Red China were more than a means of eliminating political opposition, but had become a part of a vast economic empire, run by the secret police.

The UN's revelations, coupled with the desire of Stalin's successors to win greater support from the Soviet masses, led to the gradual liquidation of the slave labor camps. Thomas and the Workers Defense League certainly could not claim full credit for this great accomplishment, but just as certainly their intervention was a major factor in bringing it about.

To help counter the communist tactic of the big lie, Thomas urged the Voice of America to undertake a campaign to refute the Soviet charge that America was an imperialist power, a charge which had gained wide currency among non-communist labor and liberal circles abroad. The Voice held an informal conference attended by anti-communist experts. Following this conference, Thomas and I conceived the idea of sending a manifesto from leading American Socialists and left-wing liberals to our friends in Europe and Asia. The manifesto was printed in *Janata*, the Socialist party paper in India, and in *Socialist Commentary* in London, and broadcast throughout the world by VOA. The signers, although affiliated with different political groups in the United States, all declared their support of democratic socialism. They included Norman Thomas; Upton Sinclair, author of *The Jungle* —whose novels formerly sold by the millions in Russia; A. Philip Randolph, president of the Sleeping Car Porters; James T. Farrell, one of America's foremost social novelists; Sidney Hook, author of *From Hegel to Marx;* Lewis Corey, author of *The Unfinished Task;* August Claessens, secretary of the Social Democratic Federation; Reinhold Niebuhr, founder of Americans for Democratic Action; Robin Myers, national secretary of the Socialist Party; labor educator Mark Starr and nearly a dozen others.

Among other things the manifesto declared that America was not imperialistic in supporting the United Nations in Korea. "The Korean war," it said, "could only mean loss of American money and, far more tragically, of American lives. In no sense did the American government act in the interest of American capitalism. . . . The outstanding conflict today is between democracy, with all its human and capitalist imperfections, and totalitarian despotism."

As to Lenin's theory that imperialism was the inevitable last stage of capitalism, the American Socialists answered: "The development of American capitalism has not led to imperialism; it does not fulfill Lenin's theory. The Marshall Plan was not a project of capitalists who saw in it a necessary condition of the survival of their system. On the contrary, many capitalists were lukewarm or hostile to the plan. Those who most vigorously champion capitalism today do not seek imperial expansion through forced investments, but are generally opposed to any great extension of American aid abroad." The American socialists added that America had spent more than 36 billion dollars on relief and rehabilitation in Europe and Asia since World War II, without exacting any economic or political concessions. In contrast, the communist rulers had imperialistically taken over five million square miles inhabited by almost 600,000,000 people.

The manifesto made such a profound impression abroad that it encouraged Thomas to accept an invitation to attend the Indian Congress for Cultural Freedom as a fraternal delegate in March 1951. The theme for the Bombay Congress was related to a statement made by Gandhi: "I want the winds of all cultures to blow freely through my house, but I do not want to be swept off my feet by any."

For Thomas, the dramatic memory of his Bombay visit was a great Socialist meeting held in a bare, treeless park in the textile district. Just before sunset the meeting began, with thousands of people squatting on the ground. Party members on the little platform were singing workers' songs. Thomas was garlanded with flowers. He began his speech (which was excellently translated) as the sun went down. Darkness rapidly covered the park, the stars came out. Thomas, illuminated by the string of lights around the speakers' platform, could no longer see the crowd, but as he spoke of socialism, peace and plenty, he remembers feeling the quiet attention of his audience as a tangible presence.

When he was about to leave India, a reporter from the *Manchester Guardian* who was an old India hand, asked Thomas to give his major impression of that country. The answer, which shocked some of Thomas' Indian friends, was that the thing he noticed most was poverty: conditions seemed to him worse than when he had been in India in 1907. At that time, India had been free of famine. Now, in 1951, famine conditions prevailed in several provinces, and India was suffering from the tragic consequences of partition as well. This might well have been one reason, Thomas noted, why many in India and other have-not nations were inclined to turn to communism despite American foreign aid. They had no understanding of or affection for communist ideology, but reasoned: "Look how poor Russia was after

255

the first World War and how strong she is now. See how poor and weak China was and how powerful she is now. What did it? Communism. We may have to pay a price in lack of democracy, but this may be what we need to get ahead. And, as an added bonus, it would enable us to thumb our noses at the western democracies which were our imperialist rulers."

Before he left India, Thomas had a private talk with Prime Minister Jawaharlal Nehru, in which Nehru expressed clearcut moral condemnation of Stalin's communism and what he called its "expansionist" policies. Nehru added that favorable Asian response to Stalin's communism sprang from the failure of the Western democracies to recognize Asian nationalism and to do more about the peasant hunger for land and food. He acknowledged that the North Koreans were the aggressors in the Korean imbroglio, and added that America was not imperialist, although he cautioned that the tensions of the arms race might lead to imperialist acts. Thomas advised Nehru that American public opinion was solidly against Nehru's proposal to admit the Chinese communists to the United Nations "with Mao's guns still smoking," and that the proposal made more difficult getting Congressional approval of increased American aid to India's famine-stricken millions.

After leaving India, Thomas went to West Berlin and Yugoslavia. There he found the most outspoken regard for, and confidence in, America. "They are the nearest neighbors of Stalin," Thomas noted wryly, "and have fewest illusions about his policies and ours."

Upon his return to the United States, Thomas reported his findings in a letter to President Truman and added: "What we now have to avoid is the danger that justifiable irritation against Nehru in America and against our Congress in India will block the sending of wheat, an action which both humanity and political strategy make necessary."

Thanking Thomas for his report, Truman nevertheless did express irritation about the vagaries of mankind. He resented the fact that Nehru had called particular attention to 50,000 tons of wheat which he had purchased from the Russians, while failing to call public attention to 400,000 tons of wheat which America had delivered free.

In 1952, with the Korean conflict still raging, Thomas agreed to make a tour for the World Congress of Cultural Freedom. He wanted to ascertain for himself how people in Asia and Europe were responding to the danger of communism. Accompanying Thomas on the first leg of the trip—to Japan—was A. Philip Randolph, Negro leader of the Brotherhood of Sleeping Car Porters. In Tokyo, the two men were invited to be guests at the huge May Day rally. They were seated on the platform when a band of dissident unionists stormed the platform in an unsuccessful attempt to force their leader as a speaker on the program. A riot ensued but before long order was restored; Thomas and Randolph joined the core of the huge throng as five parades headed for different parts of the city. Later, in front of the Imperial Palace, a bigger riot was staged by the communists.

Thomas was pleased to find that most Japanese condemned the riots as communist-inspired but was disturbed that the left-Socialists were lending themselves to the old communist strategy of divide and conquer. "I saw on May Day," said Thomas, "the beginning of an old play in new dress, a play that in many European countries has had a tragic end." He viewed the left-Socialist doctrine of "neutralism" as a spiritual neutralism which was manipulated by the communists into hostility not only against America but against the whole democratic process in Japan and Asia. It was a far cry from a praiseworthy hatred of war and arms. "Unless the Socialists and labor leaders adopt different tactics," warned Thomas, "they may end up with Beneš and Masaryk." In conversation with many Japanese, Thomas was heartened by the friendly feeling for Americans, and found himself loaded down with gifts pressed on him by a people alleged to hate Americans. Thomas used these incidents to try to persuade the left-Socialists that they were unlikely to win power unless they broke with the communists.

With General Dwight D. Eisenhower's accession to the American presidency came the truce in Korea in July, 1953, stilling the guns but perpetuating the partition of that unhappy land. Thomas was grateful for the end of the shooting war, but remained fearful lest lack of progress on disarmament bring about nuclear disaster. Nor did Thomas blame such lack of progress entirely on the Russians. Twice the United States rejected proposals which seemed to Thomas to lead in the right direction: first, in May, 1955, the proposal put forth by Britain and France to reduce conventional forces, a plan which the Russians accepted; and then, two years later, the Russian proposal for a first-step monitored moratorium on nuclear tests. When Thomas questioned Admiral Strauss of the Atomic Energy Commission as to why the U.S. had rejected the Russian proposal outright, he was told that the rejection was due to the uncertainty of means to detect violators of the agreement. However the Admiral then approved America's package proposal which included the suspension of tests and other matters far more difficult of inspection. The reason, of course, was that the administration was confident that the Russians would reject the package. Unfortunately, Admiral Strauss' confidence was justified.

Even though Thomas recognized that the Soviet Union made occasional gestures to ease the arms race, he was by no means inclined to accept Russian statements at face value. Khrushchev's 1956 accusations against Stalin of responsibility for "mass arrests and deportations of many thousands of people" plus tortures to extort "confessions" and "execution without trial" shook the theoretical foundations of communism. But if men were logical, suggested Thomas, the end of Stalin worship would have shattered the very foundations of communism, a rigid secular religion of secular salvation through implicit obedience to the party's commands.

In actual fact, none of the leaders, Thomas said, now repent; none ask forgiveness of God or man. They merely make Stalin the scapegoat, thus conceding the awful wickedness of the basic philosophy which made them his docile tools. Thus, when Khrushchev appealed for Socialists and communists all over the world to cooperate despite their past differences, Thomas replied, "I fear Khrushchev bearing gifts," and successfully urged the Socialist International to reject communist "united front" overtures. Thomas recalled the united front period of the 1930's in which

Socialists worked with communists in various countries and concluded, "The end of it was the deal between Stalin and Hitler, a deal making possible the second World War."

During this period of the "thaw" in the Soviet party line, Thomas was asked by Radio Moscow to record his approach to steps to promote friendship and cooperation between the United States and the Soviet Union. Thomas gladly accepted, maintaining that an absolute essential was Soviet-U.S. acceptance of universal disarmament under effective international inspection and control, free from any veto. He called upon the USSR to grant free elections in its Eastern European satellites and in East Germany, looking to the latter's unification with West Germany. Thomas also urged restoration to their former status of Volga Germans, Kalmuks and other peoples admitted by Khrushchev to have been cruelly exiled by Stalin, together with all possible redress to Stalin's other victims. Thomas favored a widespread exchange of private visitors, rather than representatives of governments. The talk was broadcast on August 29, 1956, by Radio Moscow—a circumstance which would have been unthinkable in Stalinist days.

Unfortunately, proof of actual Soviet intentions soon came in action, not words. In Poznan, Poland, a strike of 50,000 workers demonstrating for bread and freedom was suppressed with guns and tanks by a "Polish" Red Army in which all officers above the rank of captain were Russian.

Then came the armed revolt of the Hungarian workers and students in October, 1956. Thomas rejoiced that once again totalitarian communism had been unable to so subdue and corrupt the younger generation in the satellites as to make them perpetual robots or slaves. The Workers Defense League quickly organized an Emergency Labor Conference for Hungary, whereby 290 labor leaders representing five million American unionists pledged moral and material support for the freedom fight.

The new Hungarian premier, Imre Nagy, induced Soviet leaders to withdraw Russian tanks and troops from Budapest on November 1. Three days later, the Soviet tanks returned, shooting freely and brutally smashing the revolt. Thomas and the W.D.L., led by its dynamic young national secretary, Vera Rony, initiated a Freedom Petition for Hungary. The petition, signed by more than 200 world leaders, was presented to UN Secretary Dag Hammarskjold and General Assembly President Prince Wan Waithayakon of Thailand, by a delegation including Thomas, actress Myrna Loy and Bishop James A. Pike. The petition urged the UN to "implement resolutions condemning Soviet imperialist aggression in Hungary" and "to work ceaselessly to effect the withdrawal of Soviet troops from Hungary."

At first the petition received little world notice. Then a communist newspaper in Hungary charged that American "imperialists" were using Myrna Loy's sex appeal to influence the United Nations, and millions throughout the world who had not heard of the petition were apprised of its existence. The United Nations set up a five-nation subcommittee on Hungary to attempt to secure the withdrawal of Soviet troops and an end to persecution of the rebels. Later on, Thomas joined with Eleanor Roosevelt and Msgr. Bela Varga, president of the Hungarian Parliament in 1946–7, in backing an appeal for amnesty for political prisoners in Hungary. The appeal was partially successful. The Red Hungarian regime freed several authors and others who had been jailed for alleged complicity in the 1956 revolt.

Even during his support of the Hungarian rebels, Thomas opposed any military intervention by the United States or the United Nations which could escalate that rebellion into worldwide nuclear war. He kept pressing for action to reduce the arms race and to promote effective disarmament. He campaigned against nuclear testing as contaminating the atmosphere and being potentially responsible for the death or illness of thousands in this and coming generations.

When Professor Harrison Brown of the California Institute of Technology estimated that 10,000 persons would die of leukemia each year as a result of radioactive fallout from nuclear test explosions, Thomas caustically noted that Admiral Strauss, former chairman of the Atomic Energy Commission, might have found it difficult to sign the order for a new series of tests if he could visualize himself by that act killing before their time a whole city of 10,000 people. Instead, said Thomas, Strauss justified his action with the unlikely assumption that each new American test made it more likely that there would be no new war.

Thomas also opposed fallout shelters as an attempt to reduce fear of atomic war and a stimulus to "preventive" war. When Governor Nelson Rockefeller of New York recommended compulsory building of private fallout shelters, Thomas raised some searching questions. Quoting testimony that one "moderate"-sized attack with hydrogen bombs would kill 6,089,000 people in the New York area while destroying a quarter of our national population and half of our homes, Thomas asked Rockefeller:

"Who would get into shelters? How long would those outside the immediate area of total destruction and great fallout have to stay inside crowded shelters sustained by the supplies your committee recommends us to hoard? Would they be insensible to the misery outside the dubious shelters? What would happen to orderly processes of life and government, especially since we should have to expect a second attack to follow the first? . . . Might not the survivors envy the dead?"

The rush to compel the building of shelters, Thomas reminded Rockefeller, would be coupled everywhere with growing talk of preventive war. "May it not then be interpreted by the Russian people," asked Thomas, "that we plan aggressive war and by their dictator as a stimulus to attack before shelters are built?"

Apparently the public shared Thomas' misgivings about the Rockefeller program. It was one of Rockefeller's worst failures, garnering no legislative support even though his party controlled both houses of the New York legislature.

Thomas helped Norman Cousins, editor of the *Saturday Review*, organize the National Committee for a Sane Nuclear Policy, which called a rally in New York's Madison Square Garden in 1960 to urge an end to the testing of nuclear weapons and a war on poverty and international tensions. The rally, which played to a full house of 17,500 with hundreds more gathered outside, applauded Thomas, Eleanor Roosevelt, Walter Reuther, former GOP presidential nominee Alfred M. Landon and Michigan Governor Mennen G. Williams. Few remarked on the incongruity of the 49th St. Garden sign which read:

Save the Summit
Hope of Humanity
World Without War.
—Tomorrow Nite—Boxing.

After the rally, five thousand demonstrators streamed out of the Garden on their way to the United Nations. The apprehensive Police Inspector recognized the tall, gray-haired man in the vanguard—and appealed to Norman Thomas.

"Lead them down the sidewalks," he begged, "we'll clear the way. Just lead them down the sidewalks."

Thomas did, followed by Walter Reuther, Rabbi Israel Goldstein of Congregation B'nai Jeshurun, and singer Harry Belafonte. The marchers snaked down Broadway, over to 42nd Street and down to the sidewalk across the street from the UN Secretariat. They sang a number of songs—"Thomas is Our Leader" and "We Ain't Gonna Study War No Mo'." At one point a youth in white bucks scampered out ahead of the marchers, calling for "Three Cheers and a Locomotive for Mr. Thomas." Teenagers in the crowd responded with a will.

At the UN Plaza, in front of a Biblical inscription on a concrete wall referring to the time when men "shall beat their swords into plowshares," at one o'clock in the morning Thomas talked briefly against additional nuclear testing. Then the marchers observed three minutes of silent prayer for world peace and went home.

During this same period Thomas was infuriated by the pronouncements of those experts who deprecated the effects of nuclear war and, when discussing those effects, considered people not as human beings but as statistics. Herman Kahn, then spokesman for the government's Rand Corporation (later director of the Hudson Institute), was chief target for Thomas' indignation. Kahn matter of factly reminded Americans that "human fertility is high," and coupled this with the argument that under certain circumstances it might "be profitable to initiate nuclear war." To be sure, he was unwilling to commit national suicide. In his book, *On Thermonuclear War* (Princeton University Press, 1960), Kahn claimed that 180 million deaths "is too high a price to pay for punishing the Soviets for their aggression."

What price would be acceptable? Thomas was revolted by Kahn's answer: "I have discussed this question with many Americans, and after about fifteen minutes of discussion their estimates of an acceptable price generally fall between 10 and 60 million, clustering toward the upper number."

"Mr. Kahn's scientific conclusions," said Thomas, "make him something of an optimist. But what an optimist!"

Thomas did not challenge Kahn's conscious motivations but pointed out that in Kahn's thesis, which assumes the impossibility of disarmament, "lie the vested interests of all professionals of our enormous military establishment; of hundreds of scientists, enabled to indulge in research on a scale of which they never dreamed; of other hundreds of corporations, large and small, having a financial stake in preparation both for attack and defense, and of thousands upon thousands of workers who find in this business what they think is their best immediate guarantee against unemployment. . . . So let the cold war go on."

In an attempt to counteract such attitudes, Thomas was instrumental in setting up an organization called Turn Toward Peace. This hopefully experimental league was an attempt to coordinate the work of the many peace groups and other civic organizations, such as unions and religious bodies, generally concerned with approaches toward peace.

Turn Toward Peace began with the recognition that changes in American policies alone were not enough to produce peace; basic Soviet attitudes had to be changed as well. But current American policies were not likely to elicit such Soviet changes. TTP proposed that the United States initiate a series of American actions—not dependent on prior communist agreement—which would be real steps toward a disarmed world under law. These actions, it was hoped, would challenge the communist world to a new response, win support from other nations, and create a new world climate favorable to negotiation. In addition to steps toward disarmament, the new coordinating council proposed American initiatives in six other related areas: 1) growth toward world law, 2) development of a sense of world community, 3) economic planning for disarmament, 4) aid to just demands for revolutionary change, 5) reduction of international tensions, and 6) development of nonviolent defenses of freedom.

Thomas became co-chairman of Turn Toward Peace, with Sanford Gottlieb of SANE and Robert Pickus of the American Friends Service Committee as national coordinators. A national roster of individuals signing a declaration of conscience and responsibility for a Turn Toward Peace soon won signatures of Eleanor Roosevelt, Martin Luther King, Jr., Walter Reuther, Rev. Edwin Dahlberg, Clarence E. Pickett and thousands of other Americans.

In response to a call to action sent out by the youth council of Turn Toward Peace, approximately 5,000 students—the biggest youth peace demonstration in a decade—gathered in Washington on February 16 and 17, 1961, to press the Administration for initiatives toward disarmament and cessation of nuclear testing. Signs such as "SOVIET STUDENTS—WE CRITICIZE OUR GOVERNMENT—YOU MUST CRITICIZE YOURS—BOTH SIDES SHARE THE BLAME!" left no question as to the desire of the students to urge pressure on both power blocs. Students came from all over the nation at their own expense. A great many of them bedded down in sleeping bags in churches or the homes of sympathizers. The students presented their views not only to the White House but to the Soviet Embassy as well. Emil Mazey, secretary-treasurer of the United Auto Workers; nuclear physicist Dr. William Higginbotham; and Norman Thomas spoke from the platform of the Sylvan Theater near the Washington Monument to the thousands of students. Jan Triggs of Howard University and Tom Barton of the Student Peace Union emphasized the interdependence of the peace and civil rights movements, pointing out that those who attack the peace movement as "Communist-inspired" also use the same excuse to deny minority groups their full rights as American citizens. The rally sparked an increased concern for peace on American campuses.

During the Cuban crisis of September, 1962, caused by Soviet buildup of nuclear missiles in Cuba, Thomas feared the outbreak of nuclear war and the end of all hopes for mankind. He approved President Kennedy's offer to Premier Khrushchev of new efforts at disarmament and a detente between NATO and the Warsaw Pact, but warned that many influential Americans might assume that Washington could always afford a "tough" line; that America, being always right, could enforce its will by threats of war backed by the kind of action Washington staged in the Caribbean. Instead, insisted Thomas, "Nothing is surer than that we cannot thus indefinitely avoid war by the practice of brinkmanship. In future exchanges of threats it is certain that one side or the other will someday, out of false calculation of strength or sheer emotional madness, risk thermonuclear war which both sides, American and Russian, make more likely and more deadly by continuing tests."

Thomas continued to fear America's drift to a garrison state, which he described as one whose primary concern for security and power through military might dominates the public economy and politics, and which subordinates to itself such liberties of citizens as once had been regarded as among our inalienable rights. He pointed to the nation's ready acceptance of peacetime conscription, of loyalty oaths for students (since eliminated by Kennedy), of government security programs under which a soldier was given less than an honorable discharge simply because some close relative was alleged to have attended communist meetings when the soldier was a babe in arms.

To the question, "Isn't the garrison state a small price to pay for security against a dreadful submission to communist power?" Thomas answered that balance of terror or alleged invulnerability of retaliatory power will not forever provide a shield of deterrence for ourselves and our allies. War might come by accident. Some anonymous colonel, our enemy's, our own, might get a false report, or misread a radar, or go berserk under strain, and let loose an attack to which his opponent must instantly reply if he is to reply at all. And, as more nations develop nuclear weapons, the chances of accidents are multiplied.

It is a kind of madness, Thomas insisted, to believe that nations armed with chemical, bacteriological and nuclear weapons will be mad enough to risk war, but sane enough not at any time to use any of their most deadly weapons. (Thomas' prescient warnings were later dramatized by Euguene Burdick and Harvey Wheeler, whose novel, *Fail-Safe* (McGraw-Hill, 1962), dealt

265

with a situation where nuclear war could be touched off by accident.)

Viewing a growing military-industrial complex in America which was moving the nation toward the garrison state, and the changes in Russia since Stalin's death, Thomas has predicted that "*if* we avoid war and *if* the present drift continues much as it is in both the USSR and USA, in a generation or so the actual differences between us will be slight." He points to the abolition of the Soviet forced labor camps, a measure of decentralization and an intermittent policy of a lighter hand by the Soviet state in science, the arts and literature as showing some change for the better in the USSR. But unless America reverses its present trend of placing increased emphasis upon military might while whittling down civil liberties, Thomas fears, "The contest between us will become primarily a power rather than a true ideological struggle. Both sides will rationalize it semantically . . . In reality both will be garrison states—the U.S. probably with a larger element of individual right."

Even with such heavy odds, Thomas refuses to give up the struggle for peace and freedom. "At this moment," he wrote in *Socialism Re-examined*, in 1963, "if I looked from some distant planet on our struggles as one looks at a horse race, I should be inclined to bet on disaster, the triumph of ignorance, hate and greed. But I am not on a distant star. I have only my life to bet. Our obliteration or our social damnation is not inexorably decreed by fate, not by our gods, not by our genes. Somehow, through the ages we men have won for brotherhood victories which have kept our race alive and moving forward even when the odds against it were great."

TWENTY

The Test of Freedom

❧ A FAMOUS CARTOON by Art Young shows a policeman hitting a little, bespectacled demonstrator in New York's Union Square. The victim protests, "But I'm an anti-communist." To which the guardian of law and order replies, "I don't care what kind of a communist you are." And down goes the nightstick.

Thomas has long fought similar confusion about communism and democratic socialism. Some of this confusion has arisen because both communists and Socialists have professed to follow the doctrines of Marx and Engels. Further lack of understanding resulted from the activities of vigilantes and ultra-rightists in times of tension—during and after World War I, in the depression of the 30's, and when the Cold War started after World War II. In the name of Americanism super-patriots made and continue to make false and reckless charges, using America's fear of communism to equate democratic socialism, the welfare state and social reforms with communism. Thomas has particularly resented the fact that some corporations have not only launched political attacks in the mass media, but also have presented their smears as tax-free "institutional advertising," thus passing on the cost to the public.

One dramatic attack on Socialism occurred with regard to the American Forum of the Air, one of the oldest and best radio and television forums. In 1952 the Forum was forced to accept from its sponsor, the Bohn Aluminum and Brass Corporation, commercials which stated, "Socialism is dangerous; it leads to communism." In a certain Bohn commercial, the announcer also presented a drawing of a rose and another of a weed, likening the

267

rose to freedom and the weed to socialism.

Thomas demanded free time to reply and in a broadcast over NBC-TV, said: "I am not seriously alarmed by this childish propaganda, except that it serves as a dangerous precedent. Mr. den Uyl, president of the Bohn Aluminum and Brass Corp., is not attacking just the small Socialist Party in the propaganda commercials which we and his stockholders pay for. He is gunning to prevent any extension of the New Deal or the Fair Deal by calling them Socialist. When I hear these commercial expressions of concern for liberty I confess to considerable and justifiable indignation at the spectacle of corporations which never spoke out for freedom against the denials of free speech, free association and free assembly until they thought their own profits were endangered. Over and over I have met my socialist comrades in the forefront of the battle for freedom when the going was hard. I never met there any representatives of any brass corporation and I couldn't identify any considerable number of high-powered advertising writers."

Backing up Thomas, Sen. Hubert Humphrey wrote the Forum's moderator, Theodore Granik: "Many of our friends in Europe are Socialists and violent anti-communists . . . I know a great many of my Scandinavian constituents in Minnesota would consider it an insult to identify the governments of Sweden, Norway and Denmark as just a step away from communism and on the road toward communism. . . . It is important to fight communists and communism. If we do so recklessly, inaccurately and foolishly, however, we only do damage to our national self-interest."

Even President Truman joined the campaign against such misrepresentations. "You can hardly pick up a newspaper or a magazine these days," said the President in 1952, "without seeing an expensive full-page advertisement denouncing the 'Socialism' of our public power program." The powerful utility interests, Truman pointed out, "raised the cry of 'Socialism' apparently on the theory that if you can't persuade people, maybe you can frighten them; if you haven't got the facts, try a few scare words . . . It looks to me as though that advertising campaign itself is pretty close to 'Socialism,' because the taxpayers finance so much of the cost."

It would be pleasant to report that these protests succeeded in stopping the use of fraudulent commercials and newspaper and magazine ads. No such clearcut victory for honesty took place. There was one small gain, however. After Thomas' protest, the National Broadcasting Company (which carried the American Forum of the Air) announced that thereafter the Bohn commercials would contain attacks only on communism and omit any references to socialism.

Such misrepresentation was of course minor compared to a new wave of anti-democratic repression which swept across America and came to be known as McCarthyism. It was ironic that Joseph McCarthy should become Mr. Anti-Communist since as late as the fall of 1946, when Thomas was in Wisconsin, he saw McCarthy, a Wisconsin war veteran, accept communist and pro-communist support in the "open" Republican primary in order to defeat Robert M. La Follette, Jr., for the senatorial nomination. Certainly there was no hint of McCarthy's later approach to communism in his reply to inquiries about the communist support that won his nomination: "Well, communists have the right to vote, don't they?" And directly after his election, McCarthy repaid his debt to the communists by praising Stalin's stand on disarmament and expressing complete faith in Stalin's sincerity.

McCarthy was not alone in such views. When the Soviet Union was our ally in World War II, both Republicans and Democrats frequently praised Stalin and Russia. It was Stalin's aggressive imperialism and the rise of the cold war which ended that honeymoon. As Americans increasingly resented imperialistic communism abroad, they became alarmed at its manifestations at home.

There were two types of responses to this new threat of communist totalitarianism. One, said Thomas, was a form of political paranoia, which defined the problem as one of evil conspiracies, in which the great danger was internal. Communist plotters were assumed to have infiltrated and seized control of our government and only their exposure and expulsion would restore peace and order. This became the McCarthy line in 1950.

Thomas, on the other hand, agreed with those who felt that the chief danger was external—from communist control of Russia, Red China, and their satellites. They viewed the communists as capturing and perverting a basically progressive social revolution, particularly in the colonial movements for national liberation. The struggle against communism, Thomas insisted, must be the attempt to develop democratic alternatives for the revolutionary movements of our times.

McCarthy was totally uninterested in this latter approach. When he discovered gold in the hills of anti-communism, he mined it diligently. He extracted mainly fool's gold, said Thomas, but made it pay more than if it were 24-carat. (I was at the Voice of America when McCarthy conducted his raids there. His "pro-American" underground at the Voice fed him half-truths and lies; he repeated them with Congressional immunity before the television cameras; loyal and conscientious government servants were smeared and fired. Voice appropriations were drastically cut by Congress and the agency reduced to the point of ineffectiveness.)

Thomas was astounded when McCarthy invented the policy of reversal—if a man says he is against communism, he's a secret communist—many years before Robert Welch and his John Birch Society elevated it to a principled theory. When James Wechsler, the strongly anti-communist liberal editor of the *New York Post*, again acknowledged his youthful membership in the Young Communist League, McCarthy barked, "Your purported conversion does not convince me at all."

Wechsler pointed to a 1952 Communist Party resolution attacking "the Reuthers, Dubinskys, Wechslers et al 'who paralyzed independent political action,'" and McCarthy retorted, "Did you take any part in promoting passage of that resolution?"

Aghast, Wechsler replied, "Is this a serious question? The answer is no."

To which McCarthy said: "I feel that you have not broken with the communist ideal. I feel that you are serving them very, very actively." McCarthy added that if the Senator were head of the Communist Party and Jim Wechsler came to Moscow and turned out to be a bright young man and good writer, he would tell him to go back to the United States, say he was breaking with the Communist Party, make general attacks on communism but actually be the ringleader in attacking and destroying anyone who tried to hurt Soviet Russia.

Appalled by this outrageous smear, Thomas wrote McCarthy, reminding the latter of his acceptance of communist support in his 1946 primary victory over La Follette. "Remembering that fact," wrote Thomas, "it occurs to me that if I were secret communist commissar in America and a bright young politician and able demagogue had accepted my party's half-secret help, I would tell him to build himself as a foe of communism but actually to be the ringleader in discrediting anti-communism by methods which offend American lovers of fair play, win a mistaken sympathy for communists as martyrs, and irritate America's allies . . . At the very moment that the Kremlin's evil record is most potently discrediting communism, you create a diversion by inviting men profoundly to distrust democracy as you exemplify it . . . How often I have had to apologize for our Senate to Americans and foreigners that it permits you to be Lord High Inquisitor! And how the Kremlin must rejoice!"

Thomas was to find that world preoccupation with McCarthyism was indeed intense. When he flew to Stockholm in 1953 to attend the World Socialist Congress, he was driven directly from the airport to a party sponsored by a group of Swedish Socialists. Before Thomas could sit down to dinner, the question of Joe McCarthy was raised. Certain people had so exaggerated an idea of McCarthy's influence that they asked, "How did you manage to get the State Department to let you leave America?"

Throughout Europe, McCarthyism was an issue at every gathering and meeting Thomas attended. This fact so disturbed him that finally, at a session of the Socialist Congress, he told the delegates:

"I have already written to America of the serious damage McCarthyism is doing to the reputation of American liberty abroad. I feel I must tell you that bad as McCarthyism is, it has not revived anti-Semitism, which is at its lowest ebb in America; it has not impeded our all-too-slow progress toward ending racial discrimination. It is not as yet equivalent to the beginning of Nazism in Germany. None of us dares say in any country, 'It can't happen here.' But as of today (when McCarthy has met some checks), McCarthyism is for liberty a bad skin disease, rather than a cancer, and we are not helped in fighting it by exaggerating its evil or its power."

Thomas soon found that the skin disease could cause a bad rash. In an attempt to appease Senator McCarthy, Secretary of State John Foster Dulles appointed Scott McLeod security officer of the State Department. McLeod embarked on a campaign to remove Socialists and former socialists from the Department. Thomas wrote to McLeod who, after a lapse of six weeks, finally replied:

"I would never knowingly employ a Socialist to fill such a (policy making) position within the department . . . and whenever I become aware that any person who occupies such a position is a Socialist, I shall use my best efforts to see that he is removed." While McLeod issued this statement without consulting Dulles, the latter, when it was brought to his attention, approved of the ruling.

Thomas was in Germany when McLeod released his reply, but after hearing the letter read over the telephone from New York, he immediately wrote McLeod:

"At a time when McCarthyism at home gravely injures American leadership for peace and freedom abroad, you contribute to McCarthyism by . . . a policy of barring Socialists from foreign service to their country—except, of course, when it comes to paying taxes and fighting in its wars . . . Your partisan concept of foreign policy is manifest in your statement that you no more need socialists to carry out American foreign policy in foreign countries where socialism is strong than you need communists in communist countries."

"Here in Germany," Thomas noted, "on my way to Berlin, I find that statement particularly shocking and injurious to the American cause. The mayor of Berlin, Ernst Reuter, is a socialist who has been lauded by our highest authorities. The workers of East Berlin, whose revolt against communist oppression made June 17th a great day in history, are largely socialist. I have before me the statement of the communist official organ, the *Neues Deutsch-land*, that 'hunting for illegal Social Democrats in the Sovzone is the most important task of present SED (communist) policy.' So you encourage that policy by denouncing all American socialists as unfit . . . in any foreign country."

Thomas conceded that there are high policy making jobs in which the President has not only a right but a duty to have men closely in sympathy with his point of view. "It is dangerous, however," he wrote, "to carry the concept of policy making down to positions primarily on the operational level . . . Civil service is completely wrecked if the notion of policy making is carried down almost to the level of office boys."

When Thomas returned to the States, he wrote to President Eisenhower seeking an appointment to discuss this problem. Finally, in October, Thomas heard from one of the President's secretaries that he would be willing to meet with Thomas. On October 27, 1953, at the White House, Thomas explained to the President that McLeod and Harold Stassen (then in charge of foreign operations programs) seemed to regard a believer in TVA as some sort of Socialist, and to hold that almost any job was "policy making." To this the President listened patiently and without criticism or objection. He assured Thomas that he knew socialists were loyal and he did not dispute Thomas' assertion that the likelihood of security leaks from people who talked too much was no greater among Socialists than among Republicans. At a meeting three days later, Eisenhower directed his Cabinet that Socialists were not to be excluded from non-policy making jobs in the government. Apparently needling his Secretary of State, he also mentioned that Thomas had quoted a current saying that "McCarthy runs McLeod, and McLeod runs Dulles."

Thomas had long supported the need to protect military secrets from foreign agents, communists or fascists and others whose chief loyalty was to totalitarianism. But he maintained that Mc-Carthyism with its vicious political exploitation was no way to carry on a security system. Noting also the ridiculous extremes to which McCarthyism led, Thomas said, "I question the value of the state of Indiana's requiring professional wrestlers to take loyalty oaths before climbing into the ring, and Washington, D.C.'s insistence on security clearance before renewing the license of second-hand piano dealers."

In the industrial security programs covering more than six million workers, Thomas came upon many abuses arising directly from McCarthyism. In Buffalo, N.Y., James Schuetz, a Socialist and a leader of UAW Local 501 at Bell Aircraft, was fired as a "security risk" because his union activity showed he "lacked integrity and discretion." Thomas joined with the Workers Defense League and the United Auto Workers and testified in Schuetz' behalf, but it took five months before Schuetz was reinstated.

At this time, accused employees had no right to confront their accusers; the same policy applied with regard to military security programs. Again, some of the charges were absurd. In one case a draftee received an undesirable discharge because he was a member of a subversive organization—enrolled by his parents at the age of eight! Another was in trouble because it was alleged that his mother-in-law had been a "fellow-traveller";—however, she had died ten years before the young man married into the family. The Workers Defense League, with Thomas' help, appealed more than a hundred such cases, and was remarkably successful. Then Rowland Watts, national secretary of the League, drafted a 250-page report on the Army security program which influenced the Army to revise its security procedures somewhat.

However, the Armed Forces continued to hand out "derogatory discharges" when information about so-called subversive pre-induction activities was discovered after a draftee entered service. "While such new information may necessitate the discharge of a draftee," argued Thomas, "the character of the discharge should depend solely upon performance in the service." The Defense Department refused to accept Thomas' views, even though the Workers Defense League pointed out that a less-than-honorable discharge affected a man's earnings in a very direct and damaging way. Finally in 1958 the U.S. Supreme Court upheld Thomas' contentions and ruled that Army discharges must be based only on draftees' service records while in the Army. Similarly, the Court struck down President Eisenhower's industrial security program in June, 1959, because the program denied an accused person the right to confront a witness or examine a document used against him.

The Attorney General's list of subversive organizations, a repressive listing which both predated Senator McCarthy and lingered on after his demise, also engaged the attention of Thomas and the Workers Defense League. In this connection, Thomas was reminded of the lines from Gilbert and Sullivan's "The Mikado," when Koko, the Lord High Executioner, sings:

> "I've got a little list, I've got a little list
> Of society offenders who might well be underground
> And who never would be missed, who never would be missed."

The first Attorney General's list of subversive organizations had been set up in 1941 as a guide to government agencies in time of war. In 1947, President Truman established the list formally by executive order, and in March, 1948, it was released by Attorney General Tom Clark. None of the organizations appearing on the list had been given the opportunity for a hearing. Immediately, Max Schactman, head of the Workers Party, a small, dissident Trotskyist group which was strongly anti-Soviet, challenged the inclusion of his organization. Thomas and the Workers Defense League supported the challenge, but the Attorney General refused to change his ruling.

In 1953, the Supreme Court ruled that the list had been wrongfully compiled because the Attorney General gave no hearing to the organizations listed. Thereupon President Eisenhower issued a decree reinstating the list, but directing that groups labelled subversive should be notified and given an opportunity to be heard. The Schactman group, now called the Independent Socialist League, again asked for hearings, but they did not take place until 1955-6. Then the government produced only two witnesses. One was Professor G. T. Robinson of Columbia, who hardly seemed a reliable witness since he admitted never having heard of Schactman's group. The other witness was a former member of the Workers Party, James Burnham, author of *The Managerial Revolution*, who had traveled down the road to the far right and the *National Review*.

For the defense, the Workers Defense League secured attorney

Joseph L. Rauh, Jr., who worked without fee in support of civil liberties. As witnesses he marshalled Norman Thomas; Daniel Bell, then labor editor of *Fortune;* magazine writer Dwight Mac-Donald and the author, as former national secretary of the Socialist Party. We all testified that the Schactman group did not advocate the use of force except in the unlikely event that they should take power legally and capitalists use force to resist them. It seemed rather strange that Hearing Officer Edward Morrissey would not concede that Thomas and the other defense witnesses were experts on communism, but that Professors Robinson and Burnham were. In the face of the overwhelming weight of the evidence, Morrissey found for the government. The case did not end here. The Workers Defense League appealed to the Attorney General and on July 16, 1958—just ten years after the original appeal—the Attorney General removed from the subversive list the Workers Party; its successor, the Independent Socialist League; and its youth affiliate, the Socialist Youth League. This was the first time that any organization on the list fought its case through to a conclusion and a victory.

While Thomas vigorously opposed both McCarthyism and security hysteria, he did not exaggerate their importance in the American scheme. Noting that "our jails are not filled with dissenters; speech is still free to heretics who dare claim their freedom," Thomas reflected sadly that the worst evils in America are the drive for conformity, local censorship by voluntary vigilantes in schools and libraries, and the cowardice and apathy of the public before this censorship.

An example of conformist pressure that disturbed Thomas was a pamphlet, "So You Want a Better Job?" by Paul W. Boynton, a personnel officer of Socony Vacuum Oil Company. One passage read:

"Personal views can cause a lot of trouble. Remember then to keep them always conservative. The 'isms' are out. Business being what it is, it naturally looks with disfavor on the wild-eyed radical or even the moderate pink. On the other hand, I think you will find very few business organizations who will attempt to dictate the political party of their employees."

Thomas wrote to the company and Boynton came to see him. He couldn't understand why Thomas should object. After all, 300,000 copies of his pamphlet had been circulated for years, and Thomas' was the first word of criticism that had reached him. From the colleges and even the students he had received only applause. (Boynton ignored the fact that a student's attack in *The Princetonian* had sparked Thomas' complaint.)

Nevertheless, Thomas' attack had an effect. Some time later, C. F. Beatty, Socony's industrial relations director, wrote Thomas that the pamphlet had been revised to proclaim that "the world needs different viewpoints; blind conformity means stagnation. You won't get far unless you think for yourself."

What continued to roil Thomas, however, was the failure of placement directors at various universities to find anything wrong with the original pamphlet. One enlightened businessman told him, "You should thank Socony-Vacuum for saying explicitly what most corporations quietly cause to be understood."

Thomas received new evidence of the pressures of conformity as a result of a visit in the spring of 1959 to the Bach Festival on Lehigh University's campus in Bethlehem, Pa. While there, he was interviewed by the school paper, *Brown and White*, and urged socialization of the steel industry, then in the throes of a long strike. There were no immediate repercussions, but a few months later, when the Lehigh debating society, Delta Omicron Theta, invited Thomas to speak, university officials refused the request to list him in the official lecture series and banned the meeting. Perhaps this action was not entirely unconnected with Lehigh's current fund-raising drive or the fact that many of the university's most prominent—and wealthy—alumni headed big steel companies.

Stimulated by the unexpected proof that he was not too "respectable" to promote controversy, Thomas wrote to the American Association of University Professors chapter at Lehigh, asking whether or not he would be welcome if he attended the 1960 Bach Festival. "Would you advise me," he asked, "to seek permission either from the president of the University through proper channels, or more directly from the President of the Bethlehem Steel Company?"

277

As a result, the Lehigh AAUP chapter urged that the power to approve guest speakers be withdrawn from the university president and turned over to a faculty-student committee. The student council backed this approach and the national executive committee of the National Student Association decried the Lehigh ban on Thomas as a "violation of academic freedom."

Apart from the humorous aspects of the situation, Thomas was indignant. "In my long life," Thomas told the *New York Post*, "and I am 75, this has happened to me only four times. But it has done my ego some good. I am not just a national monument—somebody is afraid of me . . . My interest in keeping the situation alive is this. There is a great deal of censorship on campuses. The average college president lives in fear of his alumni. I think that's what happened at Lehigh."

Thomas' concern over anti-democratic manifestations was heightened by the resurgence in 1961 of ultra-right-wing groups which he called a "serious menace to the nation's democratic freedoms." He said that he was "more frightened" by the growing ties between large segments of industry, the military and radical rightists, than he had been by the McCarthyism of a decade earlier.

The movement symbolized by the late Senator Joe McCarthy, Thomas said, was a "one-shot affair, whereas the John Birch Society and the hundreds of other militant, allegedly anti-communist action groups are grass-roots movements." Moreover, he added, they give "the impression of much better organization and are therefore a more tangible menace."

In releasing a report on "The American Ultras," compiled by Irwin Suall, national secretary of the Socialist Party, Thomas charged that "extreme right-wing indoctrination of captive audiences" in the armed forces, even following General Edwin Walker's use of John Birch Society propaganda, had continued despite a Defense Department ruling barring such activity. Thomas accused Vice Admiral Robert Goldthwaite, commander of the Western Sea Frontier, of conducting a "virtual one-man crusade for right-wing extremism from coast to coast." The Admiral, Thomas continued, had recommended that sailors attending a leadership training program at the Pensacola, Fla., Naval Air Base obtain "anti-communist" materials from an extreme rightist group, We The People. Led by the Rev. Billy James Hargis, the group called for the impeachment of Chief Justice Earl Warren.

Thomas charged that American radical rightists had "strong connections with the leaders of powerful corporations; their activists are high in the military; and they can summon up community support across the nation from every know-nothing, bigoted and anti-democratic tendency in the land." Thomas did not suggest any plot theory of malevolent reaction but stressed that the problem was of greater importance precisely because the country confronted not a handful of fringe fanatics but rather significant social forces in American society moving toward the politics of radical reaction.

While Thomas has considered that the extreme right poses an ultimate threat to all Americans, he feels that its most immediate threat is to responsible conservatives. Nothing, he noted, was more certain to destroy the appeal of conservatism than its identification with the wild men on the right. One might assume that Thomas would welcome such harm to the conservatives, but that would reflect a lack of knowledge of one of Thomas' major characteristics—a sense of responsibility. He has never believed in the philosophy of "the worse conditions become, the better the prospects for change."

Thus Thomas praised, as "commendable first steps," attacks by Richard Nixon, Senator Barry Goldwater and the *National Review* upon Robert Welch, head of the John Birch Society. But he has urged conservatives to attack not only Welch but all rightist extremism. Fortunately, his advice has been at least partially accepted. Many Republican political leaders and opinion molders lashed out at the ultra-rightists. They do "devil's work far better than communists could do," charged Senator Thomas H. Kuchel of California in May, 1963. "The curious fact is that the fright peddlers, from the simple simpletons to the wretched racists, all claim to be conservatives. They defile the honorable philosophy of conservatism with that claim as thoroughly as the communists defile the honorable philosophy of liberalism."

279

Thomas commended Kuchel but warned those Republican leaders who apparently thought they could "use" the Birchites that they were making the same mistake John L. Lewis made when he thought he could "use" the communists in the early CIO days. When the Birchers and their allies captured various segments of the Republican Party, including the Young Republicans of California, the college G.O.P. of Michigan and the Wyoming Republican Party, Thomas' concern proved to be valid. While he feels that the radical right is far from taking over the country, its members are capable of creating much mischief, particularly through vigilante and censorship tactics in small towns throughout the nation. "Eternal vigilance," Thomas says, "is still the price of liberty."

TWENTY-ONE

Zionism and the Middle East

◄§ THE QUESTION OF ZIONISM and the Arab lands has been of deep concern to Norman Thomas for many years. As a man of conscience he has shared the guilt felt throughout the Christian world because of anti-Semitism and the centuries-old persecution which culminated in Hitler's extermination of six million Jews. In addition, many of his closest friends in the Socialist Party and in liberal organizations have been Jews who strongly supported Zionism. Thomas understood and sympathized with Zionist goals, but his sympathies never prevented him from seeing clearly that in their zeal for the new Palestine, Zionists themselves created problems.

As early as 1919, Thomas wrote an editorial in *The World Tomorrow:* "We must remember that . . . in this ancient land of his fathers the Jew today and for centuries past is in a minority among the inhabitants . . . The most that Zionists can ask is that Britain . . . should assure them a fair chance to create by colonization a population predominantly Jewish, with guarantees that such a state will ultimately be given complete self-government in which all elements of the population will have their proportionate share." Thomas also noted that the Prince of the new Arabian kingdom, welcoming the Zionist ideal, wrote: "We are working together for a reformed and revived Near East, and our two movements complete each other."

Thomas enthusiastically supported the proposal that Palestine

281

become a bi-national state, jointly run by Jews and Arabs—a proposal first advanced by Rabbi Judah L. Magnes, who worked with Thomas in the American Union Against Militarism before and during World War I. After World War II, Thomas' opposition to certain nationalistic features of Zionism led some Jewish and Christian pro-Zionists to characterize him falsely as "anti-Semitic"; in actual fact, Thomas has constantly sought to aid the world's persecuted Jewish minorities. He appealed to Britain's Labor Government to "honor its pledge" by repealing the British White Paper which limited immigration into Palestine, and at the same time demanded the abolition of America's immigration quotas to permit free immigration of Jews and other displaced persons into the United States. Taking President Truman to task, Thomas insisted that urging Britain to allow 100,000 Jews to enter Palestine while refusing "to open the doors of the United States to Europe's homeless Jews" was "rank hypocrisy."

Within hours after Britain dropped its mandate in 1948, the independent state of Israel was proclaimed and was attacked by Arab troops. The United Nations, through Ralph Bunche, brought about an armistice which corresponded to military lines —but the armistice never became a peace. For this, Thomas said, the chief blame fell on the Arab states, but he did not exonerate Israel of all responsibility. While acknowledging Egypt's guilt in closing the Suez Canal to Israeli shipping, as well as in organizing murderous feyadeen raids, Thomas was critical of the Israeli, British and French invasion of Egypt in 1956. He was troubled by the Arab who said to him: "You Christians and Westerners, not we, persecuted the Jews; yet you make *us* pay the price!"

Thomas thought it a great loss that liberal Jews in such large numbers had become nationalistic. "There is a quality of Greek tragedy," he added, "in the fact that homeless Jews have found a most insecure home by processes which rendered an equal number of Arabs homeless." While aware of the social backwardness of most of the Arab nations, Thomas insisted that democratic and socially progressive Israel could only become viable if a beginning was made to the slow process of reconciliation with the Arabs.

In 1956, Thomas became chairman of the Institute for International Labor Research, an autonomous organization initiated by the Free Europe Committee. The Institute asked Thomas to go to the Middle East to try to arrange for publication of translations of factual anti-communist works by reliable Arabic groups. He was also urged to make such a trip by Dr. Don Peretz, author of *Israel and the Palestine Arabs*, published by the Middle East Institute. Peretz had already been to Syria and Egypt, as a correspondent for the *Socialist Call*, to investigate the plight of Jews. In Damascus, he had been called to police headquarters and ordered deported to Lebanon immediately. When Syria's Foreign Minister, Salah el-Bitar, leader of the avowedly Socialist Ba'ath Party (at this writing Prime Minister of Syria, following the March 1963 coup d'état), learned of the deportation, he arranged for Peretz' return, gave him an interview for the *Call*, and treated him cordially. The warm reception to socialism led Peretz to believe that if Norman Thomas could be induced to make a trip to the Middle East, he might be able to help various minority groups in the area.

It happened that Bitar came to New York as the chief Syrian delegate at the next UN General Assembly. Since he was anxious to meet American liberals and hear more than the official American foreign policy views, Thomas, at Peretz' suggestion, arranged for Bitar to see Senators Hubert Humphrey and Ralph Flanders as well as Chester Bowles. Bitar found these meetings enlightening and urged Thomas and Peretz to visit Syria. Thomas accepted Bitar's invitation and he and Peretz went to the Middle East in November and December of 1957, visiting not only Syria but Egypt, Iraq, Lebanon, Jordan and Israel as well. One of Thomas' major concerns was the problem of minorities in the various countries: the Copts and Jews in Egypt, Jews in Syria, and Arabs in Israel.

During their stay in Egypt, Thomas and Peretz talked with many government officials, journalists, foreign observers, private citizens and members of minority communities, particularly Jews and Coptic Christians. There seemed to be no repressive measures in force against minorities, but considerable uncertainty about the future. When Peretz had been in Egypt the summer before, he had visited a Copt journalist with a friend of the latter, a Muslim. At that time the Copt strongly denied that there was any discrimination in Egypt. Now, however, he told of many instances of discrimination. When Peretz asked him to explain his change of attitude, the Copt replied, "What did you expect me to say then? You were here with a Muslim." This, although the Muslim was his friend and a fellow Socialist!

Thomas and Peretz met with President Gamal Abdel Nasser for almost two hours, discussing Nasser's program for Egyptian reform, minorities and foreign policy. When Nasser tried to explain what he meant by "democratic socialism," to which his National Union was committed, Thomas found him rather vague. Nasser proposed to create a mixed economy, using private and governmental capital to develop national industry. He indicated that few businessmen in Egypt understood the need for productive investment; most, he insisted, were merely speculators.

When Thomas mentioned his concern about the problem of minorities and asked whether the welfare of Jews and Copts was included in the objectives of the revolution, Nasser seemed somewhat taken aback. He pointed out that 70 per cent of the country's engineering students, and many government officials, were Copts but that Coptic leaders had often attempted to intervene when the government was considering new legislation. This he said he would not tolerate. Nasser said he agreed with Thomas on the need for separation of church and state in a democratic society, but added that conditions in Egypt precluded such an approach to ecclesiastical matters, noting his difficulties in settling differences in the Copt community over the choosing of a new patriarch.

After the attack on Egypt in October, 1956, Nasser said, there had been a popular outburst against the Jewish community because many former Egyptian Jews then in Israel had served in the invading Israeli army and the intelligence service. He had tried to halt the fear-caused mass exodus of Jews early in 1957 by issuing statements that he did not wish to distinguish between Egyptians on the basis of religion. When Jews had been expelled from Egyptian clubs, Nasser ordered that they be readmitted. He also decreed that members of minority groups must not be discharged from jobs, asking people with complaints to come to him for redress. The characterization of Egypt as Islamic in his new constitution, he termed purely descriptive and emphasized the non-sectarian nature of the state.

When Thomas and Peretz asked Nasser how decisions of major national importance were reached in Egypt, he responded with a long and involved explanation of the 1956 constitution and the workings of the national assembly. The same question was asked of Assembly President, Abd al-Latif Baghdadi. His answer was much simpler and more revealing. "There are six of us who make these decisions," he said, and named in addition to Nasser and himself, the commander-in-chief and three other former officers.

One of the leaders of the Jewish community told the two Americans that, from time to time, Jews were deprived of Egyptian nationality because they had remained out of the country for more than six months, or because they had "Zionist tendencies." (Both Nasser and Baghdadi said that the six-month regulation had been directed at Jews who had gone to Israel from Egypt.)

In Syria, the security police detained Thomas and Peretz because the latter's name was still on the blacklist following his expulsion the previous summer. But when the police phoned Damascus and learned that the two had an appointment with Foreign Minister Bitar, they permitted them to continue their journey. Bitar was very hospitable, made some suggestions of persons whom his American visitors should see, and invited Thomas to address a meeting of the Ba'ath Arab Socialist Party.

The meeting, attended by about 200 party leaders, including government officials, university professors and students, was held at party headquarters in Damascus. Bitar told the group that Norman Thomas would undoubtedly say things with which they would disagree, but he urged them to listen and to learn. At the time, the only up-to-date English language publications available in Syria were the *Egyptian Gazette* and the *Moscow News*. This being the case, when Thomas criticized the Soviet Union and communism from a public platform, where he was speaking at the invitation of the Foreign Minister, it was a significant occasion. Thomas, relating the fate of the Czech democrats who thought they could work with the communists, told of the suicide of Czech Foreign Minister, Jan Masaryk, after the communist coup d'état and reminded his listeners, "You can't have too long a spoon to sup with the devil." Thomas spoke also of the need for any Socialist Party to work for internationalism as well as minority rights. His talk was well received, and the many questions afterward were neither hostile nor argumentative.

At a private dinner meeting later with a group of Syrian socialist leaders, Thomas raised the subject of Jews by telling about the brave fight of the Jewish Socialist Bund and other Jews in the Warsaw Ghetto against the Nazis during World War II. He mentioned that he had heard that some thousands of Syrian Jews were being badly discriminated against and asked whether or not something could be done to arrange for the immigration of those who might desire to leave Syria for countries in the Western hemisphere. The atmosphere was tense and there was dead silence for a while. One Syrian party leader then said that this subject had often been brought up by Zionists to attack Arabs. He spoke of the many centuries of good relations between Jews and Arabs.

Thomas replied that he had heard that Jews, particularly those in troubled border areas, were not only economically distressed, but discriminated against both by public opinion and law. In particular, he added, he had been told that over a thousand Jews in the town of Kamishly and the villages nearby were subject to special police or military controls. Moreover, those families wanting to leave the area or the country could do so only after paying a large sum of money—which, in view of the impoverished nature of the community, made such departures almost impossible. Other restrictions to which Syrian Jews—and not other Syrians—were subjected were that they could not buy or sell property, nor could they use their bank accounts, which had been impounded.

Unfortunately, continued Thomas, Jewish populations in the Middle East, like Arab refugees and the Arab minority in Israel, were often the helpless victims of the clash between Arab nationalism and Zionism. He insisted that he was concerned with securing justice for the Arab refugees and the Arab minority in Israel as well as for Jews in Arab counties. The Arab Socialist leaders agreed to take up the matter in their party and see what could be done, since they too felt that infringement of minority rights was a matter of real importance to all socialists.

A couple of months later, when Syria and Egypt combined to form the United Arab Republic, Thomas wrote Nasser a letter of congratulation and asked, "Can you find ways to ameliorate the lot of the five or six thousand Jews still living in Syria? . . . I know how many are your burdens but the question I raise is one of humanity and seems to an outsider to afford a chance for giving valuable evidence to the whole world of the stand of your country for the rights of men as men. As you well know, I am not a Jew. I have consulted no Jew on the matter of writing this letter and certainly have not been asked by any individual or organization to write it. I am prompted to write only by my own concern as a democratic socialist and by the respect I felt for your understanding of the problem of minorities when I discussed the matter with you."

Thomas later heard that the leader of the Jewish community in Syria was visited by a government official and told not to worry, for things would be all right. The bank accounts of Syrian Jews still in the country were unfrozen, and they were again permitted to leave, but only if they left all their belongings behind them.

Everywhere in the Arab world, Thomas and Peretz found the climate of opinion such that all Arab leaders seemed to feel anti-Zionism a necessary prelude to statements on any other issue. In Baghdad, Iraq, the American visitors met with several cabinet ministers and other leaders who were both pro-American and anti-communist. Yet every anti-communist remark was accompanied by abuse of Zionism.

In Lebanon, when Thomas and Peretz visited the Maronite Catholic Patriarch, who had been for years a Maronite Catholic priest in the United States, he refrained from anti-American sentiments but reminded his visitors: "You must remember, we are a handful in a sea of Muslims." Another Catholic leader who had been frequently charged with support for extreme Arab nationalism was the Greek Catholic Archbishop Hakim, whom the two Americans visited in Haifa, Israel. He expressed sentiments similar to those of the Maronite Patriarch. Both seemed to feel that overt support for the West, or a lukewarm attitude toward Arab nationalism, would be detrimental to the continued welfare of

287

their flocks in the Arab world. In Beirut, when Thomas was talking to a group of Arab students and professors, an American made anti-Semitic remarks which several Arabs echoed. Thomas immediately reminded them of the Nazi horrors against the Jews, of the concentration camps and Jewish heroism, and showed his strong resentment.

Thomas found that even those parties in the Arab countries which claimed to be both democratic and socialist placed little emphasis on individual liberty, press freedom, minority rights, or such basic socialist programs as democratic social ownership of the major means of production, a planned economy, and the equitable distribution of national income. Instead their main themes were national liberation, self-determination and freedom from the "imperialist yoke"—which Thomas felt was frequently only a euphemism for attacking Israel. After listening to a bespectacled young Arab intellectual in Beirut rant for more than an hour about his version of democracy and socialism, it occurred to Thomas that the slogan of Arab socialists was "liberty, equality and revenge."

In one respect, Thomas' trip was quite unsuccessful. He tried diligently to find responsible Arabs to handle the literature of the Institute for International Labor Research. He found many interested, but always with this qualification: "Add attacks on Zionism to those on communism, and we'll be glad to handle it." Thomas, of course, refused to consider any such proposition.

To come to Israel, as Thomas and Peretz did, from Jordan through the Mandelbaum Gate in the old city wall of Jerusalem was an experience which made Thomas "mourn for our human folly." "Once you have walked through two control posts," said Thomas, "you are about as far from the land you have left as if you were on the moon. And you cannot go back save by a most roundabout route. I have been in divided Berlin but in comparison with Jerusalem it is a unified city. Old Palestinians questioned us eagerly about neighbors whose roofs were easily visible from their windows."

In Israel, they were hospitably received. Foreign Minister Golda Meir was friendly and receptive when she and Michel Comay, former Israeli Ambassador to Canada, received Thomas and Peretz in her home in Jerusalem. When Thomas reported on Arab fears of Israeli expansionism, she replied that her government was prepared to give guarantees against Israeli aggression. Thomas was particularly impressed by the great degree of freedom which existed in Israel to discuss controversial issues such as the Arab refugee and minority problems. He found in Israel far more tolerance in discussion of these issues than in the United States, where any public criticism of Israel or Ben Gurion brought scorn. Even government officials felt free to disagree with national policy on particular issues. Minister of Development Ben Tov, for instance, told Thomas that he disagreed with the government's attitude toward problems concerning the Arab minority and the neighboring states.

Thomas was heartened by the efforts being made in Israel to improve the civil and material status of the Israeli Arabs. But he felt that the moral problem raised by Israeli appropriation of the property of Arab refugees required Israel to press positive proposals to offset Arab and Russian pressures on the infant state. He doubted that such proposals could bring durable peace except as they might be included in the pattern of a *modus vivendi* between the USA and the USSR on the road to disarmament.

"A beginning of progress," said Thomas, "might be made if the Israeli government would say convincingly that the Arab war which enlarged her territory has not changed her willingness to work out economic cooperation or union with Jordan, which holds part of the territory in Palestine for which the UN's 1947 plan proposed such union. This action would strengthen both partners and in no way frustrate achievement of a larger Arab federation . . . As evidence of good faith Israel might urge joint patrols of borders by a mixed force of her troops and her Arab neighbors. She should hasten the process already begun of turning the Arabs who did not leave Israel into first rather than second class citizens . . . The hate and the arms race in the Middle East which it inspires can only lead to an Armageddon in which Death alone will be the victor."

What impressed Peretz most about Thomas on the six weeks' trip was the latter's unaffected simplicity and his monumental

energy. Although then 73 years old, he always insisted on carrying his own luggage and was active from nine in the morning until
late at night. Young Peretz found himself tiring more easily than
Thomas. As a prominent American political figure, Thomas had
easy access to the leading statesmen of all the countries he visited,
but seemed surprised to discover how well known he was in the
Middle East. While he had gone abroad to listen rather than to
speak, he spoke and was questioned at public student meetings
in the American universities in Cairo and Beirut, at off-the-record
conferences first with Arab and then Jewish students at the
Hebrew University in Jerusalem, at a radical "opposition" Arab
club in Lebanon and at a Ba'ath Socialist meeting in Damascus.
At the same time, he wrote his twice-weekly columns for the
Los Angeles Mirror Syndicate, read many books and articles and
managed to master the names of innumerable unfamiliar individuals, groups and parties.

Although Thomas was rueful about his failure to promote Arab
use of educational material about communism, he was heartened
by the response in both Israel and the Arab lands to his plea for
the rights of minorities, and continued his efforts to ameliorate
Middle East tensions.

TWENTY-TWO

The Lonely Quest

◦§ FROM HIS EARLIEST DAYS, Norman Thomas longed for the strength that his parents found in their high sense of relationship to God. Ethically, he felt, their religion gave them a code and a conscience which delivered them from uncertainty. Evil there might be, and suffering hard to understand, but over all was God who had His own in His care. His universe was man's home. The generation which believed this, said Thomas, "did not have to hope with the Bishop of Birmingham that 'whatever is at the heart of things is not hostile to our highest aims and ideals.' Their God was a Father; not a 'whatever is at the heart of things.' . . . They were heirs of life eternal, children of Him who was King of Kings and Lord of Lords."

Like many people, Norman Thomas went through a childhood phase of fearing death and questioning immortality. But his questioning never went very deep and his parents' reassurance somehow dealt with those fears. When he joined the church it seemed a natural step, requiring no tremendous emotional upheaval. In college and afterwards, Thomas gradually developed a more liberal view of the Bible and a feeling of harmony between science and religion. At Union Theological Seminary he shared the pragmatic philosophy whose foundation was William James' *Will to Believe*. The kind of Christianity Thomas enthusiastically accepted was that preached by Harry Emerson Fosdick and Henry Sloane Coffin. It was a religion of dignity, beauty and considerable power, but in later years he found it hard to understand how he could think it an intellectually satisfactory explanation of man's relation to the universe.

World War I made it impossible for Thomas to reconcile Christianity and war, which he termed the negation of Christian ethics. That war might be a judgment from God and a consequence of man's sins, Thomas could accept, but he could not see how followers of Christ could ever be justified in using the devil's means of war or that a God of love could require it of them. During and after World War I, Thomas was particularly bitter over the spectacle of preachers shouldering arms and spreading hate. Too often, clergymen identified their nation's aims with God's, saying, as did Sir Harry Lauder, "The Bible teaches us to forgive our enemies but not God's. And the Germans are God's enemies." One theologian, during World War I, assured his congregation that Christians who were killing each other would be reconciled and united in Heaven—which seemed cold comfort indeed to Thomas.

In the war and its aftermath Thomas could find little evidence of the God who was love. Although he argued that man's wickedness and stupidity, not God's, was responsible for the unhappy world of 1920, he could not help but ask, "Has a God of love no responsibility for the weakness of the men he had made?" And thus, slowly but surely, Thomas lost faith in a God who was at once power and love; with it necessarily went his uncompromising religious pacifism, although by no means his hatred of war.

Shortly after World War I, Thomas attended a number of conferences which finally resulted in the formation of the National Conference of Christians and Jews. One night a number of Jews, and Christians of various Protestant denominations—Thomas can't recall whether any Roman Catholics were present—explained why their religion gave them a greater sense of brotherhood. When Thomas was called upon to speak he said that he did not doubt the sincerity of his colleagues but, at the same time, it was logically and historically untrue that the religious bodies which they represented had been made more tolerant and brotherly by the intensity of their creeds. The Jews, he reminded his audience, were a Chosen People in a peculiar sense by the Act of God. As for the Catholics, outside the Church there was no salvation even though some who were not Catholic might, under exceptional circumstances, be saved. And each Protestant sect had been inclined in its day to maintain that it provided the exclusive road to heaven. All this was a consequence of differing beliefs concerning God and His way of salvation. The terrible wars of religion had a certain horrible logic behind them, and tolerance was eventually born of exhaustion and a turning from religious fanaticism rather than a triumph of Christian brotherhood. Practically, said Thomas, Americans were facing the necessity of teaching men, in the name of religion, to be more brotherly and tolerant than the churches had been, less cruel than the God they worshipped. "Why," asked Thomas, "should believers on this earth be so much kinder to infidels and heretics than their God, who has prepared death and hell for those not chosen of His grace?" His questions provoked protest but no answer, and Thomas was not invited to further conferences.

As the years went by, and Thomas started to regard churches more and more as fallible man-made institutions and to judge them as such, his respect for them rose. While he still felt them dubiously Christian according to the teachings of Christ, he thought they filled a place of great importance in community life. They brought real help and comfort to their members, and evoked sincere generosity in their support. Thomas has always refused to attack any religion or any creed, except as some of its teachings encouraged cruelty, intellectual obscurantism, or a bigoted separation of "true believers" from their fellow men. "One does not idly seek to deprive one's fellows of aid and comfort in the difficult business of living."

Thomas, who has written and published a great deal on a wide variety of subjects, has published very little on the subject of religion. For one thing, even when he was most inclined toward Marxism, in the early thirties, he never accepted dialectical materialism as a philosophy. He considered its predestination to be as bigoted and unsatisfactory as that of Calvinism, and its gospel contained no saviour nor any salvation for the individual as an individual. Moreover, he resented the shallow, intolerant atheism of most orthodox Marxists, which he felt left many important questions unanswered philosophically. Above all, Thomas' own absorbing interests were in the social order and he was disinclined to be deeply involved in religious or philosophic controversies that might dissipate his energies or drive men away from the socialism in which he believed. Yet privately he kept seeking for some answer to life's sorrows, some guaranty of its joys which would be half as satisfactory to him as the liberal Christianity in which he had once believed.

The Sunday after the Japanese surrendered, ending World War II, was a beautiful summer day in Cold Spring Harbor. Thomas wrote in his diary: "Nature rejoices with men. Soon the church bells will ring and the little churches will be crowded with thankful worshippers. I shall not be among them although all sorts of memories and desires urge me to go.

"It is not for lack of joy that the cruelest war in history is ended in our victory with my own country and my own loved ones well and safe. There aren't words to tell my happiness that I can look at Evan, home on leave, and not think: 'It's but a respite from hell. Twice he has gone, once to the African desert in the American Field Service, once in the Navy to the invasion of Europe, and returned. But to expect it the third time from the invasion of Japan is too much.'

"Neither is it from lack of a sense of the desperate importance of religion to men who have acquired with the atomic bomb a literal power to wipe out their race . . . Where shall we look but to God, if He be good, now that science has wrested from Him so much of the secret of the force that holds together the atom and the universe?

"Why not, then, church? Because, if God be omnipotent Power, I cannot praise His ordering of this war-cursed world. If He be love, how can I give Him thanks for the triumph of amoral force? Or how can He accept our adoration unless we bring to Him the sacrifice of a humble and a contrite heart? And that we shall not offer. Even our prayers will speak of our exultation in power and the pride of our vengeance. Let our enemies repent."

The failure of Socialists and liberals in all countries to build a peaceful and prosperous world made Thomas reject his earlier, almost automatic faith in a sure and desirable "far off divine event to which the whole creation moves." Nevertheless, he conceded, "There is undoubtedly a Power, not ourselves, behind the universe whom or which we may call God. The question is how far He works for righteousness. And that question stands even if one admits—as I do—that there is a goodness in the universe not easily explained without some ultimate."

The universe itself, Thomas came to think, was not immoral but amoral, indifferent to man and his hopes and fears. The origin of evil, as well as good, remained for him a great philosophical problem. "The devil of the orthodox," he noted, "must have his moments of profound despair over the virtue and kindness that all man's weakness and cruelty cannot crush. As parish minister, as political leader with many intimate contacts with the labor struggle, as a neighbor among neighbors, I have seen quite too much goodness and quiet heroism and capacity for mutual aid to accept any dogma of total depravity."

"To some men," Thomas added, "the revolt from an accepted faith has brought in itself emotional satisfactions, but not to me . . . I respected the sincere efforts of men to make a religion out of ethical culture or humanism or devotion to the community but I found in the resulting creeds poor substitutes for the kind of Christianity in which I had once found strength and hope. I hasten to add, however, my deep conviction that man as an individual and in society need not depend upon revealed religion for an ethical code of compelling power."

Indeed, Thomas has devoted his life to emulating Socrates' assurance to Glaucon: "In heaven there is laid up a pattern of such a city, and he who desires may behold this, and beholding, govern himself accordingly. But whether there really is or ever will be such a one is of no importance to him, for he will act according to the laws of that city and no other."

Sorrowed by the death of his beloved wife, Violet, Thomas wrote again of his deep longing for a belief in life after death:

"Violet's death, added to my own long standing sense of failure in most big things that I have tried to do, and—what is far worse —my growing doubt of man's capacity to achieve the good society, a fellowship of free men, here on earth, leads me back to my old yearning for some sort of personal immortality.

"I covet for myself a faith I cannot have. I am one of life's fortunate—and their number, I fear, is all too few—because I have been granted so many of the things worth cherishing. I find it easy to believe the ethics of Bertrand Russell's *Free Men's Worship*. We little men are greater than the vast impersonal universe in proportion as we understand it. And if none of us is ever privileged to play out his role, if the end for us as individuals and as a race is silence, yet there is beauty and a possible glory in the interval given us, and the loveliness of life can be enhanced by our conduct.

"More than I can tell I wish that I thought such love as mine and Violet's could live not alone in memory and perhaps in influence. Even more than that I wish I could see clearly a sure and hopeful way of deliverance—to which I might better contribute —for the generations of my children and grandchildren from the deep night of our civilization's end. I suppose—no, I know—the thing to do is to keep on, to enjoy what can be enjoyed, to do the things one certainly believes should be done, and among the uncertain to make the choices which will best give human decency a chance to live and grow. I should like a surer hope."

In essence Thomas believes that something which can fairly be called religion is indispensable to man. "The older I grow," he says, "the more inclined I am to think that my doubts of all the great concepts of God the Supreme Being, God the Ruler of the Universe, God the Father ordering each of our lives according to His plan, or God everywhere immanent in the universe and revealed by it, do not deprive me of the right to use the term as a kind of personification of spiritual values in which I do believe and for which the noblest humanism seems to me to lack an equivalent."

Thomas is willing to accept a statement by E. L. Allen, a British professor of divinity in "The Twentieth Century," that: "God is not some power that Christians aver to stand behind spiritual values and give them their worth; He *is* the realm of spiritual values." But then, muses Thomas, "I cannot explain the beauty of the earth or the effect upon me of the starry heavens in terms of physics, geology and astronomy. Still less can I explain life by biology or tell how chemical and physical processes are transmuted into Beethoven's music, or Shakespeare's verse, or a mother's love for her child. This I know: I walk in a world sometimes of pain and sorrow but a world of beauty and wonder; that if evil befalls me so does good, often far beyond my conscious desert. Is it wrong for me ever to say, Thank God (when perhaps I should thank Fate or Fortune) or to steady my heart and mind by something akin to prayer? Is this instinctive response denied me because I cannot longer confidently affirm the catechism definition of Him as a 'spirit infinite eternal and unchangeable in His being; wisdom, power, holiness, justice, goodness and truth.' I can still say with Tolstoy, 'God is the name of my desire.' "

TWENTY-THREE

Leader at Large

꿏 WHEN NORMAN THOMAS became seventy-five years old, a friend and associate, Stephen Siteman, asked him what he felt he had achieved. "I suppose it is an achievement," replied Thomas, "to live to my age and feel that one has kept the faith, or tried to. It is an achievement to be able to sleep at night with reasonable satisfaction. It is an achievement to have had a part, even if it was a minor part, in some of the things that have been accomplished in the field of civil liberty, in the field of better race relations, and the rest of it. It is something of an achievement, I think, to keep the idea of socialism before a rather indifferent or even hostile American public. That's the kind of achievement that I have to my credit, if any. As the world counts achievement, I have not got much."

To many Americans, this self-appraisal seems totally inadequate. On that same seventy-fifth birthday, the *Washington Post* editorialized about Thomas: "Above all else he has been a conscience of the American people . . . among the most influential individuals in twentieth-century politics . . . We join great numbers of his fellow Americans in congratulating the country on having him as a leader at large."

Whose judgment was more nearly right? Doubter Thomas or his kinder critics? Perhaps we can best answer if we take a look at what Thomas has done and what made him function. Certainly it is true that Thomas' six campaigns as a Socialist presidential nominee fell far short of the goal of making America socialist and of building a strong socialist movement. But they were successful in popularizing social security, unemployment insurance, public housing, civil rights and enforceable universal disarmament —all programs later acclaimed and adopted by both Republicans and Democrats. Thomas never won an election but, as this book has shown, he won many other campaigns. He initiated the charges of graft and bribery which led to the Seabury investigations of the Jimmy Walker administration in New York City. Before the smoke cleared, several judges went to jail and a mayor resigned in disgrace. When Frank Hague tried to stop free speech in Jersey City—when Indiana Governor Paul McNutt declared martial law in Terre Haute to break a strike—when attempts were made to frame Italian anti-fascist Athos Terzani on a murder charge— Norman Thomas stepped in and justice triumphed.

In a moving radio documentary, dramatist Morton Wishengrad portrayed Thomas' role in America. There is the definition, said Wishengrad, "provided by exhausted sharecroppers in the South and West; by exploited Mexican-Americans in Texas; by persecuted Japanese-Americans in California; by conscientious objectors in Federal penitentiaries; by Negroes everywhere in the United States. He is their voice. So long as he is alive and capable of standing before a public forum, those who are alienated and excluded are not entirely mute. One man articulate in the service of so many. It is beyond socialism, beyond political system and beyond economic doctrine."

Undoubtedly Thomas' greatest gift is that of oratory. Speech experts have marveled at his forensic talents, which never consist of endlessly repeating a prepared and memorized lecture. One union expert in Detroit told of listening to other speakers and thinking, "I've heard all this a hundred times before." But then Thomas would begin to speak. "He does not hash over the old ideas in a tone of soap box finality. He gives an *exploring* talk. He searches, tries to get his audience to take another peek in the corners, to look at things in a new way. Invariably he leaves one with fresh viewpoints. His barbs are fired with a smile but they hit their mark with telling effect."

Thomas' effectiveness as a speaker stems from several sources: his enormous reading over a wide range of subject matter, his many contacts with leaders in varied fields, and his superior intellect. His depth of conviction, which has caused many to liken him to the Prophets of old, impresses every audience with his honesty, his complete genuineness and his good will.

To those who conclude that Thomas' failure to bring socialism to the United States or to build a strong Socialist Party proves that he was not a successful speaker, Thomas has said, and I agree: "I do not underestimate the importance of effective public speech when I say that, given the circumstances, I could have made better speeches and still have failed, while under different circumstances I might have made worse speeches and succeeded."

After his 1932 campaign, Thomas embarked upon a career as a paid lecturer, but refused to give any lecture agency sole title to his services. He always insisted upon the right to speak without fee for the Socialist Party, unions and similar non-profit groups. Except for the period before World War II, when he took an unpopular anti-war position, there has always been a great demand from colleges and civic groups for Thomas' paid lecture appearances. His influence upon several generations of college students on more than a thousand college campuses has made him one of America's most effective mass educators. His appeal has been primarily to those whose interests ran to politics, economics and the social sciences, and he has always urged people to think for themselves rather than accept any dogma.

Nor has Thomas' influence been a result solely of his public appearances. Thousands of people have read his books—there are more than a score—and his articles and newspaper columns. Most of his books were tracts for the times rather than great literature, but some, like *Human Exploitation*, written in the depths of the depression, and *A Socialist's Faith*, written after World War II, are of enduring value. They have influenced socialist thinking throughout the world. Thomas Douglas, former Prime Minister of Saskatchewan's Cooperative Commonwealth Federation government and now leader of Canada's New Democratic Party, is only one of many who say they first learned their socialism from Norman Thomas' books, pamphlets and articles.

What is more, Thomas has established ties of personal interest and sympathy with hundreds of individuals who have sought his counsel. Many became so inspired as to change the course of their lives, entering into new activities and professions, being helped by Thomas to be more truly themselves. Over the years Thomas has opened the minds and enlisted the energies of countless thousands in campaigns for freedom. He has worked tirelessly with scores of organizations, some well-known, others small and obscure, giving not only his name but his time and his best thoughts as well. He has frequently aided people in trouble even when no problems of civil rights or liberties were involved.

Thomas has always treated people as individuals, recognizing that they are influenced by their economic and social backgrounds yet often capable of rising above narrow self- or class-interest. His innate dignity and fairness appeal to Americans in high and low places. At the 1948 Democratic and Republican national conventions I noted the deference which top leaders of both parties accorded Thomas. Presidents, Senators, Congressmen, Governors and hosts of other public officials, armed with the knowledge that they would be treated reasonably, have welcomed his views.

While Thomas has been described as a prophet, he has always been more interested in practical solutions than in any kind of dogma—theological or political. As has been mentioned, he could not accept strict adherence to the theology of Calvin. And, in applying for membership in the Socialist Party in 1918, he conceded that his socialism was not "of the most orthodox variety." He could never accept the easy assurance of infallibility that is the hallmark of the True Believer.

Even before becoming a socialist, Thomas displayed his sense of realism when he coupled his support of women's suffrage with an expressed doubt that women would vote any more wisely than men—at the same time maintaining they had just as much right to be wrong. This annoyed those suffragettes who argued passionately, "When the women get the vote, war will be ended for all time."

In a time when apathy and indifference have characterized much of mankind, one of Thomas' outstanding qualities has been his capacity for indignation at any injustice. This has been true even when the philosophies of those suffering hardship have been anathema to Thomas—Communism and ultra-rightism, for instance. "He has added greatly by prompt action to the slower-

301

moving Civil Liberties Union," notes Roger Baldwin. "Indeed he has often been a civil liberties agency all by himself, and a most effective one, with an acute sense of timing and publicity."

At the same time, it must be admitted that Thomas, in his zeal for justice, has sometimes lent his name too readily to protests formulated by others. Even when he felt that a specific protest was unwise, as in the case of some pacifist direct action programs, he gave his support if he felt that the sponsors were acting in good faith. But he is not above shifting his support if he is proved wrong. When the Arab states boycotted American concerns doing business with Israel, Thomas, influenced by the anti-Zionist *Jewish Newsletter*, at first justified the boycott on the grounds that it was not anti-Semitic but only aimed at Israel. However, when it was pointed out that the Arab boycott affected all Jews, as well as many Americans who were not Jewish, Thomas quickly acknowledged his error and wrote to the State Department in an attempt to end the Arab boycott.

In a well-written account of Thomas' activities within the Socialist Party (*Norman Thomas, Respectable Rebel*, Syracuse University Press, 1961), Murray B. Seidler argues that "almost from the beginning of his political career, Norman Thomas has been regarded as a respectable rebel." My difference with Seidler is slight, but nevertheless important. Thomas has been respected, but not always considered respectable. The difference is not merely semantic. From his earliest involvement with the Socialist Party in the 1917 Hillquit mayoralty campaign, Thomas has swung against the tide of the American majority and has been the object of slander and obloquy from the right as well as the left. Ultrapatriots in World War I and II demanded his arrest as a traitor. James W. Ford, a Negro Communist, charged in 1932 that "Mr. Thomas actually incites and justifies lynching by the white upper classes," while William Z. Foster, the Communists' national chairman, as late as 1954 (in *The Worker*) called Thomas "a darling of the Bourgeoisie" devoted to "a slick defense of the aggressive line of American imperialism" and support of "concentration camps for Communists."

Because Thomas opposed America's entrance into World War II, Wendell Willkie accused him of "narrow isolation." Others were less kind, calling Thomas an appeaser and a friend of Hitler. He was charged with anti-Semitism despite the fact that he pleaded with Roosevelt to open America's doors to save the Jews of Europe. And when Thomas balanced his criticism of Arab excesses with a call for Israel to accept Arab refugees from Palestine, some American Jews were quick to declare him anti-Semitic, even though his views were shared by certain Israeli government officials.

There were also those sectarian critics, it must be admitted, who censured Thomas for being too moderate. Dwight Mac-Donald, once a Trotskyite, then a militant anarchistic pacifist and still later a *Fortune* and *New Yorker* writer, wrote in *Politics* (October, 1944): "My objection to Norman Thomas can be put briefly: he is a liberal, not a socialist. A socialist, as I use the term anyway, is one who has taken the first simple step *at least* of breaking with present-day bourgeois society . . . His [Thomas'] role has always been that of left opposition *within the present society*, the fighting crusader in small matters (like Hagueism and other civil liberty issues) and the timid conformist in big matters (like the present war)." Here it might be added that MacDonald had suggested that the Socialist Party nominate Negro leader A. Philip Randolph for President, despite the vigorous pro-war stand of Randolph.

Leon Trotsky was another who insisted that Norman Thomas "called himself a Socialist as a result of misunderstanding." It should be noted that for Ford, Foster, MacDonald and Trotsky, all democratic Socialists were not "real" socialists but only "reformists," like Thomas' colleagues in the Socialist International.

Thomas is a public man, most at home on the speaker's platform. He enjoys an audience, relishes a debate. So great is his concern with public issues that some friends believe he has no other interests and, indeed, is incapable of relaxation. Once, for instance, Roger Baldwin invited Thomas to his country home in New Jersey and involved Thomas in what he thought was an absorbing rural project, trimming apple trees. Thomas joined the activity, but even when he was perched high on an apple limb, carried on a continuous stream of talk about current political problems. "I have never since tried to repeat the invitation," said Baldwin. "The only nature Thomas knows is human nature. That's a superior way of life, but it is not mine."

Baldwin is not quite accurate. Thomas may discuss political affairs so often because he thinks that is what is expected of him. I know that my wife and I have spent hours talking with him on an assortment of subjects, ranging from child rearing to bird watching, and on occasion we have enjoyed hearing him gossip about the great and near-great, at home and abroad. Gardening was one of Thomas' happiest recreations until arthritis made it impossible for him to continue; he and I have discussed the relative merits of putting peat moss on top or mixing it with the soil. He is no expert on art but enjoys going to art exhibits and museums, where his taste runs to representational rather than abstract art. "I get all my modern art from the drawings of my grandchildren," he says.

Bach is one of Thomas' favorite composers and he enjoys both symphonic and chamber music. He regrets his failure to develop his early interest in singing and playing an instrument, but in 1939 was given an opportunity to indulge a secret desire to be an orchestra leader. This occurred on Cal Tinney's radio show, "If I Had the Chance," over WJZ.

"When you can't get Toscanini," was the way Thomas put it, "you go to the other extreme." He had just finished conducting the most remarkable orchestra of many a year, composed of Rockwell Kent, flautist and artist; Arthur Garfield Hays, playing the mandolin; comic Eugene Howard disguised as a violinist; author Clement Wood with a ukulele; cartoonist Peter Arno and writer William C. White at the pianos; and Frank Norris of *Time* magazine at the drums.

Music lovers in the audience conceded that a certain lack of professional grace was more than compensated for by the enormous energy with which the musicians laid "Old Black Joe" a moulderin' in his grave. When Tinney, after the performance, asked Thomas if the confusion hadn't been too much for him, Thomas reminded Tinney sternly, "You forget that I have been in Jersey City."

Thomas genuinely enjoyed such forays into the entertainment field, and always informed the Socialist Party office of radio and television programs on which he was scheduled to appear—except for Alexander's Mediation Board. This was a radio and TV program which was something of a cross between an advice to the lovelorn column, a psychiatrist's couch, and a magistrate's court. Apparently feeling guilty, Thomas always managed to "forget" about these programs. He still insists, however, that the advice he gave there was at least no worse than that given by many psychologists and family counselors he has known.

Baseball was another of Thomas' interests. Some years ago, in Chicago, he unexpectedly paid a visit to Maynard Krueger, thus annoying the three young Krueger girls who had been scheduled to go to a baseball game with their father. The girls bounced into the room where Thomas and Maynard were discussing Socialist Party factional problems and one said to Thomas, "I bet you don't know who had the most home runs in the National League last year." When Thomas correctly replied, "Mel Ott" and gave the right number of homers, his stock soared.

No matter what the subject, Thomas seems to have a fund of information and is always entertaining. It is only fair to add, however, that more people have probably shared Baldwin's experiences with Thomas than the ones my wife and I have had.

In his own childhood, Thomas was aware of how frequently his mother would use the appeal of parental love in order to affect important decisions by the children. He felt that such appeals were singularly difficult for youngsters to resist and early decided not to use them on his children in order to induce them to follow his socialism, fight his causes or choose professions he favored. In later years, he wondered whether or not he leaned too far backwards, but his children bear witness that he kept his pledge. Violet once remarked, "The only thing that he requires of his family is that as individuals we think. He doesn't demand that we think his thoughts. Of course," she added with a smile, "I'm convinced he believes that if we think rightly, we'll agree with him."

Perhaps because studying and good marks had come so easily

to him, Thomas was somewhat intolerant of less than perfection in his children. At Vassar, Becky temporarily lost her scholarship when outside interests caused her to flunk a course in Spanish. Thomas sternly told Becky that instead of spending the summer vacationing, she would have to work at a summer job. She did, and soon after returning to college regained her scholarship. When Evan went to Princeton, his father warned him against flunking. Profiting from Becky's example, Evan worked hard and finally made the Dean's list in his junior year. Oddly enough, despite the tremendous stress on education in the Thomas household, only Becky among his children graduated from college. Bill took a job after a year at Arizona State University, Frances and Polly left college to marry, and Evan quit in his senior year to join the American Field Service during World War II.

Both when his children were young, and now that he has fifteen grandchildren and three great-grandchildren, Thomas has made every effort to be with them on significant occasions. If a grandchild is singing in the chorus for a school play or playing an instrument in a school concert, Thomas will try to arrange his schedule to be there. So many of his grandchildren have gone to the East Side School in Cold Spring Harbor that he has frequently been asked to deliver the commencement address there. Recently a parent said to her child, "My, aren't you lucky to have Mr. Thomas speak at your graduation?" Whereupon the youngster replied seriously, "We certainly are. He only speaks here every other year."

Of his five children, four consider themselves Norman Thomas followers, and believe his views on public affairs are more nearly accurate than those of anyone else. All love and respect Thomas and regard him as a great man.

Despite his unconventional political and economic views, Thomas lives by a strict code of individual morality. Even though he understands human failing better than his own parents did, he is still impatient of it, particularly when it affects his own family. When interviewed by the *New York Herald Tribune* on the occasion of his seventy-fifth birthday, Thomas announced proudly, "There's not one divorce among my five children and that ought to set some sort of record."

Thomas has been called America's greatest dissenter, but he has never been enamored of dissent for its own sake. "The secret of a good life," he wrote, "is to have the right loyalties and to hold them in the right scale of values. The value of dissent and dissenters is to make us reappraise those values with supreme concern for the truth . . . Rebellion per se is not a virtue. If it were, we would have some heroes on very low levels."

Thomas, who has run for many offices ranging from alderman to president, told me several years ago that the two posts that really intrigued him were Mayor of New York and United States Senator. Yet in 1933, when Raymond Ingersoll, a Fusion leader who was later elected Brooklyn borough president, approached Thomas about serving as a Fusion candidate for mayor, Thomas refused. He said he was too committed to the Socialist Party and its national program to assume a new role. While Thomas insists that he has always regretted that in public life he has been a critic and adviser with no chance for public office, one wonders whether subconsciously he has preferred the critic's role. This view is buttressed by Thomas' approval in his recent book, *The Great Dissenters* (Norton), of Socrates' statement to the men of Athens that "He who will really fight for the right . . . must have a private station and not a public one."

One essay in that book is, to an extent that Thomas may not realize, a self-appraisal of his own career. For in the book Thomas reveals how closely he identifies his own life with that of Wendell Phillips, the great abolitionist. Indeed, the parallels are striking and the differences minor.

Although Phillips was a patrician whose family inherited wealth and Thomas' family was relatively poor, the latter's marriage to Violet Stewart assured that the young couple would have no financial worries. Phillips, wrote Thomas with approbation, "did not rebel against his parents and a modern novelist would reject him out of hand as any sort of hero because all his life he devotedly loved one woman, his wife, and she an invalid. Fanatic he may have seemed to men incapable of hatred of an enormous evil, especially if that hatred should disturb their own way of life. But lovable he assuredly was. I can think of no dissenter with whom it would have been a greater joy to live and work in close

307

relations."

Like Thomas, Phillips showed no signs in his youth of a nascent radicalism. At Harvard, he was the proud leader of the aristocracy. Phillips was a great orator and, again like Thomas, he was interested in the entire human condition. He often spoke out on issues other than slavery. At a World Anti-Slavery Convention in London, Phillips argued against the inconsistency of "admitting colored brethren into our friendship" while yielding to parallel "prejudice against women." He also threw himself into the cause of those "enslaved" by the "wages system," and in 1865 championed the eight-hour day.

Wondering how easy it was for Phillips to follow his conscience in the assurance that he was right, Thomas asked, "Did he never regret renunciation of the power and position which by another course he might have attained—senator, perhaps?" Phillips told a friend that he would have liked to have been a U.S. Senator, yet, says Thomas, "He never changed his course to seek it. I question whether he could have been as happy or as helpful to his fellow men had he subdued his outspoken voice of conscience to the compromises of politics." That comment, I believe, reflects Thomas' view not only of Wendell Phillips' life but also of his own.

Now in his late seventies, Thomas still roams the land from Maine to California, from Florida to Oregon, speaking incessantly on peace, civil rights and socialism to enthusiastic audiences in which young people predominate. He makes at least three speeches a week, attends countless committee meetings, writes a semi-weekly column for the *Denver Post*, leads civil rights and union picket-lines, publishes a book every few years, appears frequently on television and radio, and spends his spare time suggesting solutions for mankind's woes. Describing Thomas in these later years, A. H. Raskin wrote in *The New York Times:* "The years have given a cavernous austerity to his patrician face, but the wrinkles of laughter still hold their own against the wrinkles etched by time. His pale blue eyes glow . . . and ideas tumble from his thin lips with the easy eloquence that used to make his campaign speeches entrancing to conservatives as well as liberals."

Recently a friend asked Thomas why he spent so much time

running all over the country when he should be lessening his activities. Thomas said he was too much the evangelist to stop. The real answer was given by his wife many years ago when she foretold that Norman Thomas would never retire until the world became "peaceful or perfect." In the present state of the world, he still has a lifetime job.

General Bibliography

Irving Bernstein, *The Lean Years*, Houghton Mifflin, 1960.
Robert J. Donovan, *Eisenhower: The Inside Story*, Harper, 1956.
Foster Rhea Dulles, *Labor in America*, Thomas Y. Crowell, 1960.
Donald Drew Egbert & Stow Persons, *Socialism and American Life*, Princeton University Press, 1952.
Raymond B. Fosdick, *Chronicle of a Generation*, Harper, 1958.
Ray Ginger, *The Bending Cross: A Biography of Eugene V. Debs*, Rutgers University Press, 1949.
Ben Gitlow, *I Confess*, Dutton, 1939.
John Haynes Holmes, *I Speak for Myself*, Harper, 1959.
Howard Kester, *Revolt Among the Sharecroppers*, Covici-Friede, 1936.
Arthur Mann, *La Guardia: A Fighter vs. His Times*, Lippincott, 1959.
Lucille Milner, *Education of an American Liberal*, Horizon, 1954.
Selig Perlman, *Theory of the Labor Movement*, Macmillan, 1928.
Joseph G. Rayback, *A History of American Labor*, Macmillan, 1959.
Karl M. Schmidt, *Henry A. Wallace, Quixotic Crusade 1948*, Syracuse University Press, 1960.
Louis Waldman, *Labor Lawyer*, Dutton, 1944.

Selected Works of Norman Thomas

BOOKS

After the New Deal, What? Macmillan, 1936.

America's Way Out: A Program for Democracy: Macmillan, 1931.

Appeal to the Nations: Holt, Inc., 1947.

As I See It: Macmillan, 1932.

The Choice Before Us: Mankind at the Crossroads: Macmillan, 1934.

The Christian Patriot: Young Friends' Movement, 1917.

The Church and the City: New York Presbytery, Protestant Episcopal Church, 1917.

The Conscientious Objector in America: Huebsch, 1923. Revised as *Is Conscience a Crime?* Vanguard, 1927.

Great Dissenters: Norton, 1961.

Human Exploitation in the United States: Frederic A. Stokes, 1934.

(with Bertram D. Wolfe) *Keep America Out of War: A Program:* Frederic A. Stokes, 1939.

Mr. Chairman, Ladies and Gentlemen: Reflections on Public Speaking: Hermitage, 1955.

The Prerequisites for Peace: Norton, 1959.

Socialism on the Defensive: Harper, 1938.

A Socialist's Faith: Norton, 1951.

Socialism Re-examined: Norton, 1963.

The Test of Freedom: Norton, 1954.

War: No Glory, No Profit, No Need: Frederic A. Stokes, 1935.

We Have a Future: Princeton University Press, 1941.

What Is Our Destiny? Doubleday, Inc., 1944.

(with Paul Blanshard) *What's the Matter with New York: A National Problem:* Macmillan, 1932.

PAMPHLETS

The Challenge of War, League for Industrial Democracy, 1924.
Conscription: The Test of Peace, Post War World Council, 1944.
Democracy and Japanese Americans, Post War World Council, 1942.
Democracy versus Dictatorship, League for Industrial Democracy, 1937.
Democratic Socialism: A New Appraisal, League for Industrial Democracy, 1953. Rev. ed., Post War World Council, 1963.
The New Deal: A Socialist Analysis, Socialist Party, 1934.
The One Hope of Peace: Universal Disarmament under International Control, Post War World Council, 1947.
The Plight of the Share-Cropper, League for Industrial Democracy, 1934.
Russia: Promise and Performance, Socialist Party, 1945.
(with Joel Seidman) *Russia—Democracy or Dictatorship?* League for Industrial Democracy, 1939.
The Socialist Cure for a Sick Society, John Day Company, Inc., 1932.
A Socialist Looks at the New Deal, League for Industrial Democracy, 1933.
A Socialist Looks at the United Nations, Syracuse University Press, 1945.
The Truth About Socialism, Socialist Party, 1943.
(with A. Philip Randolph) *Victory's Victims?—The Negro's Future*, Socialist Party, 1943.
War as a Socialist Sees It, League for Industrial Democracy, 1936.
What's Behind the "Christian Front"? Socialist Party, 1939.
What Is Industrial Democracy? League for Industrial Democracy, 1925.
World Federation: What Are the Difficulties? Post War World Council, 1942.
World Government, War and Peace, Post War World Council, 1948.

DEBATES

Lawrence Dennis, Norman Thomas, A. J. Muste, and Raymond Moley.

"Which Way America—Fascism, Socialism, Communism or Democracy?" America's Town Meeting of the Air, 1935.

Norman Thomas *vs.* Earl Browder. "Which Road for American Workers, Socialist or Communist?" *Socialist Call*, 1936.

Norman Thomas, Mme. Olivia Rossetti Agresti, and H. V. Kaltenborn. "Can Democracies Avoid Dictatorship?" America's Town Meeting of the Air, 1937.

Norman Thomas and Dr. Harry W. Laidler *vs.* Col. Robert S. Henry and Samuel B. Pettengill. "Should the Federal Government Own and Operate the Railroads?" University of Oklahoma Press, 1939.

Norman Thomas, James G. McDonald, Cesar Saerchinger, and Frederick L. Schuman. "Are We on the Road to War?" America's Town Meeting of the Air, 1940.

Norman Thomas *vs.* Frank Kingdon. "Should We Adopt the President's Lend-Lease Plan?" America's Town Meeting of the Air, 1941.

Norman Thomas, William H. Chamberlin, Raymond Moley and Raymond Swing. "Russia and America—Postwar Rivals or Allies?" America's Town Meeting of the Air, 1945.

Norman Thomas, Norman Angell, Jean Gottmann, and J. J. Singh. "Should Colonial Empires Be Liquidated?" America's Town Meeting of the Air, 1945.

Norman Thomas, John M. Devine, George Fielding Eliot, and Leif Erickson. "Is Universal Military Training Necessary for Our Security?" America's Town Meeting of the Air, 1947.

Leon M. Birkhead, Martin Ebon, Norman Thomas, and Raymond Moley. "Which Way America—Fascism, Communism, Socialism, or Democracy?" America's Town Meeting of the Air, 1948.

Norman Thomas, Bartley Crum, G. Bromley Oxnam & Louis Waldman. "What Should Be the Limits on Your Free Speech?" America's Town Meeting of the Air, 1949.

Norman Thomas, Helen Gahagan Douglas, and Herman W. Steinkraus. "What Is the Difference Between Socialism and Social Welfare?" America's Town Meeting of the Air, 1950.

Index

316

317

318